P.B.Webster

THE CAIRNGORMS
ON FOOT AND SKI

By the same Author

THE TATRA MOUNTAINS
SKI TRACK ON THE BATTLEFIELD
THE UNITY OF EUROPE

THE
CAIRNGORMS
ON FOOT AND SKI

By

V. A. FIRSOFF

*Illustrated
by the Author*

ROBERT HALE LIMITED
18 Bedford Square, London, WC1

First published in 1949

THIS BOOK IS PRODUCED IN
COMPLETE CONFORMITY WITH THE
AUTHORIZED ECONOMY STANDARDS

PRINTED IN GREAT BRITAIN BY
NORTHUMBERLAND PRESS LIMITED
GATESHEAD ON TYNE

DEDICATION

To Marjorie and little George Ingram,
my companions on the scree-fields of
life, with their fleeting suns, their small
flowers, their weariness and promise of
vast views at the skyline

CONTENTS

CHAP.   PAGE

I. THE FIRST MEETING 11

II. THE LONESOME HILLS 23

III. HEATHERS AND WEATHERS 39

IV. THE CONTORTED PLATEAU 61

V. THE ARCTIC HEIGHTS 85

VI. EAST OF THE LAIRIG AN LUI 111

VII. THE BURN'S WAY 135

VIII. ON THE LOCHS AND LOCHANS 163

IX. THE PASSING GIANTS OF THE GLENS . . . 185

X. IN THE WORLD OF PERPENDICULAR VALUES . . 205

XI. STUDIES IN WHITE 223

XII. A-SKI-ING ON THE TOPS AND "WRAITHS" . . . 237

XIII. LET'S TALK OF PTARMIGAN AND CHARS-À-BANCS, OF

PRESIDENTS AND PARKS 261

INDEX 273

ILLUSTRATIONS

1 The Author at the Pools of Dee, in the Lairig
  Ghru   *frontispiece*

                                                    facing page
2 The Glen Feshie hills   16
3 The Cairngorms from Craigellachie, Aviemore   17
4 Ben Macdhui, the highest Cairngorm   32
5 Loch Etchachan. ". . . the ground suddenly breaks
  and a gaping chasm opens before you" (p. 32)   32
6 Loch Morlich and the northern corries of Cairn Gorm   33
7 The head of Glen Avon offers a typical example of
  glacial erosion   33
8 Loch Insh and Creag Mhigeachaidh on a dull wintry
  day   48
9 Ciste Mearaid, the last of the snow   48
10 It's spring and the gean is in bloom. Loch an Eilein 49
11 On a crisp December morning. "Whitewell" and
   Braeriach   49
12 Cairn Toul from the summit of Braeriach, Coire
   Bhrochain rocks on the right   64
13 The Sgorans. The "Pinnacle Ridge" with A'Chailleach   65
14 The tortuous cleft of the Linn of Dee   80
15 Cairn Toul in Early Spring   81
16 "The sun is beating down in a concentrated blaze,
   bringing the torrent to a cold, white incandescence."
   Am Fèith Buidhe   96
17 A glimpse of Loch Avon from the rocks of Coire
   Raibert   97
18 Mullach Lochan nan Gabhar in the massif of Ben
   Avon   112
19 Dubh Lochan from Beinn a'Bhùird   113
20 The Caledonian pines of Glen Quoich   128
21 Glen Avon and the Cairngorms from Tomintoul   128

9

facing page

22 The Ben Avon heights from A'Chioch, Beinn a'Bhùird 129
23 "The Goats' Lochan is cradled in a deep secluded hollow" (p. 130) 129
24 ". . . the water had folded small, like translucent silk, in the burn's elbow by the bridge" (p. 145) 144
25 The Lairig Ghru 145
26 Glen Lui with Càrn a'Mhaim in the distance 160
27 Loch Einich from the edge of the Great Moss 161
28 Loch Pityoulish from Creag Chaisteal 176
29 The Comyns' castle on Loch an Eilein 176
30 The bleak waters of Loch Builg 177
31 Loch Morlich, the largest of the Cairngorm lochs 177
32 "Evensong." The Derry 192
33 The Woods of Strathspey in winter garb 192
34 Kennapole Hill in May 193
35 Glenmore with Meall a'Bhuachaille in the background 193
36 The Devil's Point from Càrn a'Mhaim across the Lairig Ghru "mounth" 208
37 The Shelter Stone Crag 208
38 Malcolm Slesser's party exploring the great slab 209
39 "Over my right shoulder I could see the Black Pinnacle, which seemed to be floating midway down— a dark spire in an airy flood" (p. 221) 209
40 Rothiemurchus under snow 224
41 Speyside in silver filigree 225
42 Near the summit of Sgòr Gaoith 240
43 A scissor-christie in heavy set snow (the author) 241
44 Cairn Lochan on a sunny day in February 256
45 "The sight I had been looking forward to was now before me" (p. 248) 256
46 The Great Rough Corrie of Braeriach 257
47 On the narrow snows of Coire na Ciste. The 1948 Scottish Kandahar Cup Race 257
48 Cairn Gorm from Ord Bàn, Loch an Eilein country 272
49 Càrn Crom and the Derry Forest at sunset (the inclination of the trees attests to the force and persistence of the Sou'wester) 273

Folding Map *at end*

I

THE FIRST MEETING

Glen Feshie of storm-blasts!
Within thy shelter could I wish to be;
Where I could find the whortle,
The cloud and the black berries—
Round nuts on the hazels,
And red fish in the linns.
(A Gaelic poem from *The Poetry of Badenoch*)

I FIRST met the Cairngorm Mountains after several years of London, with its hustle, its teeming crowds, its fads and affectations, and, lastly, its bombs and sirens. The old hills came like a revelation: they restored me to vastness and solitude, and helped to place things human in proper perspective in the world.

It was in the opening days of November that an L.M.S. train was hurrying me past bistre-fawn slopes, tinged with blue and deep brown, golden birches stooping over amber streams, and thin wisps of smoke rising from the grey stone houses by the railway-side into the cold air of the morning. Then the view widened into the breath-taking emptiness of Drumochter, long vistas of bare hillsides disappearing somewhere in the mist above Loch Ericht.

Surely it was *Ultima Thule!* . . . Small wonder none of the early conquerors could maintain a foothold here for long. The Legions of Rome were halted by the Picts at the mysterious Mons Graupius. The Norsemen held only the seaboard. In vain did Edward I cross this pass with his doughty army; his successor did not "keep troth", and lost the day at Bannockburn. Not until after 1746, which marked the end of "Bonnie Prince Charlie's" mad enterprise, were the wild Highlands finally subdued, with no tenderness, by the "Southrons'" might and law, leaving some Jacobite embers still smouldering under the ashes of retrospect.

At Kincraig, where I saw my blue cases appear on the platform from the guard's van, rain was pouring down in streams. Mr. Clark, looking twenty years younger than his birth certificate, was there to greet me, huddled up in a weatherproof overcoat and a sou'wester. I was a bit baffled at first by the unfamiliar accent, though the people of Inverness-shire speak fine musical English. Somehow, rather stupidly, my tired brain found it difficult to reconcile itself to the fact that " aboot " was not an article of footwear, but signified a spatial relation.

Achlean, he said, which was my destination, was a good six miles up in the hills, a long way to go, and he thought that I would perhaps be more comfortable somewhere at Kincraig. . . . My rooms weren't quite ready.

If it was a long way, a long way I would go, and we could manage it somehow. I did not expect luxuries.

I felt quite strongly about that, and this seemed to reassure him. But he had only a motor-bike, and could not take my luggage, so I had to hire a car, which he soon fetched.

My lungs filled with clear cool air, I subsided drowsily on the leather cushions of a back seat and let the driver whisk me by the gleaming waters of Loch Insh, through the forest of Feshie-bridge, up onto the moorland track of Glen Feshie. On the left, steep, scree-scarred hill-faces alternated with scraggy pinewoods. On the right, the Feshie was in spate, rolling down below the curtains of birches with the sound of distant surf.

Waves of rain were beating against the car windows.

It was a vast and lonely world, emptier it seemed to me even than the sub-Arctic uplands of Sweden, though the impression might have been largely due to the fresh contrast with London. It took some time before the car, grunting and puffing over the bumps and stones, brought me to the green flat among the heather-grown moraines where Achlean stood.

At this point let me explain that Achlean is a croft roughly half-way up the Glen from Kincraig, at the starting-point of the stalkers' path up Càrn Bàn Mòr, with which I was going to become very familiar.

I stayed there for about three months of late autumn and

early winter and, though my host's earlier surmise that I would have been more comfortable at Kincraig might have contained some truth, I would certainly not have exchanged the experience for a few ounces of additional comfort. It was cold at times and very windy; there were not always enough rabbits to supplement the war-time rations; but whatever may have been lacking in amenity was more than amply made up for in kindness, friendliness and consideration.

It is not easy for a large family to make a living out of a hundred sheep or so grazing on a wide mountain hirsel; some acres of indifferent soil where the inclement climate permits few and meagre crops, chiefly oats and hay, " 'tatties ", " 'neeps ", with possibly a little " kail " thrown in for the balance; two or three cows for milk; a handful of poultry, subject to temperamental whims in the vital task of egg-laying; and a steadily diminishing supply of rabbits, other game and fish being taboo to the crofter, whose tenancy has long ceased to include the shooting and fishing rights. And families are large, with anything up to ten " bairns " or perhaps more in these lonely Highland crofts, scattered sparsely among the once-populous glens and windswept moorlands, miles of indifferent road from the nearest shop or school. In these conditions life is hard and lays great claims on endurance, forbearance and perseverance. But for this very reason it has preserved the ancient dignity and the unjaded genuineness of thought and feeling that have often been lost by the more comfortable townsfolk and the " room-letters " of the popular tourist resorts, with their petty village scandal, jealousies and inflated ambitions.

It is difficult, no doubt, in the rough toil on the land to develop and maintain the higher cultural level of urban existence. On the other hand, without contact with stark " uncombed " Nature one is apt to lose hold of the fundamental values on which all sound judgment must ultimately rest.

Scottish education is good, albeit somewhat bookish, and the standard of information reached by a crofter's son or daughter can at times put to shame their presumptuous coevals in town finery with genteel prunes-and-prisms voices. People living amid an ocean of restless humanity may find it difficult to realize what the wireless means to those far-off homesteads; but, once they have done so, they will perhaps excuse the volume of cantankerous correspondence regarding the failings of the B.B.C. which periodically fills up the " Letters-to-the-Editor " columns of the Scottish press.

In the days of the chimney-less " black-house ", when neighbours used to gather for a *ceilidh* in the uncertain gloaming of smoky peats or a flickering " quick-fir " splinter (it had to be dry and resinous, and the Glen More Forest at the foot of Cairn Gorm was famous for such " quick-firs "), it was no easy matter to maintain contact with the outside world and keep abreast of events.   Allegiance was narrow and superstition rife.   Kelpies in the shape of white horses used to emerge from the river fords to announce to the wayfarer his impending doom and then vanish under the water with a thunderous clap of the tail. *Cailleach Bheur*, " the Fierce Grey *Cailleach* (old woman) ", a blue giantess with a black face, used to perambulate the hills after nightfall or wail pitifully at the door craving admittance, and woe to him who would let her in !   Ale and *uisga*, the " holy water ", were plentiful and cheap, and occasionally, after a visit to a hospitable Highland home, a minister would be " spirited away " by the fairies to be carried " through aether and fleecy clouds "[1] and eventually deposited, unharmed, on the doorstep of his manse.

To-day, alack, even Hogmanay " is not what it used to be ", though more than enough for the modest ways of the writer.

Still, the Old Man of Ben Macdhui continues to reveal himself at suitable moments to solitary professors.[2]   Once, passing in thick mist the headwaters of the Eidart, I turned the corner of a rocky rib where the sound of the tumbling waters suddenly rushed at me.   It seemed I heard the stamping of hoofs on the stones, and I paused, somewhat startled.   Who knows but that a kelpie might have been making off, not to be surprised in the act of fortune-telling.

[1] See Francis Drake-Carnell : *It's an Old Scottish Custom* (London, 1939).
[2] The story originated in an experience of the late Professor J. Norman Collie.

To those with attentive ears who listen to the voices of silence they will yet confide wonders, less tangible but no less worthy, which live in human hearts and in the granite heart of the Cairngorm Hills. . . .

It rained persistently my first few days in Glen Feshie and, apart from an "expedition" to Kingussie, the "Capital of Badenoch" and a small town in the Spey valley an odd eight miles away, during which I missed the only bridge on the short-cut and had to ford a minor river, I did not venture far afield. When, finally, the sky cleared and the mists lifted from the hills, they revealed the tops covered with a fresh fall of snow, dazzling white in sunshine.

In a spurt of enquiring eagerness I ran up the stalkers' path, covering the intervening three upward miles to Ciste Mearaid (Margaret's Chest or Coffin) in about an hour's time. I was kicking out steps in the crisp, firm snow with my thin "townee" shoes, which were soon filled with it, and had to be taken off time and again to remove the unwelcome wet layer from under my instep. Ptarmigan flew across the gully with the strange noise as if of a wooden rattle or a miniature machine-gun; deer peeped round the edge of the hillside; but the skyline refused to yield the summit of which every succeeding knoll and heap of stones held an elusive promise.

In the end, however, I emerged on a gentle rotundity, marked with a couple of voluminous cairns, which was Càrn Bàn Mòr itself. On one side lay the deep, blue world of Glen Feshie; on the other an extensive snow-covered plateau with the white summits of Braeriach, Cairn Toul and Monadh Mòr, which was to become my main gateway to the High Cairngorms in summer and winter alike. Of what lay beyond those summits there was no indication, and I had to wait for nearly a year before I was finally able to penetrate there; for to remind me that I was a convalescent supposed to rest, there were leaden weights in my temples and a rising temperature was glowing in the hollows between my eyes and nose. I suddenly felt cold and shrunken under the chilly breath coming from the white expanse before me, and was forced to retrace my steps.

I paid for this effort with a day in bed.

Generally speaking, my convalescence at Achlean was highly unorthodox. I borrowed a pair of old ski which, unfortunately, were not equipped with steel edges, and had very little even of their wooden edges left after the wear and tear of thirty years. Of these I made as much use as was possible, which was, on the whole, quite often, since, once the winter had secured a hold on the hills, it went on snowing heavily, though intermittently. The Sgorans, the Great Moss, Meall Dubhag and the head of Glen Feshie, all within a range of six miles, were as far as I dared venture, for my body was weak and my knees would soon get flabby under the strain of downhill running.

Still, thanks to the ski, I could explore the surrounding country far more thoroughly than would otherwise have been possible, and I also implanted the seed of ski-ing enthusiasm in the hearts of the younger generation of the inhabitants of Glen Feshie. Even Mr. Clark himself acquired a pair of ski some months later at a roup in Kingussie—for his personal use.

I remember discovering on the Coire Ruadh (the Red Corrie) side of Càrn Bàn Mòr (the Great White Hill) a slope of fine powder-snow below the white sinuous gully of a hushed-up stream. The sun glittered on its speckless smoothness, lighting here and there a prismatic beam in an ice crystal. The air had that invigorating purity of a fine winter's day in the mountains which it would be difficult to convey to those who have not experienced it themselves. A flow of strength entered me after the first run-down, as if I had tapped a secret spring of life. I felt that I still could ski; that, therefore, everything was going to be right again; that the world was a fine place, even though Tobruk had fallen and the Germans were invading Egypt.

There is a tipsy feeling about the cloud of snow-dust raised on a sunlit slope by a fast christiana swing. Ski-ing, as F. S. Smythe says in one of his books, is the nearest thing he knows to flying, beside which flying in a 'plane is a very inadequate experience. As an ex-squadron-leader he ought to be a good judge.

So down I " flew ", or rather " danced ", again and again, until

The Glen Feshie hills

it was time for the last weary climb up to the saddle in the tightening grip of the evening frost. Followed a quick glide along the snowed-up *allts*,[1] a cautious descent over heathery patches, and at last—the door.

I was once more in bed with a temperature of 100°, but in the final count this has proved to be a good cure.

While lying through the windy night on uneasy hot pillows in a state of half-consciousness, I seemed to hear the bark of field-guns, the whine and thud of shells, and the clangour of tank tracks on stones and gravel coming from the hills on the other side of the Glen. Waking up, I half-raised myself on my elbows to make sure that the Nazi invasion of Britain had not begun. But the night was fairly quiet, save for the "wuthering" of the wind in the chimney. I shut my eyes with the swelling noise of battle in my ears.

By an odd coincidence that was the night when in actual fact Monty's barrage was roaring away at distant El Alamein.

Two days later I was up and out once more.

I became familiar with the haunts of Glen Feshie and its hills.

Much of the old forest near the lodge was still standing, though the Canadian forestry troops were busy there every day felling trees. This they did skilfully enough, leaving a thin screen of pines to dissimulate the devastation; but it will take years before beauty returns to spread her green mantle over the dead stumps, decaying branches, and brown earth churned-up by the tractors. I was one of the few to witness the last days of the old firs and to seek shelter under their humming crowns from the "storm-blasts" of Glen Feshie. Snow was deep among the tall junipers at the bifurcation of the Glen, and as I passed roe-deer pranced away over the drifts and turned back to see if I was following. I found none there during a recent visit.

The nearest patch of woodland was Badan Mosach—according to the map—which is the Gaelic for "Dark" or "Dirty Grove", so called presumably by reason of the boggy ground at the meeting of the small burns in its lower part; but to me it was the "Wee Woodie", the name under which it was locally

---

[1] *Allt*—the Gaelic for stream, often used in the local place-names.

B

The Cairngorms from Craigellachie, Aviemore

known, just as Allt Fhearnagan was simply the " White Burn ".

In fact, Gaelic is nearly extinct in this part of Inverness-shire, and only once have I heard two old shepherds converse in it without visible effort.   True, most people make it a point of honour to know a few words of their ancestral language, but their knowledge does not go very far.   Even those of the older generation who profess to " have the Gaelic " (which is a sure title to respect) are often unable to give the equivalents in it of quite simple English words, and I have long given up trying to elicit from them the exact meaning of place-names, so frequently do they contradict one another.   Thus, a curious situation has arisen where the place-names are becoming more and more completely divorced from the spoken tongue and as meaningless, even to the natives, as if they were Coptic or Chaldean.   The result is continuous distortion of the old Gaelic names, arbitrariness, and anglicization of spelling, and the gradual substitution of English ones in the local usage.

This makes Highland place-names much more bewildering than, for instance, those of Wales, where the eye, if not the ear, will soon perceive a certain logical order. . . .

However, the " Wee Woodie " was the nearest patch of woodland and the usual objective of my afternoon strolls, when energy or the weather had let me down.

It was seldom really cold.   Once you had made up your mind to get to grips with the weather, it proved as a rule far less formidable than one might think watching the white turmoil through a window pane.   But the wind was fierce, and I was literally blown off my feet by a sudden blast on the way to the school-house at Stronetoper, where the " post-lassie " used to leave the mail for Achlean when it got very " wild " and " blowy ".   Yet there would also come restful, quiet days, imbued with sunshine, with the scent of spring in the air.   My last week in Glen Feshie that winter was marked by a speckless blue sky, ground frost and a great calm.

Hard-frozen snow lay deep in the " Wee Woodie ".   At midday it would get so warm there that I used to sit in a chair improvised out of my ski and sticks, with rolled-up sleeves and

shut eyes, in mild bliss under the caress of winter sunshine
for maybe an hour or more, without that chilly feeling which
one gets after a siesta in an arm-chair in front of a fire.

One such clear February day the "postie's" red bicycle
brought me the saddest news I had yet had.

As I went up the hill once more, a grouse gathered itself into
a stuttering flight, clucking with fussy agitation. A doe barked
huskily from afar. Allt Fhearnagan was washing away beneath

sheets of yellow ice and tumbling over the rocky steps. The
frozen grit by the streamside crunched under my ski-boots as I
leapt over the water from a protruding rock.

A stranger like myself among the pines of Badan Mosach, a
wintering Camberwell Beauty spread out the dark velvet of its
cream-rimmed wings floating through the still air, and alighted
on a tree trunk. There it sat basking, opening and shutting its
wings. I, too, rested my cheek against a pine-tree, and friendlier
than the touch of a human hand was its rough bark.

I took the first train south.

The weather continued fair. White down to their waists, the old lonesome hills stood above the dark strath.

I was leaving with a promise to return, the promise which I have since kept.

I have spent in all about six years in the district, which has given me opportunity to get better acquainted with the mountains and their people, their ways and peculiarities, beauties and commonplaces.

I have known the Cairngorms in friendly and in malevolent moods, and amassed a fund of experience which I would like to share with those who wish to visit these lonesome hills or to revive their memories of them. In this book I have set myself the task of combining objective information with the enlivening touch of personal approach; scenic description, supported by photographic evidence and some pen-and-ink drawings of my own, with practical hints to the walker, climber and skier.

There are works dealing with the Cairngorms, but rather few. To those desirous of studying their walks, tours and climbs I can recommend Sir Henry Alexander's guide-book, *The Cairngorms*, published by the Scottish Mountaineering Club. It is a mine of information and pleasant reading too, free from the monotony of the catalogue and the tedium of technical detail. So far, however, as the rock climbs are concerned, the book is badly out of date and various notes that have appeared in *The Cairngorm Club Journal* will be found helpful in supplementing the information it gives. Mr. Seton Gordon's *The Cairngorm Hills of Scotland* will also be found interesting, especially by those with an ornithological inclination; whereas a friend of mine, Mr. Richard Perry, has recently written a book, *In the High Grampians*, covering from this standpoint an area including the Western Cairngorms, which I would like to recommend to all nature lovers. *Walking in the Grampians* by Mr. Charles Plumb contains a description of the main Cairngorm tours.

This exhausts the list of modern general works on the district, at least to the best of my and the Inverness County Librarian's knowledge.

None of these books will be of great use to a skier, who has to fall back on the articles in *The British Ski Year Book* (one of them, *Ski-ing in Scotland* by W. R. Higginbotham, has been reprinted in pamphlet form by the Scottish Ski Club and gives useful suggestions with regard to ski-ing in the Central and Western Cairngorms), *The Scottish Club Journal* and other club publications. It is hoped, therefore, that the present work will fill this gap to some extent.

In the preparation of *The Cairngorms on Foot and Ski* I have relied chiefly on personal experience, but I am indebted in many ways to the above-mentioned authors, as well as some other works which, whenever advisable, will be referred to in the footnotes. Acknowledgments of personal help will likewise be made in the footnotes or in the text.

In order to avoid the controversial pitfalls of Gaelic spelling, I have followed throughout that of the Ordnance Survey Map, although it is often incorrect and self-contradictory, the same words being spelled differently in different place-names. In a few cases, however, I have been forced to depart from this practice, as certain place-names I have mentioned do not occur in the O.S. Map, and laying no claim to be an authority on Gaelic I can only hope that they will be sufficient for identifying the places.

II

THE LONESOME HILLS

1. Their Peaks, Valleys and Divisions

THE Cairngorms have the distinction of being the highest and wildest compact mountain area of Britain. True, the island's most elevated height, Ben Nevis, stands in the company of the Aonachs as a lonely outpost at the westernmost end of the Grampians where its huge bulk looms unrivalled, over the sea. But, after all, there is not such a lot of difference between Ben Nevis's 4,406 feet and the 4,296 of Ben Macdhui, the highest of the Cairngorms—a paltry hundred and ten feet! And Ben Macdhui, whether it takes its name from a hypothetical MacDuff or a black hog, which animal the mountain is said to resemble to a Gaelic eye, can count in its close vicinity on three supporters, all of them exceeding 4,000 feet: Braeriach (4,248 ft.), Cairn Toul (4,241 ft.) and Cairn Gorm (4,084 ft.). This, in the days of clan feuds, used to give the squatty Ben a decided ascendancy over his rival. For, be it noted, Ben Macdhui had long been thought to be the loftiest summit of the country until, in 1810, Dr. Keith's barometer dissented from public opinion giving Ben Nevis a stature higher by fully fifty feet!

The matter did not rest at that, and the "adherents" of Ben Macdhui for a long time would not give in, bearing a heart-felt grudge against the inhabitants of Fort William, who in turn spat mentally at the very mention of that other Ben. Yet justice was on the latter's side, and thirty-seven years later they carried the day. The sappers, who "paid handsomely", as the local story goes, and incidentally were responsible for the erection of the huge cairn embedding a minor obelisk on the top of Ben Macdhui, made a detailed survey of the Grampians and ruthlessly degraded the peak to second place in the orographical hierarchy of Britain. John Hill Burton is said to have been ready to go down on his knees and implore the surveyors to reverse their verdict. The dispute continued to rankle, and a project was seriously entertained of adorning the summit of Ben Macdhui with a " sepulchral vault " of such size as to out-top Ben Nevis. Mercifully, this has not come to pass.[1]

To-day this is past history, but memories are long in these parts, and I am not too sure that all the flames of the old controversy have been finally quenched. At any rate, writing in 1925, the Rev. John Stirton does not go beyond the somewhat cautious statement that Aberdeenshire includes " *Ben Macdhui*, said to be the second highest mountain in Great Britain."[2] You never know but that the surveyors might, after all, have made a mistake. . . !

However, here we are with Ben Macdhui, the three other "four-thousanders", and Beinn a'Bhùird (3,924 ft.) and Ben Avon (3,843 ft.), as the " Six Cairngorms ", which have all been *done* in one day by some sturdy spirits equipped with even sturdier legs. Bynack and Beinn Mheadhoin (pronounced Main) in the north and the hills abutting on the Great Moss, which extends west and south-west of Braeriach and Cairn Toul as far as the valleys of the Feshie and the Geldie, complete the rather amorphous system of the Cairngorm Mountains, forming, as it were, an excrescence on the main body of the Grampians at about the meeting-point of the counties, Inverness, Aberdeen and Banff.[3]

The two *Lairigs*, that is to say " passes ", once the roads of

---

[1] Sir Henry Alexander: *The Cairngorms*, pp. 114-5.

[2] *Crathie and Braemar, A History of the United Parish* (Aberdeen, 1925), p. 7.

[3] The term "Cairngorms" is sometimes used very loosely, Lochnagar and many other hills being included, which tends to blur the geographical boundaries of these mountains. Yet, although the delimitation is partly artificial as far as the outskirts of the group are concerned, the group itself is an unmistakable geological unit. My classification is based on Alexander Inkson MacConnochie, who writes: " The Cairngorms comprehend an area of about 300 square miles . . . bounded on the south by the Dee, westwards from Gleann an t'Slugain, and the Geldie; on the west by the Feshie from the Geldie to the Spey; on the north-west by the Spey between the Feshie and the Nethy; and on the east by the Learg an Laoigh to the Avon; thence, on the north, by the Avon to Inchrory; and, thence, on the east, by Glen Builg and the Bealach Dearg to the Dee."—" The Cairngorms," *The Cairngorm Club Journal*, Vol. I.

cattle and seasonal field labour in full daylight and of caterans on some more misty occasions, the Lairig Ghru and the Lairig an Lui, divide the Cairngorms into three easily recognizable parts. Between the " passes ", which in this case means passages or tracks rather than depressions between two heights, lie the Central Cairngorms, with Ben Macdhui, Cairn Gorm, Beinn Mheadhoin and Bynack as the main summits. West of the Lairig Ghru are the Western Cairngorms, which include Braeriach, Cairn Toul, Monadh Mòr, and Beinn Bhrotain (pronounced Vrotten) and the Glen Feshie hills. East of the Lairig an Lui rise the Eastern Cairngorms, Beinn a'Bhùird and Ben Avon with their attendant heights.

The north-western boundary of the mountains is well marked by the flat ground, that is the *strath*, along the Spey. Kingussie, Kincraig, Aviemore, Boat of Garten and Nethybridge are the main towns and villages of Speyside at the approaches to the Cairngorms. Aviemore, which faces the Lairig Ghru, is undoubtedly the best placed of all. The Dee rises in the heart of the Cairngorm country, and for this very reason, while Glen Dee is a natural highroad leading to its central peaks, it does not constitute a clear demarcation line in the south-east. The central, eastern and southern part of the massif are within reasonably easy compass of Braemar and Inverey on the Dee, and the latter locality forms the principal " climbing headquarters " of the district. Tomintoul is the best centre for the Eastern Cairngorms, and the northern corries and gorges of Ben Avon in particular.

All these places possess hotels and boarding-houses of varying quality and are usually overcrowded during the season, which lasts from June till September or thereabouts. Speyside lies on the direct rail route to London, and is by far the more accessible from the south. Oddly enough, the quickest way of getting from Aviemore to Braemar, a distance of twenty-seven miles, is by walking through the Lairig Ghru; a train or a car journey between the two places is a long and devious affair. There are no tourist or climbing huts or shelters in the Cairngorms.

Although sorely thinned out by the war-time and post-war

fellings, which are continuing at the time of writing, the forests
of Rothiemurchus, Mar and Abernethy still crowd, dark-green,
to the feet of the mountains. If, however, the devastation is
allowed to proceed at the present rate they may soon become
mere "deer forests", which are characterized by the intermittent presence of deer and the total absence of trees. Even
reafforestation does not altogether solve the problem, for it will
take hundreds of years to replace the old twisted Caledonian
pines, and the new trees might shoot up into the timberman's
ideal of a straight stem, which is, no doubt, excellent for the
sawmill, but not equally pleasing to the eye.

Anyway, the Giant Spectre of Glen More would do well to
cover his single eye with his bleeding hand, as the sights I have
seen there would hurt his sombre heart.

Along Strathspey silver lochs are scattered. . . .

As seen from the west, the aspect with which I am most
familiar, the Cairngorms do not present a striking outline. It
is not so much that of a comb or a saw-edge as rather of an
untidy quilt. The Braemar panorama, for which the Morrone
or Morven hill is renowned, is also somewhat uninspiring. The
hills are too near, with much intervening ground, and in consequence are flattened out. The knowledgeable people maintain that the Cairngorms look fine across the Moray Firth from
the heights on its northern side, and I have no reason to doubt
the truth of their words. But the views from Aviemore, Nethybridge, and the Grantown-Tomintoul road heights, though
nearer, disclose some of the more rugged features of the mountains, and proper lighting, snow or cloud will bring out the noble
structure of the higher peaks, throwing into relief the crag-bound
inlets of the glens and the cliff cauldrons of the corries.

On the whole, however, the beauties of these hills are un-
ostentatious, and will fully reveal themselves only to those who
go out in search of them. On a sunny summer day things seem
flat and commonplace, the lochs are just picture postcards, and
in approaching the "High Tops" one can count on a weary
grind in sweltering heat up the heather-grown slopes. It is
rather in stormy weather, spring and autumn, in the sweet fresh-

ness of the morning, or at Nature's sacred hour when the day-light is passing, that the Cairngorms have a message to impart.

There is endless fascination in watching the mountains reflect the changing moods of the weather. Quick clouds whirl and coil round the tops. Grey squalls beat on rock and scree. Piled cumuli will transform the barren slopes into a staircase to the fairy castle of luminous giants. Claret lights and russet gleams will chase over the dark blue faces, or a threatening grey canopy stoop low over the summits, indigo-black in impenetrable gloom. At night weird ashen clouds will soar up from the northern sky-line in the green sheen of the Aurora Borealis, like the vision of a shaggy Apocalypse.

And, of course, there is always the heather. . . .

2. *Their Story*

The Cairngorms are not a mountain range, but a residuary plateau; they are what a geologist calls "hills of circumdenu-dation" (or "monadnocks", if you prefer a more up-to-date term). The word is a bit of a Frankenstein monster, but it con-veys a wealth of meaning.

Sometime in the Silurian age, I do not know how many hun-dreds of millions of years ago, the part of the Earth's surface that is now Scotland was disturbed by powerful subterranean movements which ran through it in a series of titanic waves, approximately from the south-east to the north-west. They heaved up, broke and depressed masses of rock, which rose in huge billows of schist and gneiss to form a system of mountain ranges extending from the south-west to the north-east. For millions of years rain water streamed down their faces, carrying small fragments of rock into the swelling rivers below which gradually chiselled out deep valleys winding towards uncharted seas. Then a new disturbance occurred. The pressure from inside the bowels of the Earth broke through the weaknesses of the half-consolidated inner rock masses, and incandescent magma surged upwards lifting an enormous weight of land above, spread out mushroom-wise in the hollows it had opened for itself and set in hard granite "bosses", one of which now forms the Cairngorm Mountains.

Yet, an inconceivable succession of ages was required for this. What used to be dry land became sea and land again. Water, ice and wind ground down the old lofty mountains to a level table-land. Thousands of feet of rock were removed until the granite of the Cairngorm boss was laid bare. The streams and rivers continued to follow their old beds, delving deeper and deeper into the ground, till they sank into canyons: and one of these is the Lairig Ghru, another is Strathspey, and yet another Glen Dee. The mountains that might have rivalled the Himalayas had gone without a trace, but their valleys remained. Slowly more and more of the table-land was destroyed, "denuded", washed away, and as the land, relieved of the burden of rocks that had once rested upon it, redressed itself, the course of the streams quickened, their "corrasive" force increased. The table-land was broken up into segments and heights isolated by "circumdenudation".

Such a segment of the table-land was protected on the top by a layer of disintegrated rock which was removed but slowly by the action of wind and water and constantly renewed from below; but it yielded to the tooth of time on the sides and round the edges, assuming a rounded or a domelike shape. Originally its sides might be quite steep and even precipitous, but they would tend, unless other factors intervened, to get buried under the debris falling from above and thus lose their abruptness. Mountains of this type, known for their gentle outline as "subdued hills", and described by the Gaelic word *monadh* (pronounced monah), are frequent in the Cairngorms, which are nothing else but the "circumdenuded" remnants of the old plateau. Some of them are flat-topped, as for instance Beinn a'Bhùird (the Table Mountain), some have evolved into irregular domes; while their slopes and faces display various stages of the outlined development. As the weathering proceeds the hills lose more and more stuff round the crown, and are eventually whetted down into narrow crests and cones. In the West Highlands, where the rainfall is much heavier, this has already happened, but in the Cairngorms there are no real aretes or ridges, except Càrn a Mhaim, an outlier of Ben Macdhui, and the small spurs jutting out between the adjacent corries. There are, however, one or two minor conical peaks, of which Càrn Eilrig (2,435 ft.), an outpost of the Braeriach massif above Rothiemurchus, is the best example.

Our story leaves out one important stage. The Cairngorms were, so to speak, overwhelmed in the midst of their life's career by the Ice Age. For thousands of years a heavy sheet of ice shrouded the hills. Fed by copious snowfalls, it was steadily sliding down the slopes, grinding away the rocks that were still left standing above the level of the old table-land, but at the same time deepening and broadening the valleys, undercutting the flanking mountain-sides, and gouging out of them cliff-bound amphitheatrical depressions which are known in the Scottish Highlands under the name of " corries " (from the Gaelic *coire* or *choire*) and which form the most characteristic feature of the Cairngorms.

Millions and millions of tons of " comminuted " rock, gravel, sand and clay, small and big " erratic stones ", have been carried down from the mountains and spread along the valley-beds as " glacial drift ", accumulated in " kames ", " moraines " and " drumlins ", which still diversify the courses of burns and rivers, " pond back " the waters of the lochs left by the retreating glaciers and, grown with birch, pine, juniper and heather, violets and primroses, provide those fairy knolls on which the wee green-mantled folk alight from the eddies of the west wind for reasons and purposes best known to themselves.[1]

Thus, the High Tops of the Cairngorms are " subdued ". Most of their summits lack definite individuality, and are but the highest points of the fragmentary table-land. " It would be hardly an exaggeration to say "—writes Sir Archibald Geikie[2]— " that there is more level ground on the tops of these mountains than in the valleys below ", and, indeed, once you have reached the 3,500-foot contour or thereabouts in any of the three main

[1] D. A. MacKenzie: *Scottish Folk-Lore and Folk Life.*
[2] Archibald Geikie: *The Scenery of Scotland*, p. 216.

massifs of the Cairngorms, all their summits can be *done* without much climbing.   A vast undulating plateau of scree, chaotic boulders, grit and marshy ground connects Ben Macdhui with Cairn Gorm.   Moine Bhealaidh (the Moss of the Pass) is an expanse of high-level tundra east of the Lairig an Lui.   But the largest of all these plateaux is Am Moine Mhòr—the Great Moss between Cairn Toul and Braeriach on the one side and the Glen Feshie hills on the other.

The Great Moss is a realm of ice-polished granite humps, glittering sheets of water, burns twinkling away through the labyrinths of moss-grown boulders, grey or reddish scree, peat-hags, sedge, meagre grass, club mosses and the stunted growth of berries, enlivened here and there by a few Alpine flowers. Fauna, flora and climate alike are distinctly arctic, and one might well fancy oneself somewhere at the end of the world, on the very verge of the Pole.   Apart from Glen Feshie and the lower Glen Dee, the Cairngorms are quite uninhabited; the distances are great (the mountains cover about 150 square miles at the 2,000-feet contour) and it would be difficult to rival these heights for their sense of remoteness and isolation.   But on a calm, sunny day there is a great peace there; the air is like wine and you can lie down in the soft warm grass or moss, listen to the burns talking softly to one another across the corries and glens, and forget the troubles of the world.   Such days will come, and last for weeks on end.   More often than not, however, the weather is foul.   Atlantic gales range freely over the High Tops, and on a cold windy day mere survival there will tax your powers to the utmost.   In low mist orientation is difficult in featureless country which can offer but little help in path-finding where cairns have not been provided.

Wind is the dominant factor of the scene.   Everything bears its mark: the decaying boulder screes, the stretches of bare grit, the plants, the animals.   By rotating the gritty water which gathers in rock hollows the wind has worn out curious round bowls and basins, sometimes of considerable size, known as "pot-holes".   In winter the snow gets little chance of maintaining itself on the summits as a uniform cover and, save for occasional drifts, is soon blown down into the shelter of the corries and gullies, forming huge cornices on the lee side of the scarps. This state of things must have prevailed for thousands of years after the Ice Age, and to a great extent probably during and before it, contributing not a little to the development of the characteristic structure of the mountain-sides.

The snow lies deepest at the foot of the hills on their eastern and north-eastern sides (the westerly and south-westerly winds predominate) and, though there are in the Cairngorms no recognized " eternal snows ", at least one snow-field in the Rough Corrie of Braeriach is not known within living memory ever to have entirely disappeared. Many other " wraiths " without a claim to eternity endure well into the summer, and often survive until the following winter.

As the rocks weather higher aloft, loose fragments fall on the snow and slide down over it a good way out into the valley, where they are deposited in a crescent-shaped mound. At the same time the water flowing down the mountain-face works its way under the snow where it rapidly erodes the rock, weakened as it is by intermittent freezing in contact with the snow, and makes it recede at the head of the snowfield. Thus the gradient of the rock face increases, while its foot is kept free of the stones dislodged from above. When there were still glaciers in the Cairngorms and the daily and seasonal variation of temperature was much greater, this process occurred on a larger scale, but it continues in many places to this day.

The effect of this is that the snow-field, or the névé that used to feed the glacier of yore, has been eating deeper and deeper into the side of the hill, dredging in it an amphitheatrical hollow, bound on three sides by precipitous rock walls which tend to become steeper and higher with time until they have reached the very summit. Slice after slice of rock has been removed from the mountain by denudation, but, since the debris could not accumulate immediately at its foot, the face has preserved its virgin abruptness. In this way the corries have come into being and are able to perpetuate themselves. Only where the original snow-fields disappeared did the gradual accumulation of detritus begin, and the sides of the rocky cauldron were eventually over-run by the screes, showing only the top edge of the cliffs and sometimes not even as much. Such what one may call "dere-lict corries" are to be found in many parts of the Cairngorms, most often on their western faces. In some cases even the screes have become overgrown with vegetation, so that nothing but the shape is left to remind us of what they used to be. Many others, however, are still preserved in their pristine glory, and all the High Cairngorms have their arrays of corries with sheer mural precipices of anything up to 800 feet in height, which provide the wildest and most magnificent scenery of the massif.

As you walk along the levels and gentle declivities of the High Tops the ground suddenly breaks and a gaping chasm opens before you. Black and forbidding, the jagged granite falls down in pinnacled buttresses and polished slabs towards the desolation of the screes or a small tarn contained by the mound of debris at the bottom of the gigantic cauldron. Farther down, the deep gash of a glen follows the foaming waters.

Many of the Cairngorm glens are deep, with sides over-steepened by the vanished glaciers which have undercut the flanking mountains and carried away the protruding spurs, so that only triangular rock faces remain to show where they used to be. As a rule, the shaded side of the glen, which in most cases is also the lee side, where ice and snow have maintained themselves for a longer period, offers a higher and steeper scarp, while on the opposite side the cones of debris have already engulfed most of the crags. Another typical effect of the glacia-tion is that the bottom part of the mountain-side is often both more uniform and steeper than the pre-glacial slopes and rocks above. At the head of Glen Avon and Gleann Einich, which form excellent examples of such scenery, the terminal moraine of the retreating glacier has dammed the waters pouring down into the trough-like depression from the surrounding escarp-ments and produced large lakes which reflect the black rock ramparts and the grey rivers of scree rising in their gullies.

Apart from these two, there is a host of minor lochs and

Ben Macdhui, the highest Cairngorm
Loch Etchachan. ". . . the ground suddenly breaks and a gaping chasm opens before you" (p. 32)

" lochàns " (tarns) scattered through the corrie-land, on the flat heights, and at the foot of the hills.   The narrow valley of the Dee has little to show in the way of lochs, but the wide strath of the Spey is favoured with a cluster of beautiful sheets of water within the wooded area north-west of the Cairngorms.   Loch Morlich, with a sandy beach sheltering among the knobby pines of Glen More at the foot of Cairn Gorm and its rugged corries, is the largest of these, though it has a close rival in Loch Insh near Kincraig at the entrance to Glen Feshie, which affords, I think, even finer views.   Loch an Eilein is chiefly famous for the Comyns' castle on a small island in it, from which it takes its name (the Lake of the Island). Its surroundings have suffered much through war-time fellings, but some old Caledonian pines still mingle their sombre graces with the feminine lightness of birches on the rock-studded slopes of the westward hills.   Loch Alvie and Loch Pityoulish are two other large lakes of the Aviemore district.

Though the annual rainfall of the Cairngorms (30 ins.) cannot compete with the wetter regions of the west, and Speyside has a Scottish reputation for dryness, there is no shortage of water either on the hills or below them.   Springs and marshy ground will often be found near the very highest tops, of which the Wells of Dee on the plateau of Braeriach are the most famous example.   Thence the young river gathers part of its waters (the other part comes from the Pools of Dee in the Lairig Ghru), and hurls itself over the edge of the escarpment into the Rough Corrie, shooting down " the grisly cliffs that guard the infant rills of Highland Dee "—in the words of that oft-repeated quotation which makes you almost feel that in all " phantom fairness " Monte Rosa ought also to be " hanging *there* ".[1]   But it is not so and, albeit the cliffs are quite impressive, I have found the view somewhat disappointing.   The waterfall, high as it is,

---

[1] Just as there is hardly a description of the Cairngorms of any length that fails to invoke the " grisly cliffs ", so have, for some obscure reason, the writers of general mountaineering works found it incumbent upon them to tell you

> " How faintly flushed, how phantom fair
> Was Monte Rosa, hanging there."

C

Loch Morlich and the northern corries of Cairn Gorm
The head of Glen Avon offers a typical example of glacial erosion

seldom carries much water. Perhaps publicity has done it a disservice.

Being what they are, that is to say the " circumdenuded " fragments of a table-land, the hills have no clearly marked watersheds with mountain tops spaced pat at the heads of the main valleys, as in those well-behaved Austrian and Italian ranges to which one is referred by the geology manuals. As a rule no peak crowns a Cairngorm glen, and it ends in the sharp escarpment of a high plateau with summits rising round its edges. In most cases this is not due to the " beheading " of the valley by the neighbouring stream which has worked its way through the intervening ridge; the peak has simply never been there. There is, however, at least one good example of " river-capture ". The Feshie has insidiously broken through the hillsides towards the Eidart and " captured " its waters from the Geldie, a tributary of the Dee, into which the Eidart used to fall.

The trickles, rills, burns and torrents flow from the Cairngorms in all directions down the outward slopes of the plateau, forming what is known as a " radial drainage system ". Owing, however, to the fact that the granite boss out of which the mountains have been carved is tilted to the south-east, so that it attains its highest elevation in the north-west, their waters show a natural preference for the eastern rivers of the Dee and the Don. Thus, the Spey would have had less than its fair share, save for the already mentioned exploit of the Feshie and the similar trick of the Avon which, having found along the Builg Burn near Inchrory a band of soft limestone, has opened through it a channel towards the Spey and deserted the Don.

3. *Their Rocks and Stones*

As has been repeatedly intimated, the main massif of the Cairngorms is composed of granite, which weathers into characteristic pillow-shaped blocks and, disintegrating along its regular quadrangular joints, often falls apart into even slabs resembling the gigantic bricks of some Cyclopean building. As its power of resisting the elements varies considerably from place to place,

one finds isolated outcrops of rock scattered over the rounded
backs of the hills. These are the so-called "tors", known also
under the more homely name of "warts". Seen in the mist,
they can easily be mistaken for houses or "bothies", and are
for this reason sometimes referred to as "barns", of which the
Barns of Bynack are the most noteworthy.

Schistose rocks appear on the outskirts of the massif, but peter
out about Loch Morlich, just east of Glen Feshie and north of
the Dee, where the southern outliers of the Eastern Cairngorms
are composed largely of quartzite, gneiss and felspar porphyry.[1]
Limestone and conglomerate enter some of the glens on the
north-eastern fringe but do not penetrate deep into the hills.
The main peaks are all granite. The acid granitic soil is responsible for the general barrenness of the Cairngorms, though
heather flourishes on it in the lower reaches up to some 2,500
or 3,000 feet, depending on local conditions.

Cairngorm granite may differ in texture and composition, but
the typical variety is pink or brick-red owing to the colouring
of the felspar it contains, coarse-grained, with little or no black
mica. It weathers easily. The dark "black" granite, richer in
mica and of finer grain, which is much tougher, also occurs and
is responsible for many of the more rugged features of the hills.

The coarsely crystalline character of the Cairngorm granites
is the result of slow cooling in great depths under the pressure
of the overlying rock strata. Thanks to this they are rich in
quartz veins which contain large nests of mountain crystal.
Transparent "white" crystals are of little value, but when
tinged with iron oxide they assume an amber or honey, and
sometimes blue, colouring and are much used for ornaments
under the name of Cairngorm stones. Search for these used to
be one of the popular occupations of the "ghillies", shepherds
and cowherds[2] when off duty, and at one time regular mining
operations were carried on on Ben Avon. To-day, however, all

---

[1] T. F. Jamieson: "A Geologist on the Cairngorms," *The Cairngorm Club Journal,* Vol. V (Aberdeen, 1908).

[2] In the old days, before the coming of sheep, cattle and horses used to be grazed on the Cairngorm pastures, and summer "shielings" were scattered over the glens and corries. They have left behind a rich crop of place-names.

the more obvious veins have been badly overworked, and much luck and/or skill is needed for a really worthy find.

The Statistickal Account of Scotland published in 1795 speaks of " pellucid stones, of the nature of precious stones, equally transparent, beautiful in their colour, and some of them, particularly the emerald, as hard as any oriental jem of the same kind ". Emeralds are very rare. Amethysts are encountered more often, but beryls and topazes used to be fairly plentiful and some fine specimens of these stones have been found in the past.

Owing to the reddish felspar, granite screes, when not overgrown with lichens, often appear red, and the large areas of bare grit that cover the wind-swept high plateaux of the hills are usually distinctly pink. This is reflected in the frequency of " Red Corries ", " Spouts ", " Burns " and " Passes ", and was responsible for the old name of the mountains.

Cairn Gorm, or properly *A'Charn Guirm*, meaning Blue Mountain, originally designated only the hill which is still so called, whereas the whole massif was known as Monadh Ruadh, that is to say the Red Mountains, as the counterpart of the Monadh Liath, the Grey Mountains of schist and gneiss which stretch in craggy hummocks and dreary moorlands to the northwest of Strathspey. Only during the last century did the new name come into general use.

As to its appropriateness there need be little doubt, for, seen from afar, the hills at most times appear blue: dingy cobalt on a warm hazy day, intense purplish blue after a rainstorm, indigo at an evening hour. But autumn is the season when the complementary yellows and browns serve to bring out the blueness of the shadows and distant ranges.

Then there will come the days of peculiar clearness and windless calm with which the summer bids farewell to the Cairngorms. Or else a turmoil of cloud will break upon their brows, casting blaeberry shadows down the slopes, and the low sun will smite the sombre corries with shafts of yellow light which deepen their murk to a bright marine blue. Tender and subdued in the gradations of colour, stark and ominous in magnitude and form, the old hills roll and swell up the horizon in a mighty symphony caught in the silence of brooding time.

When sunset descends from the west the burnt-out glories of heather are relit in the brilliance of polished copper, among which sapling pines stand suffused with a rich green glow. The birches are golden lamps on the background of dark blue lochs. Each tree is etched finely in shadow and light, a distinct individual in the forests that rise tier upon tier towards the sun-imbued mountain-sides. Perched high at the skyline, the corries lie, pools of darkness, and still higher aloft the pinnacled rims of their buttresses stand out sharp against the pale jade of the waning eastern sky.

Then the world sinks into chilly blue depths. The mountains become featureless silhouettes, cut out of dark slate, and the primrose glare of the west spreads its spell over the sleeping waters. . . .

III

HEATHERS AND WEATHERS

South wind, heat and produce;
West wind, fish and milk;
North wind, cold and tempest;
East wind, drought and withering.

(A Gaelic saying)

1. *The Weathers*

THE usual Highland spring is not a clearly marked season; it seeps in imperceptibly. Slowly it grows warmer and warmer; blizzards alternate with spells of hot sunshine. A flower opens out here, a green leaf appears there, and the eternal youth of the world is renewed once more, the winter having tapered out into summer in a series of concentric waves that eventually flatten down and die out.

The first intimation of the approaching change comes in the midst of frost and snow. Grey cloud, edged with foxy russet, overspreads the sky. The air grows limp and muggy, and yet somewhat heady. The snow sags and loses its lustre. It will be drizzling, or the wind from the west will roll billows of cloud over the hills.

At such times the visibility assumes a sombre fullness. The nearer hills darken to damson, and now and then subdued dun lights blossom forth on their sides from some hidden source and fade out again. Farther away there is no structure in the mountain faces; they are like a grey-blue decoration supporting a greyer sky. Dense gloom gathers in the corries. Mist whispers on the boulders and is blown into dim shapes, grey and white, escaping over the snows. There is a suggestion of mystery about the scene: it would seem that at any moment strange animals might descend from the tops into the brown snow-streaked glens, or a band of ghostly warriors pass by on a secret foray.

I do not know whether the Highlander of to-day, used as he

39

is to his surroundings, falls under the spell of nature. But in
the old days, when there were no newspapers, no "pictures",
no wireless, and even the modest invention of the paraffin lamp
was absent from his murky home, he simply had no escape
from it, to which a rich legacy of haunting Gaelic tales bears
witness. . . .

A few days will pass and winter will reassert itself in black
and white. Yet the snows continue to recede into the shelter
of the gullies and windy heights, and by the end of March
even on the High Tops their cover is broken, only large fields
and "wraiths" surviving well into May or even June. The
pulse of mountain life quickens. Dark spots and patches appear
on the white winter coats of ptarmigan and blue hares. Birch
twigs turn a deeper wine, buds grow turgid with suppressed life.
Tortoiseshell butterflies emerge from their winter sleep, a mountain ringlet may flutter up among the heather, craneflies and
midges begin to stir, and a stray bumble-bee will buzz along in
search of early flowers.

The drama of the spring and of the Cairngorm climate
generally is dominated by the trial of strength between the
south-west and the north-east wind, the one a spirit of lax moist
warmth, the other of stern crystalline cold. The westerly and
south-westerly winds are the most frequent; they are associated
with a semi-permanent system of low atmospheric pressure in
in the region of Iceland; while both they and their opposites
follow the main lie of the land, with its south-west to north-east
valleys and mountain ranges.

The land-drained south wind may be penetratingly cold when
the southward hills are under snow, and a south-easterly gale,
fresh from the wide northern seas, will scatter snow squalls over
the High Tops. An east wind which comes often in the wake
of a passing cyclone is bitter on the Eastern Cairngorms, chilling
in the Lairig Ghru, where, compressed both vertically and
horizontally, the river of air gathers tremendous force, but ineffective on the western slopes. The north wind, on the other
hand, spends itself on the vast mountain-land of northern Scotland, and by the time it has reached the Cairngorms is relatively

mild and dry, often bringing clear fine days of warm sunshine, at least in the shelter, though the nights may be icy enough. A north-western wind may contribute a quota of rain or snow (a foot of the latter is equivalent to an inch of rainfall), until it shades into a west wind, the little brother of the great Sou'-Wester.

All these other winds are, however, but passing visitors. The age-long feud is between the North-East and the South-West. The two winds come early to grips with one another. It will blow persistently from the south-west and west during the early winter, just out of spite, to drift and thaw up the snow and sweep it down into the north-eastern corries, so that the Nor'-Easter should see his work ruined and be goaded into a rage. This will come as sure as day, and he will fling himself down on the hills in a paroxysm of anger and fretful energy to spread his Arctic dominion over top and glen, to drive the people, sheep and cattle into the shelter of roofs and walls, until, satisfied and exhausted, he abandons the world to moderate southern winds with pale veiled skies and "inverted" temperatures. Then it will be much warmer on the High Tops than in the glens below, where the cooled air will collect each night bringing the temperature lower and lower, as low perhaps as 50°F of frost. Slowly, very slowly, a new depression will form over the Atlantic and give the Sou'Wester a chance to break through, tear to shreds the high *cirro-velum*, mix up the steady layers of cold and warm air, and bring relief to man and beast. This will be the Sou'Wester's first attempt at spring, but it will not last.

Seeing his old enemy taking heart, the Nor'Easter will be stirred to new efforts, and the tussle will go on. It will be summer-warm in mid-March and early April; then a spell of bitter north-easterly weather will cap the hills with snow. This is the period of the so-called "Lambing Storms" which—so wisely has Nature contrived—seem to assist the ewes in delivery, or so an earnest crofter insisted. A warm sunny spell will follow in May but, if the usual writ runs, the end of the month will be cold and heavy snows will revisit the Cairngorms. This time they are no earthly good to anybody, not even to a skier, just a plain "darned" nuisance. It is these late May snows and frosts, coupled with an excess of Lambing Storms, that are apt to spoil the local crops, to singe the young leaves, and nip the promise of fruit and berry in the bud.

From a mountaineer's standpoint these two months and the following month of June are probably the best of the year, for their average rainfall is only about one third of the annual average. The precipitation being generally higher in the hills than on lower ground, its reduction to one third makes a proportionately greater difference.[1] Sunny weather prevails, the air is dry, so that climbing, even with a heavy pack, is considerably less like hard work than at other times.

2. *The Spring on the Tops*

It was hot on March 31st, 1946. Even at nine in the morning as, shouldering my skis, I set out for the stalkers' path up Càrn Bàn Mòr and the Ciste Mearaid snow-field, there was in the air a distinct suggestion of heat. A light haze was veiling the thin blue of the sky. Curlews, forgetful that the Gael had christened them "birds of sorrow", were skirling merrily, and the larks soared above the moors to ring in the coming spring.

At the lower reach of the snow, where I paused to put on my skis, a sturdy brown moth caterpillar was negotiating the odd fifty yards of the white finger which the Ciste Mearaid "wraith" pointed at Auchlean. The sun struck the snow from above at a small angle, and it was still quite firm, with an icy crust on it, but grew rapidly softer on my way up the gully. Amid the white expanse a couple of ptarmigan were sitting on an "island" of clear ground, grown with crowberry and heather. They took little notice of me until I was not more than five yards away, when they got up reluctantly and pushed down the steep snow, sliding on their fluffy breasts. They thus "glissaded" a good way before taking wing and floating over to the undisturbed side of the gully. The glissade had given them the necessary start and they hardly moved their wings in flight.

[1] Gilbert Thomson, F.R.Met.S.: "The Meteorology of the Scottish Mountains," *The Scottish Mountaineering Club Guide-Book*. (Edinburgh, 1933.)

It was calm on the Great Moss, the air just stirring at the edge
of the snows, which were much more patchy than was usual at
this time of the year, so that I had to choose my way carefully
to avoid uncovered ribs. Mossy cyphel and club mosses were
preening themselves in the warm sun, and even the golden-moss,
whose most common appearance is that of grey suds, had about
it a greenness that distantly smacked of gold. Invisible golden
plover were voicing the solitude of the melting snows to the pale
sky, and some small birds which might have been snow
buntings darted along the obtuse hill crest in the direction of
Meall Dubhag.

Having crossed the snowless top of Càrn Bàn Mòr, I started
down at a fairly good speed towards Loch nan Cnapan; but the
sunshine was strong and the surface of the snow was getting
sodden, which was highly unwelcome, especially in view of the
fact that *Klister*[1] still remained unobtainable after the war.
Ptarmigan, all paired off, the cocks speckled with black, but
the hens white, fluttered up at my passage like huge butterflies.

The burns were rumbling ominously underfoot, with here
and there a dark " pocket " gaping open or a miniature crevasse
marking the danger zone. On the way back, the snow actually
collapsed under my weight, and I landed in a narrow " chest "
of moss-covered rock, some three yards deep, with swirling water
rushing furiously underneath. Not without difficulty did I
lever myself up on my arms, and my hands were shaking when
I had re-emerged on the surface.

Pools of blue water lay in the snow hollows among the rocky
knolls beyond the loch, which was partly free from ice: the
type of scenery that naturally conjured up the vision of a white
bear chewing a small porpoise.

Towards noon it became scorchingly hot, especially above the
snow, and one could easily have undressed to the skin, save for
the fear of the after-effects. The long gully of Allt Luineag was
like a white furnace. Tuareg-fashion, I wrapped thicknesses of
white cloth round my head, protecting my half-naked body with
a hooded camouflage wind-jacket of white parachute silk. I

---

[1] A Norwegian ski-ing wax used on wet spring-snow.

shut my eyes and plodded on, counting to a hundred, in the hope that, on reopening them when the hundred was over, I should find myself visibly nearer the Angel's Peak—so named by a godly mountaineer "in order to keep the devil in his place", for native fancy has dedicated the bastion of ice-polished rock on the opposite side of Cairn Toul to the latter personality. . . . However, my eyes had to be shut and reopened many times before, having slaked the agonies of thirst with a few sips of cold tea, I eventually stood on the Angel's Peak in a state of utter exhaustion.

There, a small black pug, a typical member of the Cairngorm moth fauna, came drifting up in a weak ascending current of air above the snow-packed corries. A plover called from Cairn Toul. The squatty mass of Ben Macdhui was just visible in the steely haze; the outlines of the more distant hills had entirely dissolved, leaving their snows as though suspended in mid-air. Northward An Garbh Choire Mòr (The Great Rough Corrie) spread out magnificently before me, its black rock buttresses immersed in nearly perpendicular snows which rose towards the wavy frieze of overhanging cornices. The waterfall of the Dee was plastered over with snow, only a small oval "hatch" disclosing the pillar of darkly gleaming water. Intermittently stones were falling with the sound of rifle shots: the work of corrie-building was still in progress.

3. *The "Heathers"*

The 1946 April followed with the usual suns and showers. The Nor'Easter triumphed once more and clad the hills half-way down with a thick mantle of snow, burying under it the budding plants.

Breaking out of the Highland norm, the spring came with a catch in the air and a swish of greenery, fluted in by the silvery notes of the thrush and the tinkling chirping of the chaffinch. In a few days the birches were shimmering in the green gold of small leaf that seemed to ring in the scale of light like glass carillons. Wood anemones scattered their tender whiteness over the braes stooping to the swirling amber of the burns, and primroses came out in great profusion in the woods and on the dun sides of the lower hills. Bearberries burst into bloom, but in vain did I search among the pines of Rothiemurchus for the musk-scented one-flowered wintergreen which is said to have been common there before collectors had applied themselves to it.

A word about the wood anemone: this shy, graceful flower is the "recognized bed" of the fairy who sleeps between its folded petals (only very small fairies are eligible).[1]

The second week of May ushered in another period of windless and cloudless sky. On the 9th, as I was making my way up Sròn na Lairig, there was still a lot of snow on the summits and in the northern corries. The burns were full, but the ground was parched and avid for rain. Little colour enlivened the brown moors. Emerging suddenly from a gully, I came upon a company of hornless stags (only one of them had a little stump of an antler left) in a very poor and bedraggled condition. They veered wearily away, tossing their heads as they ran as if anxious not to forget how to carry their antlers when these had grown once more. Ubiquitous meadow pipits were on the wing, and the snow-bellied wheatears flitted up the *allt*, almost skimming the ground. The heather was swarming with small beetles of lustrous green, and there was an abundance of tortoiseshells. Occasionally, a heavy female northern eggar, early this year, for they are not due till June, or perhaps an emperor moth would zigzag in unsteady flight. On the summit of Braeriach the air was hot and motionless, somewhat steamy with the melting snow, and the minutest of moths, mere specks of dust, were working hard with their tiny wings without, however, making much headway, thus serving further to emphasize the complete absence of wind.

Lochan Uaine and Loch Coire an Lochain (the corrie is called after the loch and the loch—after the corrie!) were both unfrozen, though a miniature iceberg was beached on the latter's outward shore.

When "contouring" Corrie Beanaidh along the scarp of Sròn

---

[1] Francis Drake-Carnell: *It's an Old Scottish Custom* (London, 1939), p. 239.

na Lairig I came across carpets of purple saxifrage in livid bud
on the point of opening, but as yet without a single fully blown
flower. Cushions of moss campion were a pale glaucous green,
and the alpine lady's mantle was spurting out gracefully from
the gravel in clusters of tiny white-edged leaves.

The arctic plants of the High Tops, which, together with the
blue hare, have stayed behind after the passing of the Ice Age,
exist on hard terms of survival.[1] The inclement climate heaps
on them excesses of all kinds: drought, frost, deluges of rain,
deep snow, or bitter gales scouring the ground with sharp grit.
They manage as best they can. Most are perennials, just in case
one season would not be enough to complete their life cycle.
Tall stalks would not stand a chance, so they grow low, clinging
hard to the ground to withstand the wind, and develop long,
powerful tap-roots which allow them to exploit to the full what
little the stony soil, alternately chilled and overheated, has to
offer. The cushionlike growths of moss campion, purple saxifrage, mossy cyphel, crowberry and heather at its upper limit,
with minute stalks and thick hard-coated leaves crowded close
together, affect a kind of " collective security " where each shoot
protects its neighbour against the wind, frost or dessication.
The " woody " plants, which are in fact nothing else but minute
trees, like the carmine-flowered creeping azalea, the dwarf
willows, dwarf juniper, cloud-berry and the high-growing plants
of bilberry, all common on the Cairngorms, have adopted the
" espalier " device: their short stems and strongly ramified
branches sit embedded in the small scree and gravel, only the
leaves, flowers and fruits showing above the surface.

The fertilization of the flowers is a difficult problem, and had
they to rely on insects alone many plants might fail in the vital
task of perpetuating their kind. For this reason vegetative
reproduction is frequent among the alpine and arctic plants.
But the common ruse resorted to by these hardy specks of life,
which makes them particularly endearing to the eye, is the size

[1] James W. H. Trail, M.A., M.D., F.R.S., F.L.S.: "The Flowering Plants and
Fern-Allies of the Cairngorms," *The Cairngorm Club Journal*, Vol. I (Aberdeen,
1896). Also—F. O. Bower, D.Sc., LL.D., F.R.S., "Scottish Mountain Botany,"
The Scottish Mountaineering Club Guide-Book (Edinburgh, 1933).

and bright colouring of their flowers, by which they seek to entice the insect visitors. In this also the " collective-security " cushions are helpful, since for all its size and red-purple colour an isolated flowerlet of purple saxifrage or a pink star of moss campion would be hopelessly lost in the grey Saharas of the High Tops. When, however, there are hundreds of them within a square foot or so they make a splendid splash of colour which almost takes your breath away as it suddenly blazes out on a bare hillside or a rocky ledge.

The usual flowering season is from July to September. But the purple saxifrage is an early flowerer and in the lower reaches of its zone, that is to say about 2,200 feet, will be in full bloom, weather permitting, as early as the second half of April. The higher-growing plants follow in May, and just as their last flowers peter out at the 3,000-foot contour a pink flame sweeps the *eau-de-nil* cushions of moss campion, ascending from 2,500 feet to the highest tops. According to Seton Gordon, white specimens also occur in the Cairngorms, though very rarely, and I have never seen one. The azalea will be out in July, tinging many gritty and gravelly mountain-backs with its wine-red glow.

Apart from the arctic purple saxifrage, several other species of the breed are found in various districts of the mountains, the starry saxifrage being the most plentiful of all. The rosettes of its bluish leaves are scattered in moist places all the way from the 1,000-foot contour to the High Tops. Rose-root appears sporadically on the broken cliff ledges, which are also graced by the ubiquitous lace of the alpine lady's mantle. The white dryas spreads out here and there its glossy indented leaves, adorned in June with handsome eight-petalled white flowers, on the middle heights and outliers of the Cairngorms. The globe-flower, *Trollius*, that king of the buttercups, out in June and July, grows on the high moors, among others on Braeriach, up to 3,000 feet or so; and the purple foxglove ascends high up the glens and corries, maintaining itself in flower from the end of June to the beginning of September.

Of the " berries " first comes the orange-fruited cloudberry, the raspberry's near relation. It is quite common in " cloudy places " on the high-level tundras of the hills, has a distinctive taste, and produces a rare jam to which I am very partial. Blaeberry, whortleberry or bilberry, which are all more or less one and the same thing, grows abundantly at all levels as high up as the Wells of Dee, though it seldom produces any berries at that height, and some botanists and botanizers maintain that it has got there by unfair means, the seeds having been conveyed by birds. I, however, have seen, plucked and eaten fully ripe, albeit somewhat tasteless, blaeberries at 3,750 feet on Braeriach, and am inclined to think that the poor plant has been unjustly maligned. True it is, however, that the leaves are usually much more in evidence than the berries, which we need not necessarily regret, as the former have a very winning way of turning bright scarlet after the first autumn frosts.

Now you would not readily mistake a bear for a cow, but the same clarity of distinction does not apply to bearberries and cowberries, which are so much alike that they are both popularly miscalled " cranberries ". Both plants have very similar leaves, very similar fruit, and almost indistinguishable flowers, looking like minute waxen lampshades, and both mingle with the heather up to an odd 2,000 feet above sea-level. Here, however, the resemblance ends, for the bearberry, most appropriately, outstrips its bovine relative by some 200 feet in climbing power; its leaves are smaller and darker, and the reddish stems and shoots trail on the ground like the spokes of a bicycle wheel. The cowberry, on the other hand, grows upright, singly, and flowers about a month later than the bearberry, which already in May hangs down grey boulders its graceful garlands of small pinkish bloom.

Cranberry proper is a marsh plant, rare in the Cairngorms, though it apparently occurs in Coire Etchachan.[1]

Crowberry is abundant in the " middle Arctic zone " and shows a disconcerting resemblance to the cross-leaved heath at the lower end of its spread and the creeping azalea at its topmost range, which is 3,500 feet for both plants. Even its pinkish

[1] James W. H. Trail: " The Flowering Plants and Fern-Allies of the Cairngorms," *The Cairngorm Club Journal*, Vol. I.

*Loch Insh and Creag Mhigeachaidh on a dull wintry day
Ciste Mearaid, the last of the snow*

flowers simulate those of the azalea, but unlike the latter it bears black watery fruits which recall the buttons common towards the end of the last and the opening decades of the present century on feminine and infantile footwear.

Cross-leaved heath is the first of the three heathers to show colour when its pink " ant's eggs " appear along the burns and on marshy ground. It is not very showy, and does not much exceed the altitude of 2,000 feet. The bell heather comes out about a fortnight later when the first thunderstorms cool down the air after the brief heat-wave with afternoon cumuli in the blue sky. It climbs about 500 feet higher than the cross-leaved heath and grows more abundantly among rocks and boulders, especially where the deluge of ling has been temporarily checked by the spring burnings. Its flowers shade from deep beetroot to pale claret, and often edge the slopes with a thin crimson glow as sunshine breaks through the retiring rain in dispersed silvery radiance.

The common ling or cat heather is the main feature of the country. The moors are claret-brown with it in late autumn, grey-brown in winter, green-brown in spring and the first half of the summer. Officially it does not overstep the 3,000-foot contour, but you will find isolated cushions of its dwarfed growth sheltering in the gravel hollows at much greater heights. The flowering season of the ling is short, from the end of July to the beginning of September, but while it lasts the hills are ablaze with purple.

An isolated starlet of ling is pink with just a touch of lilac; so, too, does a distant heather-slope appear pink in diffused light. Yet the effect of massed ling in bloom is often intensely purple, particularly in juxtaposition to green grass, junipers or trees or on an evening with an overcast sky. In the first case, the complementary greenness serves to bring out the purple element in the colour of the heather flowers; in the second, the apparent change of tint is due to what is known in physics as the Purkinje effect. In ordinary strong light the human eye's greatest sensitivity falls within the yellow part of the spectrum; but as the intensity of the lighting decreases it shifts towards the purple. In the evening you may cull a sprig of ling or a scabious

D

It's spring and the gean is in bloom. Loch an Eilein
On a crisp December morning. " Whitewell " and Braeriach

which appears exceptionally bright and find next day that it has mysteriously faded during the night.

This may, of course, be a trick the fairies play on credulous humans, but I strongly suspect that the explanation proffered above gives the true cause of the transformation. On the other hand, there is *no* denying that the existence of white-flowered ling is due to their agency, for whenever a fairy steps on a heather twig all its flowers are instantly bleached, which makes them very lucky. Occasionally a fairy will also tread on bell heather, but cross-leaved heath seems to be studiously avoided.

June is one of the dry months, and the first part of July perpetuates as a rule the tendency to fine weather. As, however, the " season " develops and visitors begin to throng in, grey clouds envelop the hills and cold mists spread over the pewter lochs. The 12th of August is, as is well known, a great day for the " sportsmen " who delight in slaughtering wild living things. Though appreciative of the fact that it discharges in Nature's economy the function of the exterminated wolf-packs, I do not hold with this kind of amusement and prefer the stillness of the hills undisturbed by shooting. The weather seems to take a similar view, for it is usually pouring with rain on the 12th . . .

And after the hot spell when the sun lies scorching on the nape of your neck and quivering eddies raise dust on the parched roads, you will feel the beauty of a grey day.

The thin " Scotch mist " has filled the air, like a diaphanous veil hung down from the low clouds onto the hushed world. Green, secretive dusk has crowded up into the forests, drowsing in restful communion with Earth the ageless goddess, from whom all things fleet of limb and green of leaf take life. Silence is great among the rough columns of pine. Star moss is soft and dark. The heavy dew has diluted the verdure of grass to a pale silken brightness. The hand of autumn has already touched the bracken with gold, and the ling is in full bloom. The eye can revel in its amethystine glow for mile after mile of hollow and brae, until it fades out, pink in the distance, at the grey edge where the tops and the clouds meet.

Sketched lightly in pastel shades, the hills are a glimpse of life's forfeited promise, within perpendicular gates of white mists slowly travelling by, the hills of a dream or the hills of a saga, their feet in the heather, their brows in the sky.

Boletus edulis.

4. *"To Dress a Dish of Fungee"*

This is the time when detachments of fungi, including many edible kinds, come out in the woods. First the apricot-scented, fluted chanterelles pearl out of the ground, like the tips of tiny fingers along the ditches and paths, to grow up into pale-orange wavy funnels, three to four inches across. The blusher, a "warted" agaric with a cocoa-coloured cap and tender white flesh which turns dull brick or corned-beef red when bruised or attacked by insects, will follow in a week or two. It is common in the Cairngorm forests.

Both these fungi are excellent food.

At the end of August or earlier, they are succeeded by the edible bolet (*Boletus edulis*), which can best be described as a penny bun sitting on a small milk bottle, the latter covered at the base with a brown hair-net. When fully matured it often attains the impressive diameter of nearly a foot. It has firm, white, non-colouring flesh with a nutty flavour. Its somewhat smaller kinsman—the rough-legged bolet (*Boletus scaber*), easily distinguishable by its grey-brown suède or terra-cotta caps poised on longish black-streaked " legs "—belongs to the most typical local species and will be found at considerable heights (I have encountered some specimens well above the 3,000-foot contour). The rough-legged bolet is also edible.

Finally, in September and October, the pinewoods and the heaths rich in pine humus are visited by " fleets " of orange lactaries. This fungus, with its orange " milk " and flesh turning, when bruised, a venomous-looking verdigris, may be rather frightening to a novice but it is quite harmless and fully deserving of its Latin name, *Lactarius deliciosus*. In fact, I hold it to be much more palatable than the " real " mushroom (*recte* : meadow agaric). Small lactaries resemble grey-brown overcoat buttons but sometimes, when very small, are almost turquoise blue. They have a dimple in the centre and usually display a system of brownish or greenish concentric rings. In older specimens the fleshy orange, which is the colouring of the stem and gills, spreads also to the cap.

I have found these " toadstools " a useful addition to my Cairngorm diet; but only seldom could I persuade any of my hosts to taste them, for they held that such things were not " meant to be eaten ", and anticipated my speedy demise.

It is indeed noteworthy that while all the fungi listed above, as well as many other species, are commonly known and eaten throughout Europe, they are out of favour with the British public, except for a few travellers, eccentrics and mycologists. I venture to surmise that the knowledge and practice of fungus-eating has gone the way of the old forest-lore after village culture was laid low by the twin giants of Puritanism and the Industrial Revolution. So far I have been unable to find any definite evidence to support this view, but M. C. Cooke in his admirable book, *British Edible Fungi* (London, 1891), quotes an early seventeenth-century recipe, which you may try out if you feel so disposed:

" To Dress a Dish of Fungee
   " Take them fresh gathered and put them between two dishes, and sett them on a Chaifing Dish of Coles, and there lett them Stewe, but put nothing to them in the first Stewing for they will Yeald Liquor enough of them selves, and When all the Water is stewed out of them, power the Liquor Cleane from them and put a good quantitye of Sallitt Oyle unto them and Stewe them therein. Wringe in the joyce of one or two Leamons, or else putt in some Vinniger and put in a little Nuttmegg and two or three Blades of Mace.
   " If your Lord or Lady Loves not Oyle, Stewe them with a Little Sweete Butter and a little White Wine."

Such was ye olde way. It is not clear from the description with what kind of " fungee " the lords and ladies of those days used to regale themselves, but the odds are strong that these were not " mushrooms ". I simply fry them with salt, pepper and " a little Sweete Butter " if available (I " Love not Oyle ") for about half an hour.

The coming and going of fungi, as well as of the flowers of the green plants, is much affected by weather. Cold or drought may retard their appearance; warm, moist days will extend their season; and if the autumn brings, as it often does, a long spell of fine weather they may have a second " fling ".

5. The Autumn

August and the opening weeks of September are among the worst times of the year for weather, wet and windy, with midges and " clegs " abroad in millions; but the close of September and October are often marked by days of crystal calm and wide horizons. The nights are already chilly and hoarfrost will skim the summits at dawn, melting into glittering dew in the morning sunshine. It will often be hot at noon, but never oppressively so, and the mountain shadows are already cool with the promise of winter.

In fact, September and October are excellent for mountaineering. The days are still long, and the " gloaming " evening skies provide several hours of pleasant twilight. The only fly in the ointment is that it is the mating season of the deer and the stalking season of the men who come to shoot them, and the latter feel strongly about their prospective quarry being frightened away from the plotted position by the passage of a mountaineer; while bullets go a long way and are apt to be blind in the choice of accidental targets at their extreme range. However, there is no law of trespass in Scotland, nobody can or dare object if you use the right-of-way paths and the stalking takes place in the glens and corries, not on the summits of the hills.

The 1945 autumn was exceptionally fine.

In October the birches near the burns had turned to dark bronze stained with patina, but far from the water they were still green, even high up the glens, and only lightly tipped with gold. Not for a long time had the pines been so richly green-blue, nor had there been so many " lamp-shade " flowers on the cowberries of Rothiemurchus. On the Great Moss bog asphodel was still showing its golden stars, and yellow saxifrage was in bloom along the Feshie streams. On the rocks of the Lurcher's Crag, dropping sheer into the deep gap of the Lairig Ghru, threads of gossamer were glittering in the bright sunlight of the Indian Summer, and here and there the creeping azalea, disguised amid the crowberry growth, had been tempted to unfold its carmine-tinted petals. Bell heather was also having a second lot of flowers.

On the 17th it was so warm on Braeriach that I felt quite comfortable in a short-sleeved Aertex shirt. The Dee gathered the pale blue of the limpid sky into pools of dark cobalt and carried it away into the precipice of the Rough Corrie. Cairn Toul and Sgòr an Lochain Uaine (Angel's Peak) were towering in cool shadows, only a slender beam of the sun lighting the edge of the Green Lochan on its lofty perch. Below, Glen Dee, deep and dark, was winding past the cliffs of the Devil's Point.

Fast on the wing, a golden plover cut through the air like a whip and plunged into the corrie . . .

In the west, beyond the dark mirror of Loch Einich, the Sgorans reared up in the 1,800 feet of rock, grass and scree. Their concave corries caught the roaring of the stags into their acoustic foci, and it welled up, booming like enormous bassoons.

Small herds of deer, ten to twenty hinds, an old stag, and some "staggies" in attendance, were scattered over the Great Moss, in the corries and over the lower mountain-sides. On the tops only solitary "outsiders" would sneak through or, occasionally, a big stag would climb up from below on the look-out for approaching rivals.

Stags do not often fight. They prefer to roar away at one another from some rock or knoll a few hundred yards apart, working themselves into a paroxysm of stertorous leonine coughing, which sounds quite intimidating, but only very seldom do they cross the intervening distance to test their mettle and their horns at close quarters. At your approach they will move away reluctantly, then halt, discharge at you a few angry coughs, and again withdraw, roaring furiously from a safe distance, so deep is the fear of man and his portable thunder implanted in their hearts; which is perhaps just as well for a solitary rambler.

I have read of cases where a stag plucked up sufficient courage to attack people, though I have never heard a first-hand account of such a happening. It is the sort of thing that happens somewhere to somebody at an indefinite date. Nevertheless, the stag remains a potentially dangerous animal and the gamekeeper's assurance to the contrary must be taken with a pinch of gunpowder—which he always has about him, ready for use.

Wild creatures observe a kind of etiquette, the practice of which it may be useful to acquire, and do not worry one another without a good reason.

The next day awoke, unruffled by breeze, on a pink morning with thick, silvery dew. Creeping willows showed yellow in the matted moss of Càrn Bàn. Below the summit of Sgòr Gaoith two coveys of plover whirled up at my approach and "peeled off" downslope, steering with their pointed wings.

The English equivalent of Sgòr Gaoith would be Windy Point, and windy enough it is as a rule. I remember how once I was nearly blown off its rocky promontory into the gaping chasm below, where white mists were boiling over the soot-black loch. This time, however, there was hardly a puff of wind there, and I sat for two hours in the warm sunshine doing a pen sketch, lightly dressed, without feeling in the least cold.

When, about four, I reached Geal Chàrn, the westering sun had spread above valley and hill a wake of silver dust, in which the streams and pools of water were glittering like fragments of a gigantic mirror shattered by the angry hand of some forgotten goddess of the Druidic past. Mountain ranges paled away in the distance, blue shadows in the blue sky, until they were lost in it. Westward, golden-moss, the colour of slag, shimmered like hoarfrost and, tipped with the first dew of the evening, the scarlet leaves of blaeberry shone like rubies lavishly scattered along the ridge. From Allt Ruadh came the faint aroma of resin, mingled with the acrid scent of sun-heated herbs.

The ticking of my watch was the loudest sound. Then a fly buzzed, a stag's call rolled down from the Black Sgoran, and from somewhere aloft descended the chirping of little birds heading south on their migration flight. But, strain my eyes as I might, I could see nothing. My way led down the steep ruins of rocks, grown over with mats of crowberry and golden-moss, from which white ptarmigan rose on whispering wings and glided in an oblique curve down into the cool shade of the lowly pass. The sun was setting red when I reached the edge of Creag Mhigeachaidh (Craig Vigayhay). Loch Insh lay below, a dull silver tray among the curly blond heads of the birches.

The scramble down the screes through scraggy pine thickets was laborious and slow, and dusk was gathering quickly in the broad glen. When there, the golden ghosts of a birchwood closed round me, trying to confide to me a lisping tale of joy or sorrow, the key to whose meaning I had lost with childhood.

The road wound pale over the darkening moor and the rabbits, frightened by my footfalls, scampered off, their white flags twinkling in the heather.

6. *The Coming of the Snow*

Soon after, the weather broke over the hills, though it remained fair over Strathspey. The persistent south-easterly winds blew a fleece of cloud along the High Tops, staging a minor *föhn* effect on the north-western rim of the Cairngorms. Cataracts of cloud rushed down the north faces of Braeriach and Cairn Gorm, dissolving in sleet and rain, and disappearing almost without a trace. I had to face a furious onslaught of wind in the Lairig Ghru, and was drenched and numb with cold in a matter of minutes at the Pools of Dee. The icy blast drove me back from Sròn na Lairig, but it was dead calm and the sun was bright and hot on the top of Càrn Eilrig, only two miles to the north-west. The northern corries of Braeriach were already grey with the first snow.

Quite heavy falls of snow occur at the close of October and in November, and sometimes the country will be white all the way to the sea. One may even get a day or two of ski-ing on the tops. This is, however, but a flash in the pan, and a few days later it will be " black earth " once more.

Old Yule is more often black than white. November and December are cold, humid, dark and gloomy. They make one weak of body and torpid of mind. Soon after noon a leaden hue filters into the ebbing daylight. Grey western mists trail ruefully over the faded tapestries of steaming mountain-sides.

Yet the lights of Nature are still burning. The tawny bracken is bright against the bluish screes, and in the dank forest you may chance upon a small cushion of moss of the greenest green that ever was. There, among the fawn-coloured thickets of rushes and ferns by the stream, watchful eyes will follow your steps. The reddish coats of deer match to perfection the autumn woodland tints, and would remain unnoticed save for the stamping of agile hoofs in the hasty rush of escape. Wild cats and foxes may be aprowl, but they are in no hurry to be seen, and only the sharp smell or tracks in the thin melting snow will reveal their presence.

The hips are red on the burnet and even some of the leaves are green. Note the delicate poise of the twigs and the pattern of thorns on the umber background of withered grass! I would pass my hand lovingly over the rich greenness of the heart-fern tongues, let it linger on the edges of frosted rocks, high above the forest, for everything seems so much more precious for its scarcity in the bleak sadness of the lowering sky and the chilly dampness of November air.

An icy breeze will hurry small breakers over the seemingly endless lochs under the shivering mantle of fog. For a while the hidden sun will disclose itself by the copper lights and steel-blue shadows among the rolling clouds, then slowly die out in the deeper gloom of night.

Winter seldom takes secure possession of the Cairngorms before the New Year, and the Sou'Wester reigns supreme until the second half of February. Then the contest of the winds abates and the High Tops have a thick cover of snow; but the lower, heather-grown slopes are barely negotiable on ski. The snow precipitation varies greatly from year to year, but in most winters there is at least a week or two of really heavy snow and frosty sunshine some time in February or March.

Then you may test the somewhat paradoxical truth that "it is warmer when it is colder"; for the specific heat, and therefore the cooling power, of water vapour is far greater than that of dry air, and the colder the air the lower its saturation point with steam, so that with a sharp frost the air is much drier and does not chill you to the same extent as the warmer but damper atmosphere. Most houses are badly equipped for the winter. They have very inadequate and uneconomic heating systems, utterly unsuitable for the local conditions, and are addicted to periodical pipe-bursts, for which there is no excuse but the incompetence of the plumbers. This tends to make the winter a bit trying. Once out of doors, however, you are free from the rigours of house life, and can enjoy the blue shadows and the sparkling snows without discomfort. When ski-ing you are more likely to feel too warm than too cold, but the climate is somewhat treacherous and I would not advise you to yield to the temptation of dressing lightly. On the tops, at mist-lifting time, that is to say about 1 or 2 p.m., G.M.T., a sharp wind will often spring up in midwinter, as it were, out of nowhere, and ski-ing against it may be a very exhausting affair. For this reason it is prudent to avoid being caught napping in the middle of the wide, open plateaux of the Cairngorms by the early afternoon, however fair the morning may bid.

The history of the Cairngorms gives many instances of people perishing, overtaken by a sudden snow-storm; for example, the three tailors commemorated by the Clach nan Taillear[1] in the Lairig Ghru. Yet a competent mountaineer will be able to deal with such situations without mishap, or at least have the sense to avoid getting into them.

[1] The Tailors' Stone. See Seton Gordon, *The Cairngorm Hills of Scotland* (London, 1925).

Bearberry

IV

THE CONTORTED PLATEAU

1. *The Western Cairngorms*

THE Western Cairngorms, contained between Strathspey in the north and the Geldie in the south, and between the Feshie in the west and the Lairig Ghru in the east, illustrate better than any other part of these mountains the truth that they have been eroded out of an ancient high-level plain or " peneplain ", that is to say near-plain, by the combined action of running water, flowing ice and blowing air. In fact, the Western Cairngorms still are but a contorted plateau, based massively on the 40-square-mile expanse of the Great Moss (Am Moine Mhòr), which does not sink much below the 3,000-foot contour and whose upraised rims provide the main summits. This plateau has been badly chivvied and mauled by the glens and corries, especially in the north and east, and sculptured by the streams into contortions and convolutions which have given it the present shape of a squat octopus. The outlying edges, built of schistose rocks, have yielded more rapidly to the weathering than the main granite mass and produced a system of minor *cairns* or *carns*, which name designates heap-like hills, and *creags* (crags) where one side of the *cairns* has been shaved off by a glacier. But the core of the system and the peaks along the defile of the Lairig Ghru are composed of granite. It is on granite that the vast Moine Mhòr now sits, and it is from this rock that the corrie-building process described in Chapter II has carved out the main tops, with their cliff ramparts, boulder-screes, spurs, ribs, shoulders, faces, and other parts of mountain anatomy.

Braeriach (4,248 ft.) and Cairn Toul (4,241 ft.), the twin giants of the group, rise in its most corrie-worn north-east corner, towering some 2,500 feet above Glen Dee and the Lairig path. The highest point of the Lairig Pass itself is only 2,773 feet above sea-level and the summit plateaux on both its sides are less than a mile apart, so that it forms a deep cleft between Braeriach in the west and Ben Macdhui in the east.

Incidentally, lest you should fondly imagine that the mere memorizing of the visual appearance of these names admits you within the precincts of Gaelic "mythology", I would like to add that Braeriach (pronounced Brayreeyakh), which means "The Speckled Hill", is only a corruption of the original Gaelic *Am Braigh Riabhach*; whereas Cairn Toul (pronounced Carn Towel), signifying "The Barn Mountain", ought really to be spelled *Càrn an t-Sabhail*. The latter name is due to the appearance of the mountain from the Great Moss, whence, indeed, it shows a striking resemblance to the roof of a house or a barn. From the north and east, however, Cairn Toul is an impressive sight, and both the designation *carn* and the comparison to a barn are an insult to the peak.

Gleann Einich enters deep into the northern flank of the residuary table-land, separating the massif of Braeriach from the Sgorans, which face it, frowning with 2,000 feet of black rocks and steep screes across the dark mirror of Loch Einich (the Marsh Lake) that rests at the bottom of a two-mile mountain recess. On the other, eastern, side Braeriach is well defined by the wide system of corries, extending from it to Cairn Toul and known collectively as An Garbh Choire Mòr, *anglice* the Great Rough Corrie, down which shoots the waterfall of the Dee, and which was in the days of yore regarded as the natural and, no doubt, eminently suitable lair of the "She Devil". This personage has since departed, but something of her character still survives in the desolation of the wide scree-fields and the gloomy barrenness of the cliffs.

A very substantial neck of gently sloping ground links up Braeriach with the Great Moss, but farther north, above Loch Einich, the westward spurs of the mountain have been carried away by the old glaciers, to which the characteristic triangular rock faces still bear witness. In one of these Am Bodach, the

Old Man, of whom more later, has chosen his permanent abode.
The western corries of Braeriach are of the " derelict " type, only
the top rims of the rocks showing above the long and steep scree
slopes; but in the north it has three well-shaped corries. The
first of these, counting from the west—Coire Lochain—shelters a
large moraine tarn (*lochan*), filling its entire breadth. The cliffs
girdling this corrie are not as imposing as the black granites
of the Rough Corrie, but still nearly 200 feet high and, in
combination with the dark turquoise loch below and the steep
banks of snow that endure there well into the summer, offer
a fine composition in light and shadow, as well as some possibilities of moderately exacting climbing. The next two corries,
Coire Ruadh (the Red Corrie) and Coire Beanaidh (Corrie of the
River Beanaidh), have hardly any " live rock " left; and, though
their sides are very steep, they are composed almost wholly of
grey-pink boulder-scree, piled up into fantastic buttresses that
seem ready to tumble down at the slightest touch, but somehow
go on standing. Only here and there some harder granite mass,
such stuff as the " tors " are made of, has resisted the weather
and sits among the screes like a huge piece of black iron, rusty
with brown lichens, as though welded into the mountain with
sulphur, truthfully imitated by yet another species of lichen that
has a way of growing where loose stones and live rock meet.
These black rock outcrops, often met with in the Cairngorms, are
suggestive of an old-fashioned kitchen range, a railway engine,
and faintly—of hell, with a tendency to assume a vaguely
sinister significance when seen by a weary walker through the
drifting mist. . . .

However, Coire Beanaidh has progressed so well with headward erosion that it has approached a col leading to Deeside
and dividing Braeriach from the flat-topped Sròn na Lairig with
its pink grit. In fact, the encroachments of the corrie have
reduced the highest part of Braeriach to a fairly narrow crest
which breaks off abruptly to the east in the black precipices of
Coire Bhrochain—the Porridge Corrie, the northernmost recess
of the Great Rough Corrie and probably the most impressive
piece of rock-work in the Cairngorms. The summit cairn of

Braeriach stands directly above its main rock face, which serves further to enhance the " airiness " of Cairn Toul and the Angel's Peak, enclosing the cauldron of the Rough Corrie in the south, as they rear up in majestic steepness over the Green Lochan (Lochan Uaine) which rests on the shelf of a hanging valley above the thin streak of the young meandering Dee.

The green lace of alpine lady's mantle graces the dark buttresses of Coire Bhrochain, in which mists are often caught, and come up swirling like the steam rising from a porridge pot, whence apparently the name, though different explanations have likewise been proposed. The rock is mostly disappointing from the climber's standpoint. The pinnacles are made up largely of holdless, rounded " cheese loaves ", offering difficult pitches with uninviting stratification. The direction of the joints is often downward, the traverses are moss-grown and soaking wet, while the slanting slabs are overlaid with loose gravel and precariously perched blocks.

To the west of the main summit, Braeriach widens into the usual flattish stone desert, enlivened by occasional cushions of moss campion and little oases of sedge and grass. Golden-moss, seldom golden save in a rainy summer, and black-moss, ranging in tinge from bright yellow to Indian ink, but almost pure purple in June and July, line the trickling rills which gather in the ill-defined hollow in the middle of Braeriach's plateau. Here two fairly abundant streams bubble up from a number of springs, the Wells of Dee, and pursue their course in rocky beds towards the edge of Garbh Choire Dhàidh—the Rough Corrie of the Dee with its " grisly cliffs ".

The crags of the Rough Corrie peter out in ordinary scree slopes some way south of the main summit, but recommence before the fall of the Dee. It was there that in 1810 Dr. George Keith Skene made the first recorded Cairngorm climb, following up the watercourse. The rocks are apparently sound and reliable but rather slabby and featureless. In most seasons the waterfall is a thin affair, though of considerable height.

As we continue southward the ground rises into an indistinct prominence of 4,149 feet above sea-level, which is Braeriach's

Cairn Toul from the summit of Braeriach,
Coire Bhrochain rocks on the right

South Top. Flanked by a fairly formidable buttress on the side of the Dee, the Great Rough Corrie forms here its largest recess, inside which lies a crescent of eternal or semi-eternal snow. The rocks are broken up by screes and largely " vegetated ", as this is called in climbing parlance, but when their imperfections are concealed by the steep snows and the overhanging cornices packed into the corrie by the obliging west winds from the sweeping grounds of the Great Moss they form an inspiring alpine sight, especially as seen from below or from the flanking mid-slopes, so that the overtopping flatnesses remain invisible.

From the South Top Braeriach spills itself over into the Great Moss, just as the rocky scarp of the corries swings east towards Sgòr an Lochain Uaine (Point of the Green Tarn, known also as the Angel's Peak) and, after another semi-circle of ruinous cliffs, to Cairn Toul. If one follows the edge of the scarps all these peaks can be climbed easily, without much loss of height. Below the Angel's Peak, between its north arete and a shoulder of Cairn Toul, there is a deep hanging corrie which contains Lochan Uaine, contributing yet another burn to the Dee. A small corrie nestles under the very summit of Cairn Toul: this is Coire an t-Sabhail (Corrie an t-Owl). Still farther south the regular semi-circle of the rocky Coire an t-Saighdeir, the Soldier's Corrie, enters deep into the mountain's body, reducing it to an obtuse ridge which falls in a concave grassy slope towards Glen Geusachan in the south and the green, berry-and-heather-grown and rock-streaked Coire Odhar (Corrour), a prelude to the naked ice-worn promontory of the Devil's Point dominating the upper reaches of Glen Dee, in the south-east.

Glen Geusachan, whose wide mouth is flanked by the cliffs of the Devil's Point in the north and those of Beinn Bhrotain in the south, is a kind of spacious rock-bound box with a flat bottom occupied by a green wet meadow, probably a silted-up loch, now a favourite deer grazing, across which a substantial stream, fed by the waters of Loch nan Stuirteag and the burns foaming down the steep hillsides, winds in a silver ribbon.

This glen is a deer sanctuary and the main natural gateway from the Central Cairngorms to the Great Moss. Its Gaelic

E

The Sgorans. The " Pinnacle Ridge " with A'Chailleach

name means in English the Valley of Pines. To-day, however, Glen Geusachan is utterly devoid of trees, and only the bleached trunks, roots and stumps buried in the sward are still there to show the reach of the old forest.

Braeriach sits enthroned massively over the Aviemore sky-line, a sprawling but noble peak, its northern corries outlined finely by the evening light or the snow cornices that fringe them till the beginning of July. From this side there are two main routes of approach. From Coylumbridge and the pines of Blackpark one can either take the walking "right of way" path to the Lairig Ghru and Braemar (27 miles) and gain the main summit of Braeriach from the highest point of the Pass, with a traverse of Sròn na Lairig on the way as an alternative; or else follow the "public driving road" past the Tullochgrue cottages and thence to Gleann Einich, all the way to what used to be the "bothy" which by the wish of a past Grant of Rothiemurchus was always to contain some meal for benighted travellers, but is now but a charred chimney stack at the lower end of Loch Einich. From the ruin a stalking path climbs across the steep western scree and heather slopes of Braeriach to Coire Dhondail (pronounced Ghountall), where it imperceptibly peters out, though fragments of it reappear somewhat higher up. From that corrie the lower southern summit of the mountain and the Wells of Dee are easily reached by the milder incline on the side of the Great Moss.

The first alternative provides the shortest way, though a circuit of at least twenty miles is involved; the second is some five miles longer, but much of the tedium of the foreground approach can be eliminated by using a bicycle, which may be left near the "bothy" and recovered on return. The same device can be employed on the first route if instead of following the "right of way" from Coylumbridge one combines the "driving road" with the road from Loch an Eilein to Loch Morlich and Abernethy, once used by the cattle raiders from Lochaber, and regains the "right of way" at the approaches to the Lairig.

Another way of getting at the hill is from Glen Feshie by the stalking path to Càrn Bàn Mòr and over the Great Moss, where it is advisable to keep to the march cairns on the south side to avoid the peat hags and the broken ground near Loch nan Cnapan.

From Deeside the usual way is to take either of the two variants of the Lairig path, one by way of Glen Luibeg, which join opposite the Coire Odhar of Carn Toul, cross the Dee near Corrour Bothy and, using the steep but interesting track up Coire Odhar, combine the ascent of Cairn Toul with that of Braeriach. This is a much longer tour and a bicycle is of little use beyond Derry Lodge.[1]

As the mountain is generally easily accessible, except for the rocky parts of some of its corries, there exist innumerable possibilities of varying the route of ascent and descent, though some of them necessitate tiresome scrambling over steep screes. Yet, whichever route is used, it is a long and exacting job, unless one chooses to camp somewhere in the heart of the hills, which is not always an easy matter.

What has been said of Braeriach applies also to other Cairngorms, and to Cairn Toul more particularly, which is approached by the same routes.

2. *The Sgorans*

The scenery of Loch Einich belongs to the most magnificent in the whole of the Cairngorms. The loch lies at the 1,700-foot level and the western face of Braeriach, steep, if not rugged, heaves ponderously above it to over 4,000 feet. At the head of the glen another Coire Odhar abuts on an abrupt step, fully a thousand feet high and crowned with a frieze of broken cliffs and ice-polished rock knobs, down which the waters of Loch nan Cnapan pour from the Great Moss in a number of waterfalls. West of the loch, the Sgorans tower 2,000 feet in ramparts of black granite, oversteepened at the base by the mighty glacier that once used to flow down Gleann Einich, grey rivers of

---

[1] The exact distances and approximate walking times will be found in Sir Henry Alexander's guide-book, *The Cairngorms*.

scree, cones of debris, and the grassy corries suspended among them.

Sgòr Gaoith (the Windy Point—3,568 ft.) and Sgoran Dubh Mòr (the Great Black Crag—3,635 ft.) are the two main eminences of the Sgorans, which fall fairly gently in short, subsequent glens, towards Glen Feshie in the west, but in the east, on the shadow side, form an abrupt rocky scarp some three miles long.

Sgoran Dubh Mòr certainly deserves the epithet "black", though its neighbour might justifiably object to its other title. Its soot-black granites shoot up threateningly above the lower end of the loch—in two buttresses, dedicated respectively to "married" and "unmarried men", and divided by the downward triangle of the Great Gully. All of them provide good rock climbing, which has claimed some victims, and pass over higher up into ill-defined aretes converging on the obtuse sugar loaf of the summit. The rocks of Sgòr Gaoith are broken up and consist of a system of ribs and isolated outcrops, interspersed with grass and scree. The gullies between these ribs afford moderately exciting routes of descent to the loch.

In the northernmost black arete of Sgòr Gaoith there is a pinnacle, about fifty feet high which, seen from the summit, resembles a gaunt stooping figure with its hands folded in prayer. This is A'Chailleach, the Old Woman.

But don't let her pious gesture mislead you, for her granite heart is wicked! In fact, according to one version, she is no other than the Witch of Lynchat who, turned into stone, forever presides over a scene of wild grandeur, casting an evil spell over the elements. In the old days of Gaelic fancy she was said to entice solitary travellers to their doom and harass the fishermen on Loch Einich.

Fortunately, however, she is not alone, for she has a counterpart in the person of Am Bodach, the Old Man, who faces her in the rocks of Braeriach. They are no friends, and engage in "everlasting battle", each taking a turn to putt a boulder at the other across the loch, and are said occasionally to descend to verbal invective in which A'Chailleach is particularly skilled.

True to the tradition of Lady MacBeth and the glimmerings of the matriarchal past still noticeable in the Highland present, A'Chailleach is the more formidable and malicious of the two; whereas Am Bodach is of a more genial disposition and will often extend protection to the people she persecutes.[1]

However that may be, I always hold with the old Bodach and have no good word for the Cailleach—a witch she is and there is no knowing what she is up to . . . and take my advice, this is the safer way!

The outliers of the Sgorans, as also the conical Càrn Eilrig at the head of the dreary moorland north of Braeriach, offer fine views of the mountains and the lochs of Strathspey, and it may be worth your while to walk down from Sgoran Dubh either to Geal-chàrn and Creag Mhigeachaidh (pronounced Vigayhay), or northward over Creag Dubh to Loch an Eilein.

Creag Mhigeachaidh, the most rocky of the three *creags* above Glen Feshie, commands a rare prospect of Loch Insh, sheltering among the forests of birch and pine. It breaks off towards the moors of Glen Feshie in a rapid, scree-scarred face, with a few rock ribs protruding from the heaped boulders. Most of the old trees along Allt Ruadh (the Red Stream) to the south have been felled by the Canadian foresters; but a thick growth of gnarled birches, scraggy pines and rowans, still climbs up the screes in picturesque confusion, and ferns burst out from among the stones in green explosions of life.

The other two *creags* are Creag Ghiubhsachan (Yewsahan—of the Pines) and Creag Leathan which dominates the Achlean view in the north. A geologically interesting rift, probably a fault in the floor of an old pre-glacial valley, since cut by the subsequent streams flowing into the Feshie at a lower level produced by glacial erosion, separates the three *creags* from the rest of the shoulders whose terminations they form. Tiny tarns nestle in the hollow passes formed by this rift behind the last-mentioned two *creags* (or *craigs*, either spelling is used), and thin pinewood covers their sides.

[1] D. A. MacKenzie: *Scottish Folk-Lore and Folk Life* (London and Glasgow, 1935). Also—Seton Gordon, *The Cairngorm Hills of Scotland* (London, 1925).

3. *The Glen Feshie Hills and Corries*

The flattish, rounded back of the Sgorans is joined by a wide, concave pass with the table-land of the Great Moss and the bulge of Càrn Bàn Mòr (the Great White Hill—3,443 ft.), which has often been referred to in the preceding chapters. The summit is strewn with loose stones and golden-moss forms its chief vegetation. Càrn Bàn Mòr, the neighbouring Meall Dubhag, Mullach Clach a'Bhlàir and Diollaid Coire Eindart, hardly deserve to be regarded as separate mountains: they are far too closely integrated into the Great Moss and form simply the most elevated points of its generally upraised western and southern rims.

The stalking path leading from Glen Feshie to Ciste Mearaid and Càrn Bàn Mòr gives the easiest access to these hills. Another path follows the course of the Eidart to the Great Moss.

The most interesting feature on the Glen Feshie side is the wild recess of Coire Garbhlach between Meall Dubhag and Mullach Clach a'Bhlàir. It is the only corrie in the Cairngorms facing west that displays rocks of any importance. True, the shape of the corrie is atypical, and it presents from above a pear-like outline, narrowing at the entrance into a cliff-flanked defile, down which a burn churns and foams over a stony bed. But at its head the corrie assumes the characteristic amphitheatrical structure, crowned with a broken frieze of rock pillars immersed in steep screes. In the north another minor corrie—Fionnar Choire (the Cool Corrie) intrudes upon Coire Garbhlach and affords the easiest way of descent into it from the surrounding heights, though the scree-shoots between the rocks at its head are likewise quite practicable.

A green secluded meadow, where deer often graze, spreads at the corrie's bottom and, protected by the rocks around and the winding gorge below from the chilling winds of the autumn, many plants, including foxgloves, will be found there in flower when they are over elsewhere. It is an example of the local climatic variations in the Cairngorms, which are often strongly marked, the vegetation being usually most luxuriant on the

south-easterly slopes which are sheltered from the prevailing
winds.

In the rock shoulder enclosing Fionnar Choire from the west
there is a shallow cave, some large boulders inside which suggest
an outpost of an army of giants watching your progress down
the defile. I know of no story connected with them, but I
strongly suspect that there must be at least one.

The rock in Coire Garbhlach is gneiss and schist, but granite
boulders lie scattered along the burn, indicating that we are
near the junction between them and the granite of the Cairngorm " boss ".

Farther south the hills form a number of terraced gullies
which afford good ski-ing but are of little interest to a walker.
Druim nam Bò throws up a few rocks, and at its foot lies a little
tarn—Lochan nam Bò (the Cattle Tarn); both these names are
a reminder of the times when the Cairngorm grazings used to
support large herds of black cattle. Below, Glen Feshie " tri-
furcates ", its main branch forming a rock-rimmed bottle-neck
which shelters a remnant of the Caledonian Forest. Here the
crags and screes of Creag na Gaibhre face those of Creag na
Caillich. None of these are of any particular height or difficulty,
but they combine with the clear stream of the Feshie, where
salmon will be seen leaping in the autumn, and the old knobby
pines in a scene of haunting beauty. A very large specimen of
the golden eagle is in residence in the rocks of Creag na Caillich,
and you may see its huge shadow travelling along the slopes
long before you have spotted the bird itself, so well does its fawn
plumage match the brown hues of the hills.

As we move on southward the hills dissolve into a featureless
moorland, which forms the undistinguished watershed between
the Feshie and the Geldie, and hence the Spey and the Dee, and
marks the southernmost reach of the Western Cairngorms.

4. *The Great Moss*

The core of the group is the Great Moss, Am Moine Mhòr, a
wistful dun-grey stretch of high tundra, over which mists are

driven by the south wind that will lash you with blinding rain in the summer and biting ice crystals in the winter, desolate and bleak, and yet not without its own charm.

Despite the name, there is not much moss there, except on the west side. Most of the area is grown with sedges and rough grasses, yellow-grey and red-brown in the autumn, matching to perfection the coats of the red deer. The river Eidart, captured by the Feshie from the Geldie, has gnawed deep into the plateau of the Great Moss by headward erosion towards Loch Einich, and reduced its width in the middle part to about a mile and a half. The Eidart is fed by three burns, Caochan Dubh, Allt Sgairnich and Allt Luineag, which radiate through the plateau like the three fingers of a bird's foot. The river's glen, with a rock-rimmed corrie (Coire Mharconaich) on the west side, is about a thousand feet deep at its head and, together with Glen Geusachan farther east, separates Monadh Mòr (3,651 ft.) and Beinn Bhrotain (3,795 ft.) into a distinct mountain massif, sometimes described as the Southern Cairngorms.

The upper course of Allt Sgairnich is boggy, as it flows here through a vast area of peat-hags, that is to say the sort of ground where most of the overlying soil has been washed away and only isolated crescents, strips and islets of it still rise, grown with grass, cloudberry and sedge, above sticky peat mud and gravelly pools. Waders thrive on it, but the leather-shod human foot will do well to shun it, unless it is frozen and snowed-up.

The centre of the narrowest part of the Moss is a land of rock knolls, that is to say the *roches moutonnées* of geological language. Here, in a hollow, sits Loch nan Cnapan (pronounced Crapan)—the Lake of the Knolls, a welcome landmark on a misty day. The loch's waters issue in a burn which tumbles down over the precipitous walls of Coire Odhar, about a mile to the north, into the gap of Gleann Einich.

Between the loch, the edge of Coire Odhar and the lower slopes of Braeriach, which rises insignificantly, a low, rounded hill above the Great Moss, extends a miniature lakeland, composed of rock ribs, ice-polished hummocks, winding watercourses and a multitude of unnamed and unmapped tarns, ranging in size from

mere pools, though often of considerable depth, to quite substantial lochans, not much smaller than Loch nan Cnapan itself.
This ground is almost equally troublesome as the peat-hags, and
if you are in a hurry keep to the south until you reach the high
knoll above Allt Luineag, in which the boundary cairns of the
deer forests of Glen Feshie, Rothiemurchus and Mar will assist
you. Yet, if you have no designs on the higher peaks, the place
is worth visiting for its own sake.

Its rocky intricacies, patches of grassland hemmed in among
the boulders, ribs, bare slabs and water-filled hollows, rills, pools
and glistening tarns, will tempt you to a quiet hour in the sunshine. In the distance, beyond the gap of Coire Odhar, the
dark Sgorans rise menacingly, a sterner world where A'Chailleach reigns. The deer will be there with you, the white-winged
ptarmigan and the plovers' calls, among the chaste solitude of
rock and water; and if you venture to the edge of the step with
which the Great Moss breaks off towards Loch Einich you will
be rewarded by a wide and mighty Alpine view.

On the west side of Coire Odhar an indistinct path zigzags
from Càrn Bàn down to Loch Einich.

The origin of this "lakeland" is clearly glacial. The ice
descending from the Braeriach plateau has removed the grit and
soil overlying the weathered rocks and polished up the latter into
rounded knolls and flat slabs, on which the scars left by the
sharp stones embedded in the ice can still be seen. Generally
speaking, the outcrops of rock have been smoothed on the side
facing the glacier but have developed a rough edge at the other
end where the ice has torn off fragments from their mass in its
passage over them. Simultaneously the streams running under
the glacier during the warm season have worn out grooves and
cavities in the exposed rock surfaces. These have a general
direction across the main slope of the Great Moss and thus form
natural reservoirs, in which the water from the rains and melting snows collects on its way down. Some other cavities may
be of later origin and due to the development and subsequent
decay of vegetation, the organic acids of which disintegrate the
rock, forming a layer of light soil which is readily removed by

the wind once the vegetation has died owing to a change in the original climatic conditions.

The eastern part of the Great Moss is occupied by marshy grazings rising imperceptibly towards the grass and scree slopes of Braeriach and Cairn Toul. Between the latter hill and the first ground swell of Monadh Mòr, delimited by the ravine of Allt Luineag on its way to the Eidart, there is a hollow filled with another lake, Loch nan Stuirteag—that is to say, the Lake of Black-Headed Gulls—which, indeed, used to have a colony of these birds.

The loch itself, which is a true "rock tarn", and the slopes below it giving access to Glen Geusachan, are also typically post-glacial. The ground falls down moderately steeply in ice-worn hummocks, slabs and grassy stretches and forms an "assembly point" for the deer herds when the animals become alarmed by the approach of people. Above the glen, Monadh Mòr displays a few rock ribs and a scarp of no great height. The green Coire Cath nam Fionn, a small hanging valley undercut by Glen Geusachan, and a narrow col link up Monadh Mòr with the higher and more impressive Beinn Bhrotain.

Coire Cath nam Fionn is the Gaelic for the Corrie of the Battle of the Fingalians, the "romantic" name which, not being versed in the Fingalian legends, I am unable to explain and have to refer those interested to Seton Gordon's writings.

5. *Over the Hills to Inverey*

The weather was uncertain, with mists trailing over the High Tops, when I left Achlean at about half-past nine in the morning of 16th June, 1946. There was a cool breeze on the well-trodden path of Càrn Bàn, which was rather pleasant when climbing with a heavy rucksack and dressed to meet the sterner clime of the heights. Near Ciste Mearaid midget marsh marigolds were lining the burns and a single cushion of moss campion showed a few pink starlets. From the outer mound of the Great Moss a bleak panorama opened before me. Braeriach and Cairn Toul were decapitated by cloud but the summit of

Monadh Mòr, my immediate destination, was clear. Wisps of mist came drifting up from the dark-blue hollow of Glen Eidart at the confluence of the brown slopes on the right.

I was moving down swiftly, half walking, half running along the march path. A herd of deer—hinds and fawns—having sighted me, came galloping in a long line from the peat-hags among which they had been feeding, to outstrip me on the way to Glen Eidart, disappeared among the hummocks of Loch nan Cnapan, crossed the Luineag burn and spread out fanwise on the lower slopes of Monadh Mòr, some two miles ahead.

A shower of pulverized rain rushed in from the south and passed over the plateau.

Marsh violets, the small pale kinsmen of the purple lowland kind, were growing abundantly along Allt Sgairnich. A most ubiquitous plant, it is found in any wet place from the lowest valleys to the Wells of Dee, 4,000 feet above the sea.

I crossed Allt Luineag and made for the eastern shoulder of the gentle Monadh Mòr, promising myself a view of Glen Geusachan, the Devil's Point and Ben Macdhui beyond, in which, however, I was soon to be disappointed, as the cloud ceiling dropped lower and enveloped the upper half of the hill. The sparse rain was gathering strength and I had to put up the hood of my windjacket.

Here and there a few pink flowers smiled at me from the cushions of moss campion.

On the top the cloud spread a thick blanket of silence which seemed to swallow even my own footsteps. I was walking without a compass, an example which does not deserve imitation, but which did, however, add a little interest to my otherwise uneventful progress. Keeping the south wind on my right cheek I could be fairly sure of the direction so long at least as the mountain, so to speak, ran straight. The rock joints, too, especially marked where quartz veins appeared, were useful for orientation as they all crossed the hilltop from approximately south-west to north-east. Finally, the deer tracks from glen to glen and pass to pass could be used as a pointer, and at the edge of the hill the greater brightness of the mist would indicate empty space and, combined with an ascending air current, might mean a precipice.

Thus I was able to navigate successfully enough and at 12.30 reached the summit cairn, which loomed enormous in the surrounding whiteness, the only object to catch the eye. The second cairn followed duly, but afterwards the situation became somewhat complicated, as the mountain fell away steeply towards the col connecting it with Beinn Bhrotain, with nothing to hint at the latter's position. The only way seemed to be to keep in sight of the rock outcrops of Coire Cath nam Fionn, where the rumbling of the torrents and the white streaks of snow glimmering through the mist indicated the whereabouts of Glen Geusachan.

Yet practice proved more difficult than theory, and I found myself endlessly traversing steep gravelly slopes which, incidentally, offered some of the finest displays of moss campion in the Cairngorms, though the season was too young and most of the cushions were still in bud. This did not seem to bring me anywhere and a moment arrived when I noticed that I was too far on the Geldie side and had to retrace my steps. The white streaks of snow reappeared, somewhat larger and clearer, but there was no sign of the col. Wearied by the ineffectiveness of my search, I decided to drop onto the Geldie side below the cloud ceiling and sum up the situation from there. Accordingly I made a quick descent down an abrupt green hillside, and in a few minutes was clear of the mist. One of the snowfields proved to be a patch a couple of yards across! . . . The deep, green corrie of Allt Dhàidh Mòr lay at my feet, and at the edge of the cloud on the left I could see the col. Beinn Bhrotain, however, was completely immersed in the grey canopy which showed no intention of lifting, and it seemed both more prudent and practicable to follow the *allt* down to Glen Geldie and reach the Linn of Dee, my ultimate port of call, by way of the White Bridge.

The road before me appeared interminable. The dark grey clouds sitting on the hilltops ended in a straight line some miles to the south to give way to a faint radiance which might have

meant rain or diffused sunshine, possibly both. The hills across
the glen were outlined eerily in silvery mists. There was something astronomical about them, as though they were on another
planet, viewed distantly through an immensely powerful tele-
scope. You might have walked for ever and always seen them
like that before you.

However, I was moving down fast, following the sward along
the burn—a green ribbon winding among the brown heather
moor. On the shoulder of Beinn Bhrotain, to the left, stags
appeared dimly, magnified by the mist and distorted into strange
heraldic shapes. The sward ended and I had to take to the
heath, which meant slower progress, until I found another burn
which had gone completely underground and was overgrown
with grass, with only here and there a treacherous hole, the
trap for an unwary foot. The moors below were alive with deer.
Everywhere I could hear the thumping of their hoofs as they
were making off and down at my approach.

In about an hour's time I reached the land of the eerie light
which had seemed so enormously remote and the nature of
which I had correctly diagnosed. It was drizzling and sunlight
was seeping thinly through the clouds which gathered into a
dark mass on meeting the High Tops.

I regained the Allt Dhàidh Mòr by a well-marked deer track,
enlivened with white and pink lousewort, stray buttercups, the
blue flashes of milkwort among the grass, and mauve butter-
worts clustering on the peaty banks that marked the maximum
width of the burn in spate. Here the white skeletons of pines,
long buried under the heather, had survived on the wide bleak
moor, where deer were grazing in puckles.

As I sat down to have my " tea ", whose main ingredient was
absent, by the clear tinkling water, the sun broke through for a
while and the clouds lifted from the bulky shape of Beinn
Bhrotain. This made me feel rather sorry that I had hastily
exchanged the shorter and more attractive hill walk for the
long detour over the marshy heaths.

The brightening weather encouraged me to cut across the
moor towards the Duke's Chair, thus saving a mile or two of

walking. When nearing this isolated outcrop of rock I came
across a large herd of deer. The stags reared up to have a better
look at the dangerous biped, or so at least they thought, then
swung round on their hind legs and made off in haste up the hill.

Half an hour later I struck the road in Glen Geldie which
connects Glen Feshie with Glen Dee and makes a long and
rather dreary trek. It started raining again, though the hills
remained clear.

I walked past the abandoned crofts to the White Bridge, where
a small car was parked and steam was rising attractively from a
boiling kettle. Inside the car a young couple had abandoned
themselves to the "duolitude" of the hills. The sound of my
heavily shod feet on the road failed to arouse them to a sense
of reality, and when I was finally noticed . . . well, they didn't
invite me to tea.

At the approaches to Inverey I passed a company of seven big
stags at a distance of a few yards. They were amazingly tame
by comparison with the wary beasts of the open hills, and hardly
raised their heads from their feed to give me a casual look. The
"velvet" on their brand-new horns, on which the rain had
settled in drops, outlined them with a shimmering halo in the
evening light.

It was still raining as, at 6.15, I staggered wearily to the door
of the lodge at the Linn of Dee, having covered some thirty
miles or more of rough hill ground.

Reinforced by an ample dinner of soup, fried salmon, pud-
ding, scones, cheese and tea, and an equally regal breakfast,
including an egg and bacon, I faced the next day and the return
journey in an enterprising mood. The weather had slightly
improved, but showers were still passing and clouds boiling on
the tops. The choice before me was between the long and
monotonous trudge through Glen Geldie and Glen Feshie and
the more ambitious venture of proceeding to the Corrour Bothy,
climbing the Devil's Point and recrossing the Great Moss to
Achlean. It all depended on how the day would declare itself.
Tentatively I followed the road to the White Bridge. As I was
leaving the Linn a stag waded across the Dee where the river,

having burst through the narrow rock gap, spread out in wide shallow pools.

On reaching the White Bridge I cast caution to the winds and turned north along the lower Lairig Ghru path. At the Chest of Dee, with its square rocks, clear waters and quivering aspens, the sun smiled on the scene and again hid behind a white veil.

Based on the far-flung portals of its *cairns*, Beinn Bhrotain loomed up, billowing above Glen Dee; then the Devil's Point appeared in the V-shaped gap of the valley—a grey wall of rock overtopped by streaming cloud.

Where Glen Geusachan bursts upon Glen Dee, both of them old pre-glacial valleys, there is a wide space; one might call it the Hall of the Cairngorms. Bleak and stern, the great *bens*, Cairn Toul, Braeriach and Ben Macdhui, stand around in the hush or turmoil of the weather.

The north and east faces of Beinn Bhrotain are rocky, stripped bare by ice which must have been coming from three different directions, for huge slices have been taken off the mountain as if by a gigantic file at three clearly marked angles, giving it a somewhat artificial appearance. The Devil's Point north of Glen Geusachan also bears witness to the Ice Age. It offers a face of broken and then solid rock nearly a thousand feet high, composed of huge iceworn slabs as yet little sculptured by running water.

The grey slabs of Beinn Bhrotain were glittering dully in the rain, but they were dwarfed by the Devil's Point's flight of cliff that stood out dark against the background of boiling cloud engulfing the summit of Cairn Toul. Beyond and above, the rugged edges of the corries were separated from the mountain mass into sharp-pointed peaks disappearing somewhere two and a half thousand feet above the glen. The eye involuntarily sought to prolong the lines of the slopes to their natural apices, suggesting enormous mountains concealed in the mist; while the rain served to exaggerate the distances, and the steep screes seemed to recede into miles of Alpine grandeur.

I reached Corrour in good time.

The bothy, though utterly devoid of furniture, is of solid

construction, and still affords good shelter. The roof, it is true, leaks a little, but this minor inconvenience has been parried by those who use the bothy by spreading mackintoshes on ropes strung below the rafters.

The rain stopped but the clouds were hanging low and, abandoning the ascent of the Devil's Point to save time against future eventualities, I climbed up Coire Odhar and in just over half an hour regained the level of the Great Moss, though I still had a good way to go before reaching the Moss itself.

On the slopes of Coire Odhar, grown with heather and all manner of berry plants, solitary white flowers of cloudberry, rather similar to a large wood anemone, were sparsely scattered. Above the corrie, where I was greeted by a chilly blast coming from the Moss, creeping azalea was bursting into carmine bloom and some white-flowered saxifrage, which I failed to identify, grew in mossy places. The sides of the burn were padded out with wet cushions of black-moss, as though with thick, dark purple velvet.

Clouds were racing over my head as I made my way across the grassy slopes of Cairn Toul towards the Loch of Black-Headed Gulls.

At this time of the year hinds and fawns, unattended by old stags, stay high up in the hills, while the latter pasture on the lower grazings.

Near the loch I walked into a company of anxious matrons who picketed me as I sat down on a rock waiting for good light to take a photograph of Glen Geusachan and Beinn Bhrotain. The light was most disobliging, as is the way of " lights ", so that they were kept in suspense for over fifteen minutes, uncertain of my intentions.

When I got up and continued on my way I was still watched keenly from every knoll and shoulder. The fawns were bleating and seemed curious to see what sort of beast I was. I could well imagine the " conversation " that was going on.

" What is it, Mummy? "

" It's an ogre . . . an ogre . . . you keep going, my little one! "

The tortuous cleft of the Linn of Dee

As though to justify the name of the loch, a prolonged *crew-crew* came from above and I assumed, perhaps wrongly, that its source was a black-headed gull. . . .

The weather on the Great Moss was rather unfriendly, particularly on A'Chailleach's side (it would be!). Golden plover ran round me and piped plaintively as I took refuge in the shooting butt on the big *cnap* between the Luineag and the Sgairnich, to brace myself with a sandwich and a biscuit for the coming contest with the wind.

It was about 5 p.m. when I began the ascent of the final rise leading to Càrn Bàn Mòr and its filthy bothy. Suddenly a hen ptarmigan appeared at my feet, trailing her wings on the ground as though wounded. I stretched out my hand to her, but she took off at once in perfect condition. I realized that this was the mother-bird's time-honoured ruse by which she sought to head me off from her cheepers. My heart softened.

I did not follow the ptarmigan and she soon returned, alighting a few yards in front of me. Then I noticed two tiny things, the size of sparrows, which followed their mother in unsteady flight with a thin querulous *cheep-cheep*. She flew away with them and again returned. As she saw me walking up the path, she too ran in front of me from cairn to cairn, sometimes only a couple of yards from my nailed boots.

The bird kept me company for at least half a mile, after which she must have decided that she had done her duty and floated back to her charges in an effortless glide—ptarmigan are fine fliers once on the wing.

At 5.30 I left Ciste Mearaid behind on my way down to Glen Feshie.

The rain had ceased and the wind had quickly dried up the moors. Pale, phantom-like clouds came sailing from the west, hanging down octopuses of snowy drift and grey beards of showers.

The western sky was aglow with white light, while in the south the clouds were as if drawn with a soft pencil on glossy paper of smooth cerulean blue. The brown heather slopes offered perfect, though simple, compositions with the green and blue

F

Cairn Toul in early spring

distances and the gleaming waters. Now and then the silver searchlights of heaven would sweep over the glen, lighting the birchwoods with pale green flames on the curved inclines of corrugated copper, and the pines below would be ink-dark by contrast.

It was cool; but I took off my boots, washed my feet in a stream, and lay down on my back in the heather, watching the

sky and a hawk poised above the glen. For a few seconds it stood quite still in the air, then flapped its tail rapidly as though gathering the wind under itself, and its wings trembled fast, very fast at the tips; but it could not maintain itself there for long and soon glided off in a small curve, darted a little way, and again hovered, repeating the manœuvre.

As I shut my eyes I could still see the hawk with amazing distinctness, although it had already gone out of sight. . . . There it was, scooping the air under it with its tail feathers.

Great peace and contentment descended upon me. I was feeling myself one of Nature's things, like the deer and the rabbits, the burns and the flowers. My bare toes were tingling with the memory of sixty miles of top and brae covered in the last two and a half days, but the sensation was not unpleasant and the sun said that it was good to be alive. . . . My eyelids dropped, and when they came up again it was chilly and my watch was showing a quarter to eight.

V

THE ARCTIC HEIGHTS

1. *The Central Cairngorms*

BOUNDED in the east and west by the two Lairigs, which
meet at the junction of Glen Lui with Glen Dee above
Inverey, the Central Cairngorms enter in a deep wedge
between the western and eastern parts of the mountains. In the
north Strath Nethy, a country of thinned-out pinewood, bogland and scattered pools, marks the limit of this group, which
throws out on the north-west a wing of minor hills stretching
almost to the very banks of the Spey. There these hills, diminishing in height with each successive top, end abruptly and
picturesquely in a loch, dammed by a low whale-back hillock
which separates it from the river's valley.

Between this wing of heights and the River Druie, rising in
the Lairig Ghru, lies a vast area of forest and moor which conceals Loch Morlich, the largest of the Cairngorm lakes, at the
foot of Cairn Gorm and its northern corries.

Generally speaking, the Central Cairngorms do not form so
compact a unit as either the Western or the Eastern. Here the
old table-land has been largely worn away by erosion. The
glens and corries have bitten deep into it, isolating a number of
segmentary heights and whale-back ridges, comparable in
structure to the Sgorans in the west and grouped somewhat
artificially under a single heading. The core of the system consists of the Cairn Gorm-Ben Macdhui massif, from which chains
of *cairns* and *creags* radiate north, north-west and south-east
along the main valleys. Beinn Mheadhoin and the Bynacks
stand by themselves as separate heights, resembling in some
respects the Eastern Cairngorms. Finally, between the Pass of
Ryvoan with its Green Lochan and Loch Pityoulish extends the
already mentioned wing of hills, which do not seem properly to

belong to the Cairngorms, though usually counted as part of them, and look as if a section of the Monadhliath had been grafted on to the outliers of Cairn Gorm.

The lower level of the Cairngorm peneplain, corresponding to the Great Moss, is represented by the relatively insignificant stretch of flattish ground which rises to a gentle prominence of 3,345 feet, called A'Choinneach, between Bynack Mòr and Cairn Gorm. On the other hand, this part of the mountains contains the largest residuary expanse of the high upland from which the main summits have been carved out, as typified on the other side of the Lairig Ghru by the region of the Wells of Dee and the almost level top of Sròn na Lairig.

The country between Cairn Gorm and Ben Macdhui may bear a superficial resemblance to the Great Moss, but it is much higher, with an average elevation of 3,800 feet above the sea, in consequence of which it belongs to a different climatic zone. If the Great Moss is sub-polar tundra, these heights are distinctly Arctic; while the fiercer east gales rather than the west and south winds hold sway over their moods.

The hardy growth of creeping willows carpets thickly the loose grit of the Cairn Gorm-Cairn Lochan "ridge", if it is permissible to apply this term to a long strip of plateau. Here and there patches of sedge and grass maintain themselves in the teeth of the wind. It is too high even for the blaeberry and creeping azalea, though they may occur at the edges of the high ground. Cushions of moss campion are scattered sparsely; dwarf cudweed, the little brother of the Edelweiss, and starry saxifrage complete the list of the more conspicuous flowering plants. The rest is moss and lichen: golden-moss at first, with club mosses raising their soft green fingers, then black-moss only as we ascend towards the top of Ben Macdhui, the highest of the Cairngorms (4,296 ft.), which bulges up heavily, wistful and senile, above the eternities of boulder-scree, naked slab and barren grit.

Ben Macdhui is lost among the spread of undulating table-land to the north and north-east of it—a disappointing peak, as many highest peaks are; little more, in fact, when approached from this side, than a summit cairn and a viewpoint. In this latter capacity, however, it has no rivals, owing to its superior height. Not only can one see from its top all the remaining five "Cairngorms" and most of the lesser Cairngorm summits; on a fine day, with good visibility, the eye ranges from sea to sea over Scotland's famous hills, to help in identifying which the Cairngorm Club has erected a "mountain indicator"—that is a stone pillar carrying a flat round earthenware plate on which the directions, names and distances of the peaks that can be seen are marked.

The visibility varies greatly from day to day and season to season, which provides a fruitful scope for controversy as to what one does or does not see, and many a bitter word has been spoken on this subject in jest and in earnest, for Scots people take their opinions seriously.

At most times the distances are somewhat hazy, and the reality is liable to fall short of the Indicator. On the other hand, the Indicator itself is based on photographic panoramas and on some occasions is outstripped by the eye, especially when this is aided by a good glass. It is in winter and late autumn that the best effects are obtained. In fact, summer can never rival the pellucid clearness of a fine autumn day, its wide-stretched horizons and the bright relief of its chiaroscuro. . . .

The 1945 autumn was in many respects exceptional, but a spell of fair weather is usual at this season.

It was decidedly hot climbing up on the lee side as one day in early October Richard Perry and I were making our way up Ben Macdhui. Yet, although the sun had swept the corries clear of snows, and even the semi-eternal snowfield of Garbh Choire in Braeriach had shrunk to a thin crescent at the base of the cliffs, at this height there was a cold nip in the air. On the summit a chilly draught came from the north, hissing on the weathered boulders.

Sparse tufts of spiky sedge and black-moss, touched up in places with green, red and purple, formed the only vegetation, and the stone windbreaks erected round the cairn by the train-ing troops—like the sappers' roofless bothy lower down, probably a permanent addition to the peak's "equipment"—did little to relieve the windy solitude.

The visibility was superb.

Far, far out, beyond the lower Cairngorms and the Speyside hills to the mist-shrouded sea, was spreading a vast panorama of grey-blue mountain ranges. In the north a steep, lofty peak was capped with cloud like a smoking volcano, and as you swept the western skyline with field-glasses there came into view three tall, tapering shapes, pale, but unmistakable in their airy beauty —the Cuilins of Skye.

However, the cold was so penetrating that we had to abandon the attempt at identifying the other distant hills, and struck down towards Loch Avon.

The grim wreckage of a crashed 'plane was scattered wide over the stony waste. Somehow, at least to me, it did not seem to clash with the surroundings where it had come to rest amid the melancholy majesty of geological decay. It was as if the old rocks were mocking gently the brief span of human life and the fragile machine. For long thousands of years since the ice had first released its grip upon these heights they had lain here, lashed by rain and hail, swept by fierce snow gales and scorched by fierce suns. Freezing moisture burst their crevices, weather ate away the softer felspar, leaving behind a gritty surface of quartz. Rocks fell apart into boulders, boulders lost their edges, crumbled to gravel and coarse grey sand.

On the right, Loch Etchachan lay like the gigantic blue wing of some exotic butterfly, in sharp contrast with the colourless slopes of the "warted" Beinn Mheadhoin and the bleak cone of Derry Cairngorm; then the sinuous Loch Avon itself appeared below its buttresses of rock.

The cushions of moss campion had for the most part withered to brown mats, and the dwarf willows, those tiniest of trees, just large enough for the wee fairy folk to play with, had turned the yellow of birches.

Steeped in gloom, the precipitous face of the hill fell sheer to the grey screes. . . .

2. *The High Plateau*

Above the Lairig Ghru, Ben Macdhui bulks huge, with seem-ingly interminable slopes of steep livid scree, but the prospect is too limited to allow one to take in the structure and the real proportions of the mountain. The more distant western views reveal the Ben as massive but rather shapeless. Glen Luibeg in the east is the only side from which the peak displays a majesty appropriate to its rank of the second highest mountain of Britain. The whale-back chain of heights which separates this glen from Glen Derry and the Lairig an Lui, and the cone-crowned summit of Derry Cairngorm in particular, forms the natural grandstand from which to admire the high rocky scarp of Coire Sputan Dearg and the Green Lochan of Ben Macdhui, the latter some-what higher but otherwise closely similar to its namesake in Cairn Toul.

The wide, shallow corrie rises steeply about a thousand feet above the terminal concavity of Glen Luibeg. It is rimmed with a frieze of cliffs, supported by impressive buttresses of black granite up to 600 feet high, while the main east face of Ben Macdhui consists of strongly inclined ice-polished slabs, broken up with scree and grassy ledges. The name of the corrie, which means in English the Corrie of the Red Spouts, is derived from the gullies filled with reddish scree. In the south it is flanked by a rocky outlier, Sròn Riach, up which leads one of the paths to Ben Macdhui from Deeside. The other most used track follows the Lairig an Lui through Glen Derry up to the rock-hemmed recess of Coire Etchachan, where the Ben Macdhui path separates, running along the burn which descends from the invisible Loch Etchachan, above the corrie. A little short of the loch it turns south-west along the slopes of an easy shoulder of Ben Macdhui and so to the top. The path is clear and comfortable, but it will repay trouble to climb to the crest of the shoulder, which affords fine views of the Corrie of the Red Spouts and the Green Lochan, glistening among the screes on a broad shelf of Sròn Riach, and recapture the path above the main gully, where the shoulder merges into the mass of the hill.

In early summer a large snowfield lingers above the tarn and the corrie's clefts and gullies are packed with deep drifts which long resist the heat of the morning suns.

Beyond Sròn Riach the rocks peter out and Ben Macdhui drops in rapid, ponderously fluted slopes to a flattish pass which links it up with Càrn a Mhaim. Although this hill measures only 3,329 feet, it forms a conspicuous and unique feature. It flanks the Lairig Ghru as the eastern counterpart of the Devil's Point, and has been whetted by the stream which rises high above Sròn Riach—and has, therefore, great corrasive power—down to a narrow ridge. The ridge is of no climbing difficulty, but nearly a mile long and the difference in levels between it and the glens on both sides exceeds a thousand feet, so that it makes an airy walk, with fine prospects of the Devil's Point and the Rough Corrie.

Apart from its eastern aspect, Ben Macdhui is a dull peak and rests content with the part of a " grey eminence " amongst some of the noblest scenery of the Cairngorms.

The three-mile stretch between it and Cairn Lochan is featureless, desolate and drab. A tiny tarn, Lochan Buidhe (Yellow), which enjoys the distinction of being the highest (3,683 ft.) sheet of water to rank as a lake in the Cairngorms and the whole of Britain, nestles in a shallow marshy depression that delimits the "spheres of influence" of the two hills. Thence issues a fairly abundant burn, the Fèith Buidhe, to the north-east towards Loch Avon; while another stream, the March Burn, which here marks the boundary between the Deer Forests of Mar and Rothiemurchus, rises a little below and pursues the opposite course to the Lairig Ghru. Along it runs the usual route of ascent of Ben Macdhui from Aviemore, utilizing in its lower parts the Lairig Ghru "mounth"[1] and thus identical with the approach to Braeriach. It has many variants, as the subsidiary ridge along the defile beyond Cairn Lochan can be easily gained at several points on either side of the rocky bastion of the

---

[1] A public path or road crossing the hills.

Lurcher's Crag (Creag an Leth-choin, 3,448 ft.), from which some fiery hound once leapt to death in the heat of a deer chase. The chief difficulty is deep heather, wading in which up a steep hillside is a slow and laborious affair.

There is also a path linking the Lurcher's Crag with Glen More. It follows the left bank of the Allt Creag an Lèth-choin and then Allt Mòr, which is crossed by a foot-bridge below a little bothy at the forest's edge, where the path joins the Cairn Gorm "right-of-way". A broad stretch of grass-grown upland, the Lurcher's Crag Meadow, connects this peak with Cairn Lochan and the Cairn Gorm massif.

The top of Cairn Lochan is easily the flattest part of the whole high plateau of the Central Cairngorms, and on the half-mile stretch from the summit cairn to the edge of the March Burn's ravine the drop does not exceed fifty feet. North and east of Ben Macdhui the ground becomes more diversified. It is typical post-glacial country, with rounded undulating outlines, slabby rocks arranged in amphitheatrical terraces above boulder-filled hollows harbouring small meadows, where deer often graze, strips of mossy bogland, rills and streams cascading over giant staircases, and small pools and lochans scattered here and there, though nowhere forming anything like the "lakeland" of the Great Moss. As we move farther away from the summit the tempo of the landscape quickens. The burns swell into roaring torrents, rock steps steepen, until a sudden precipice opens before us at the edge of the dreary Càrn Etchachan. Foaming waters streak with white the slabby incline on the left and below, guarded by formidable flights of granite, lies the Sleeping Beauty of the Cairngorms—Loch Avon, still, long and narrow like a fjord, with miniature sand beaches gleaming in the sun, if such be the mood of the fickle weather.

On the right another lake, Loch Etchachan, wide and rounded, occupies the width of a green corrie, rimmed by rocks, unmarked on the Ordnance Survey Map, but none the less deserving of respect and in places inaccessible.

Loch Avon is hidden in a deep cleft, some two miles in length, which divides Cairn Gorm from Beinn Mheadhoin (pronounced

Main), and abuts upon the vertical rock step of Càrn Etchachan, whose main feature is the four-hundred-feet-high Shelter Stone Crag, and the semi-circle of cliff and slab scooped out by the elements in the side of the high granite plateau that spreads in grey desolation a thousand feet higher up. The surface of the loch is 1,600 feet below the surrounding summits, from which it is invisible, for, true to the pattern of glacier erosion, the lower mountain-sides are here much steeper than the pre-glacial slopes above. The loch can be gained from Ben Macdhui by following the way of the vanished glaciers, either on the right side of Garbh Uisge—the Rough Water—to the Shelter Stone, or to Loch Etchachan and thence over the low rim of its broad bowl between Càrn Etchachan and Beinn Mheadhoin. From Cairn Gorm there are three obvious routes: Coire Domhain at the head of Loch Avon, Coire Raibert about a mile farther down, and The Saddle, a low pass dividing Cairn Gorm from the Bynack massif. A descent from Beinn Meadhoin presents no particular difficulty, though the slopes are steep and throw up considerable rocks at the opposite sides of the hill. Finally, from the Lairig an Lui and Glen Avon the course of the River Avon leads naturally to the place where it is born, sparkling-clear, from the loch's green-blue depths, hemmed in by beaches of coarse-grained pink sand.

The Saddle is probably the best approach, as here the whole scene is suddenly revealed to the eye from a middle height, which throws its essential features into due relief, without over-emphasizing any of them.

The moods of the place follow those of the elements. In winter the hills are clad in the ermines of snow and rock, and the loch is inky-black, as only in very severe frosts are its waters locked with ice. The wind will blow eddies of white gleaming dust down the corries and the icicle-fringed torrents will rumble menacingly in the deep white hush. On a wet, dull day grey mists chase over the high solitudes and eerie lights creep over the wet slabs. The loch is pale, shivering with the gooseflesh of rain ripples and lapping plaintively on the stones. But in the warm sunshine of the summer the personality of the scene has about it a sternly feminine touch. The clearness of the waters and the soft promise of the sands are restful and inviting. Little sheltered bays are tucked up coyly between promontories of blae-berry-grown stones and heath. The vivid greenness of the grass slopes caresses the eye and tinges the cliffs with warm blues. Yet the crags are haughty and grimly predatory; the high plateau sulkily aloof.

3. *On the 17th of August, 1946*

The morning of the 17th August, 1946, was flooded with hot sunshine, but soon clouds began to gather over the hills.

I was late, and left Glenmore Lodge at eleven after a relay journey from Boat of Garten. The last train in that direction was leaving Aviemore at 7.20 p.m. Aviemore itself was over-crowded, and had no "bed and breakfast" to offer. Accord-ingly, having designs on Beinn Mheadhoin, I was faced with a typical Cairngorm problem and had to walk rather faster than was pleasant or healthy.

It was intermittently scorching-hot when the streaming clouds released the captive sun, and damp-cool as I entered the forest by the right-of-way path to Cairn Gorm. The air was slightly sultry and dead still. The Fiacaill of Coire an t'Sneachda (pro-nounce Corrie an t'Reeyakh, if you please) loomed ahead as a sharp-pointed peak, with wisps of cloud coiling and uncoiling round its edge.

This path is much used, as Cairn Gorm is the most climbed of the local peaks—especially since the motor road to Glen More was repaired—and is clearly visible and well marked with cairns. It leads straight to the summit at an easy angle over the four miles of the Aonach shoulder, and its most remarkable feature is three large perched blocks. The biggest of these, Clach Bhar-raig, was used during the war as a mountain artillery target, and two direct hits were obtained, which disclosed its pink inside but barely chipped the main mass of the stone. The perched blocks provide convenient windbreaks for a short rest on a "blowy" day.

Spotted orchis and bog asphodel mingled their pale pinks and chrome yellows with the beetroots of bell-heather at the height of its flowering show which richly decked the slope.

After a two hours' brisk effort I approached the summit, but this time the top cairn with its tourist sediment of broken bottle glass[1] held for me little attraction and, heading for The Saddle, I cut across the slope towards Ciste Mearaid.

This Margaret's Coffin must not be confused with its name-sake in Càrn Bàn Mòr. Hers is a wandering legend, and opinions differ as to where the jilted shepherdess succumbed to exhaustion after her aimless trek over the Cairngorm heights; or did she only hide her Cairngorms under the snow? Anyway, the Cairn Gorm Ciste Mearaid is the more interesting of the two, as it has a pocket of eternal snow, whence a copious stream issues through a tunnel.[2] Around it the foot sinks ankle-deep in the loose grit where moss campion and saxifrages have established themselves in places.

Fifteen minutes later I was "falling economically", as G. W. Young describes it, down the south side, where a fairly distinct path led to The Saddle along the Ciste Mearaid burn, until it became lost among the boulders and heather of the lower slopes. A large herd of deer, all hinds, dispersed at my rapid approach.

With a short rest thrown in for lunch, I reached The Saddle at two o'clock and, having negotiated some boggy ground on the loch side of A'Choinneach, waded the young Avon at fifteen-past-two. It had rained heavily that month and the month before. The stepping-stones were quite submerged and the water proved much deeper than it appeared at first sight, for, as the old saying goes, "The water o' A'an, it rins sae clear, t'wad beguile a man o' a hunder year". Cold it was, too. Icy eddies lapped round my knees. Twice I had to pause in shallower places to rub my numbed shins, and it was a thrill when

---

[1] Regarded as "geological rock", this material possesses remarkable power of resisting the agents of denudation, and will endure for centuries and perhaps millennia without any visible change.

[2] The source of the stream is the Marquis's Well higher up, below the very top of Cairn Gorm.

my bare foot felt under it the warm rough sand of the little
beach.

By that time the clouds had thinned out and the midday sun
was pouring down in dry, aseptic heat. The water of the
miniature bay was shallow, of that transparent aquamarine tinge
peculiar to the high mountain streams and lakes, with low,
glowing ripples criss-crossing the murkier deep farther offshore. I lay down on my back and abandoned myself to a
hasty *dolce far niente* while my legs were drying in the sunshine.

Blaeberries grew around, luxuriant, temptingly laden with ripe
fruit of lustrous indigo. Yet mine was the high way along the
sodden sward of a burn trickling down the heather slope, so off
I set without delay. Alas, the undines played on me a practical
joke, for half an hour later, when I was already near the crest of
the hill, I looked for my watch and there it was—on the beach
by the loch; at least, it did not seem to be anywhere else.

Ach aye, nae Beinn Mheadhoin for ye the day!

The watch was easy enough to find but not the time. What
was the use of all that rush? Would it not have been better to
stay on the beach and drowse for a quiet hour?

I recompensed my disappointment with blaeberries, and
followed the moor path to the Shelter Stone.

A heron rose heavily from the loch and soared in a wide arc
—a huge grey bird. . . .

Great blocks of tumbled rock lie in chaos at the foot of Càrn
Etchachan's crags. One of these, a square granite mass which,
it has been computed, weighs 1,361 tons,[1] has come to rest on
minor boulders so as to form a fairly spacious cave which has
been improved by human agency and rendered nearly wind-
proof. This is the Shelter Stone, though there are several other
small shelter stones scattered around it, which have been equipped with dykes and are also regularly used for bivouacking.

The Shelter Stone has been known for centuries, and in the
boisterous days of yore was said to provide sleeping quarters for
eighteen armed men. These must have shrunk since, for now

[1] Henry Alexander: *The Cairngorms* (Edinburgh, 1928).

there is hardly enough room for half the number, unless it be that people were smaller in the past, to which view medieval armour may lend support. However, the Shelter is conveniently situated and a useful refuge in these hut-less hills. It is, unfortunately, infested with mice and more than rather dirty.

I did not stop there, but continued on my way up Coire Domhain.

The sun was seeping in shimmering vagueness through the thin white veil which had sailed in from the west, with occasional bursts of brighter light when a gap occurred.

There seemed to be something unfriendly about those heavy splinters of rock below, and the Shelter Stone Crag shot up in black, wicked fierceness, the Forefinger Pinnacle pointing its ragged " nail " at the white sky. The waters pouring down the corries had a warning and threatening ring.

An eagle swooped from above, trembling with agitation. I could sense in the bird's movements a thirst for fresh blood; I could almost feel the feathers on its body, so near me did this live thing suddenly become, though hundreds of yards away. . . .

These rocks are wicked! I cannot define it. It is just a fancy; but then we are our fancies, and our fancies are more enduring than flesh, itself but a fancy of a Godhead, or a maniacal consonance of atoms.

Quarter to five, twelve miles to go, and a long climb still ahead. Shall I be in time for the train? It all hangs on the problematic lift from Glen More—a lorry or no lorry?

The sun has found another hole in the veil and is beating down in a concentrated blaze, bringing the torrent to a cold, white incandescence as it swishes down the sinuosities of its slabby bed. Spray rises in a silver halo over the wet stones. The crossing is tricky, as the slabs are wet and strongly inclined. Tiny drops settle on my face, and my ears are filled with the rush of the waterfall.

Coire Domhain is green beneath the pink-grey cliffs on the left, where moisture comes trickling down in gleaming streaks. Ferns grow high up here, for the place is sheltered and well

" The sun is beating down in a concentrated blaze, bringing the torrent to a cold, white incandescence." Am Fèith Buidhe

watered, and even harebells raise their slender stalks at 3,000 feet, the height that in other localities would sustain but moss and hardy Alpine plants.

To the north-east Loch Avon is pale and sad amid the barren hillsides.

Here one can drink of the cleansing solitude, with the senses wide-awake, and the mind open to super-awareness. The air is full and somehow round. . . . We don't get enough air in our stone or brick-and-mortar boxes. . . .

Down below, the foaming streams join their courses in Dairy-maid's Meadow and plunge into the stillness of the loch. The pink slabby cliffs are unscalable, rounded and slippery, like the surfaces of interlocked fish bodies. Blaeberry still bears fruit at this altitude.

" *Guarda e passa* " . . . Is it Dante?—I am a poor dictionary of familiar quotations.

Ten to five . . . Come on, will!

Boulders are piled up steeply along the burn, a staircase for the knowing foot, a trap for the unwary.

I wonder what others have felt and seen here before, and what those who will follow me will feel and see. The Shelter Stone Crag will still be there, wickedly black and sheer, and the ferns will be bright green among the boulders. . . .

I reached the rim of Coire an t'Sneachda at five to five. The descent into the corrie took me fifteen minutes, but I lost much time in the deep heather farther down and arrived at Loch Morlich at half-past six.

There *was* a lorry going down.

4. *The Blue Hill*

From Cairn Lochan the Cairn Gorm massif runs north-east at right angles to the Lairig Ghru, backing towards Ryvoan in a wide arc. It displays a fairly advanced stage in the career of water erosion, and its regular system of subsequent drainage will please an orderly geological mind. The residuary table-land has been greatly encroached upon and moulded into a wavy line

G

A glimpse of Loch Avon from the rocks of Coire Raibert

of heights and hollows, which beyond Cairn Gorm gradually
narrows into a ridge and then breaks up into a series of obtuse
hills, ending above Ryvoan in the rocky scarp of Creag nan Gall.
The slopes are steep and often rocky and precipitous on both
sides, but more uniformly so in the east along Loch Avon and
the narrow glen of the Nethy, which rises as Garbh Allt (Rough
Stream) just a little below The Saddle, and divides the Cairn
Gorm massif from the Bynacks. In the west, towards Glen
More, the hills throw out a number of gently inclined shoulders,
one of which, Sròn an Aonaich, carries the path to Cairn
Gorm.

Cairn Gorm itself (4,084 ft.) rears up in a regular dome some
350 feet above the average elevation of the massif. This gives
the peak a distinct personality, especially when seen from the
north and east, and goes some way to explain why its name has
come to designate the whole of the mountains.

In the north-west, above the wide Loch Morlich and the remnants of the once-magnificent forest of Glen More, devastated
for timber during the two world wars and only partly replanted,
the Cairn Gorm massif begins with a heather-clad ground swell,
traversed by the ravines of concurrent burns. This rises gradually towards the array of corries, of which there are five. The
westernmost two, Coire Lochain (the Tarn Corrie) and Coire an
t'Sneachda (The Snowy Corrie), are rocky and form conspicuous
features of the Aviemore and Glen More landscapes. They are
divided by the short but steep Fiacaill Ridge, which flaunts a
real rock arete, an infrequent adornment of the Cairngorm
scene.

Coire Lochain, a counterpart of its namesake in Braeriach,
enters deep into Cairn Lochan's shapeless bulk, so that its
summit cairn stands at the edge of precipitous cliffs, riven by a
scree-filled gully which farther below runs into a formidable
chimney blocked by a chock-stone. This is the way of the rain
waters trickling from the top on to a huge gleaming-wet slab, the
birthplace of the old glacier which is clearly visible from Aviemore and often mistaken for snow. The scarp is not very high
and its rocky part does not exceed 300 feet; but the sudden

contrast between the flatness of the top and the nearly vertical drop below is almost overwhelming, so that the eye tends to exaggerate both the sheerness and the height of the crags.

In the east of the corrie rock gives place to steep reddish screes, down which a deer track leads to the sheltered, restful hollow where two small tarns are tucked up among the moraines. A foaming stream descends from the green slopes of the Lurcher's Crag Meadow in a frayed ribbon of white silk, and the dark cliffs of the corrie stoop frowning above the screes and the small grassy flat, a favourite haunt of deer herds.

Another deer track crosses the narrow gap in the Fiacaill Ridge, just below the point where the arete begins, from Coire Lochain to Coire an t'Sneachda.

The arete itself, abundantly grown with cloudberry which forms thick mats on the top of some of its steps and pinnacles, is very short and of no great climbing difficulty (I have been up and down it with a heavy rucksack and a walking stick), but quite exposed in places, as the cliff-face on the east side is nearly perpendicular. The rocks can be entirely evaded by the scree slope on the Coire Lochain side, and the lower part of the ridge is wide and bouldery.

If Coire Lochain is restful, its neighbour strikes one as empty, haunted by the wind and the echo. Here, too, there is a strip of sward; two tiny tarns, mere pools, glitter among the heaped stones; and deer will often be seen grazing. But I venture to submit, with the perversity of Man who always seeks to attribute his own feelings to animals and things, that they feel more at home in the other corrie. The Snowy Corrie is the more rocky of the two, though its rocks are less compact. Red strips of scree and disintegrating granite steps lead steeply down between black, holdless pillars. On the west side of the corrie there is no clear scarp, and the slope subsides gradually into the face below, down which a deer-track winds through the intricacies of broken cliffs, bands of slab, scree-shoots, gravel, grass and moss. Red deer are no born cragsmen, and the track is easily practicable in well-nailed boots, at least when clear of snow; but in the absence of

nails it should not be attempted, as the incline is steep and a slip
on wet moss or grass may be difficult to check.

Coire Cas is tucked up under the left " arm " of Cairn Gorm,
and Coire na Ciste under the right, this if we assume that
Aonach is the peak's "body"—there is no mistaking the
" head ". Neither of these is particularly remarkable, but in a
snowy winter they afford good ski-ing and the left " armpit " is
usually fringed with an enormous cornice which takes a long
time to melt. Occasionally the Scottish Ski Club slalom is run
in Coire na Ciste. The last of the five corries, Coire Laogh Mòr
(the Great Calf Corrie), displays a partial rock frieze. Farther
north a small lochan sits on a glacial shelf above the forest.

If you wish to reach the country beyond Cairn Gorm without
the additional effort of climbing the peak itself, probably the
best way is to follow the path up to the top bulge of Sròn an
Aonaich and then cut across the slope above Coire Cas.

This is what I did on August 28th, 1946, heading for Loch
Etchachan.

That morning the glass stood low, the hills were hazy, and
grey woolly clouds were spilling over the tops from the east, but
the weather had not declared itself. Two parties, of three and
four people respectively, were a good way up the Cairn Gorm
path, and more people seemed to be farther ahead, defying the
freshening wind which was driving rain spray down the
slopes.

About noon I dropped on to the Coire Cas side, rather earlier
than I would ordinarily have done, in the hope of getting some
shelter from the east wind. And I was well rewarded, for on
the steep slopes below the summit the air was almost still.
Coire Cas, the brown-grey saucer-like hollow at my feet, was
empty of deer—a bad weather sign. Some young ptarmigan in
grey, speckled coats ran unconcernedly in front of me, and
" periscoped " at me with their flexible necks. They seldom
took wing, and would slither down the boulders on their bellies
and take to their heels rather than disclose their white inner
plumage.

I was already wet, as the wind had driven the thin rain right through my supposedly waterproof jacket. A strong east wind is no fun in this part of the hills, and I had a queasy feeling in the pit of my stomach. Clouds were racing furiously over the edge of the high ground above the corrie, and such brighter intervals as did occur did not amount to much. All this combined to make the prospects of my ever reaching the intended objective more than doubtful, barring a sudden change in the weather. Nevertheless, I went on.

No sooner did I emerge on the open plateau than I was assaulted by an arctic blast of gale force which lashed my face with stinging rain and what felt like lumps of ice. The rocks of the Snowy Corrie loomed hazily on the right, magnified to Himalayan proportions. Cairn Lochan seemed so remote that I at first mistook it for Ben Macdhui. There was no shelter anywhere, and one could not hope to survive for long on the open heights without polar kit. I persevered for a few hundred yards to get the satisfaction of having made an honest attempt before turning back, which I did with alacrity.

With the wind behind me, going down was quick and easy, though it continued raining and I was getting more and more thoroughly soaked.

As I reached the ravine of Allt Mòr the rain eased somewhat and there was a flitting promise of sunshine. The bothy at the edge of the forest seemed inviting and I decided to wait there for a lull.

Like all Cairngorm bothies, this one was in a dilapidated state, though not so filthy as some. There was in it nothing remotely resembling furniture, and portions of the boards on the sides had been torn off for fuel. The roof, however, was still solid (one can't make a fire with corrugated iron) and the place was reasonably dry.

The expected lull did not come: instead, the rain swelled into a deluge. Waves of water pulverized by the wind came tumbling down from the sky. The stream was rushing by, a foaming fury. I stood in the doorway watching the thick bole of an old birch swaying gently from side to side under the pressure of the wind. Downwards, the burn, the slender foot-bridge, the scattered outpost pines and birches of the Glenmore Forest, the dim outlines of the hills, and the clouds streaming through the haze of the downpour, composed a picture of rare and delicate beauty. Ling was in full bloom.

A ground subsidence on the steep north bank of the stream had disclosed the underlying boulder clay. Here they were— the bones of the Earth, weather-worn and bare, amid the rush of surrounding plant life.

Strangely, drawn by some hidden similarity, my thought wandered to meetings and official occasions, with gravely stepping middle-aged gentlemen and slightly overdressed ladies past their prime. It served as an evocative symbol of civilization, as though a light key had been turned somewhere in my mind and a huge, heavy gate swung open. I chuckled inwardly at the incongruity of the unexpected juxtaposition and the fungoid effervescence of mankind. It seemed impossible to take it seriously.

Lace curtain after lace curtain of thin throbbing moisture were borne past the scene . . . and here they were, those weather-worn bones of the Earth.

The laughableness of human affairs, struggles, hatreds and conceits, the essential inadequacy of human knowledge, with its atomic bombs, wave mechanics and psychological gropings, and the unfathomable mystery of the " simple " things we take for granted, forced themselves upon me with penetrating intensity. There seemed to be a deeper meaning in things than either science or religion would proffer, and a different one. Its all-importance and all-pervasiveness were around me: the heather, the boulders, the rainstorm were alive with it, with the story of cosmic forces and the tenderness of little lives. And yet the meaning itself remained tantalizingly unattainable.

The thick birch bole was still swaying from side to side. The rain continued. My clothes were wet and cold. I decided to go.

As I was nearing the forest clearing before the Glenmore Lodge the sun came out. A dark, dingy blue bank of ragged cloud was piled up high, receding to the west beyond the loch;

but new clouds were already gathering on the tops. The heather was unbelievably bright purple in the sudden blaze of light, and the pines rose, fluffy and robust, above the moor, raindrops glistening on their needles.

Later the B.B.C. weather report described the rainstorm as the worst of the year.

5. *The Lesser Heights*

In the south-east, Cairn Gorm forms a broad shelf which breaks off abruptly in a craggy scarp to Loch Avon, about a thousand feet below. The scarp is discontinuous, and two shallow corries, Coire Raibert and Coire Domhain, enter into it in grass-grown depressions; but some of the buttresses are 500 feet high. Along the four miles between The Saddle and Màm Suim the mountain-sides are uniformly steep and undifferentiated. They are covered with rich vegetation and pleasantly green after the dull barrenness of the north-westward heights. Rapid torrents wash down the beds of slithery, moss-grown slabs. A fragmentary scarp continues with intervals, ascending to the tops as they diminish in altitude, but in most places it has given way to scattered boulders and isolated rock outcrops, among which are hidden patches of level sward, far more inviting as camp sites than the boulder chaos of the Shelter Stone.

The pass of Ryvoan separates the Cairn Gorm massif from Meall a'Bhuachaille (the Shepherd's Hill, 2,654 ft.), the highest point in the chain of hills which thence extend westwards to Loch Pityoulish.

Meall a'Bhuachaille is a gentle but fairly regular cone and, rising as it does well over a thousand feet above its immediate surroundings, it forms a conspicuous landmark of Glen More and Abernethy in the north. Craiggowrie (2,237 ft.), with its rounded hummocks of schistose rock, is the most outstanding of the remaining heights of this group, which gives shelter from the bitter north-easterly winds to the wooded tracts hugging its steeper south-western slopes. Over the low pass, An Slugan,

down which the Milton Burn flows into the Spey, a Forestry
Commission road runs from Loch Morlich to Boat of Garten.
Loch Pityoulish marks the farthest reach of the hills in the
west. Surrounded by green knolls and birch groves, this lake
lies in a rural landscape of ploughed fields and meadows that
belongs to a milder world than the stern arctic heights of the
Cairngorms.

The crest of the hills, taken either from Loch Pityoulish or the
Slugan (about 5 miles in all), makes a pleasant walk which,
apart from Meall a'Bhuachaille, does not involve much climbing.
The north side of the hills is of little interest, but Queen's Forest
in the south contains some of the noblest woodland scenery of
the district, though there are few old trees left and most of the
area has been replanted by the Forestry Commission only after
the first world war.

It was sultry and the going was heavy one day in July when,
after negotiating a maze of fields, fences and birch groves, I
gained the freedom of the hills above Delbog on the way from
Boat of Garten to Craiggowrie. On the right, true left, side of
the Craiggowrie Burn the old heather had been burnt, together
with most of the pinewood that used to cover the craggy face
of the hill. Only in the deep ravine of the stream had the trees
escaped the conflagration. The ground was still charred and
showed little green, so that the black-face hoggets were hard put
to it to find anything to eat this side of the deer fence, which
cut across the wide gully up the rock bluffs to the very top.
They were scattered wide over the hillside and tripped daintily
away, like black-stockinged ballerinas, when they judged their
security compromised by the nearness of an unfamiliar human.
Above the fence, the hollow—you would hardly call it a corrie
—was like a palette on which some giant artist, engaged on a
predominantly green subject, had been mixing his oils. It was
daubed with brownish-green and almost blue blobs and patches,
streaks of yellow and very bright vernal verdure. This is probably why the next hill bears the name of Creagan Gorm, that
is to say a "Little Crag" which might be blue or green, accord-

ing to taste, for the Gaelic word *gorm* covers both these colours, while to add as it were insult to injury, there is another word *uaine* which specifically denotes the lighter shade of green. All this, however, is but a matter of habit, and one must reconcile oneself to the fact that different people have different habits, coupled with a strong conviction that theirs are the only right and proper ones.

Walking over the " blasted heath " was easy, and the slender white bones of the heather had little success in catching my sharp tricouni nails unawares. When, however, I had crossed the fence I soon began to regret having lightheartedly strayed from the beaten track. The heather was deep and troublesome; the ground marshy, grown with russet-tipped sedges and pink cross-leaved heath; and the great abundance of cloudberry leaves formed a meagre compensation for my toil, as it was still too early for berries. Midges were on the wing and mosquitoes were pinging piercingly about my ears. To escape from this company I struck off direct towards the top of Craiggowrie.

On the top there was a sharp, rather tiring breeze, and it was trying to rain without much conviction. Below, spread the dark pinewoods, with the glaucous rectangles of young planta-tions advancing up the hillsides. Loch Morlich showed as a pale, glittering streak, above which the big hills rose, grey-blue and misty. Clouds were rolling over the tops and boiling in the corries, the sun casting an occasional patch of watery sheen now here now there. All the " four-thousanders " were present, including Ben Macdhui and Cairn Toul, just peeping out above the funnel-like hollow of the Lairig Ghru and the Lurcher's Crag with its rock " pimple ".

A half-hour passed in a vast acoustic void as I sat munching my " pieces " behind an outcrop of gneiss. The creaking of my weatherproof cape was amplified by the silence to the clanking of steel, as though ancient claymores had met in contest some-where behind me, and were biting into warm, soft, trembling flesh. I even turned round to see what was happening, but there was nothing, unless it were an echo of some long-forgotten past when the Grants had been evicting the Shaws from Rothie-

murchus, or a bunch of Lochaber " rievers " had been ambushed
by the angry locals who had missed a couple of stirks.

A stray moss-carder bumble-bee came zooming through the
wind, alighted on a clump of ling and busied itself on its pink
flowers. Oddly enough, the stunted heather plants at the upper
range of its zone were in full bloom, while the lower-growing
ones were barely in bud. Was it that the wind had aided in the
opening of their buds by shaking them, or was the greater intensity of sunshine the real cause?

Meall a'Bhuachaille was quite a pull, for it rears almost 600
feet above the pass dividing it from Creagan Gorm, and its
summit was far too breezy to linger there for any length of
time. Followed a steep descent to the edge of the dilapidated
cliffs beneath which the Green Lochan suddenly appeared, like
a huge dark emerald set in the grey platinum of the screes,
where pines clung precariously to the abrupt hillside. Above
was Creag nan Gall with its frieze of rocks in thin sunshine,
then Màm Suim, marked by a glacial shelf where the ice had
once halted, and farther away a dark blue triangle with an indented rim trailing a wake of heavy cloud—Bynack More.

This was obviously the way to see the loch.

The hill-face below was steep and awkward, overgrown with
deep heather and scattered with boulders, always a trying combination. Nevertheless, I scorned the detour to the Ryvoan
shieling and continued down dead straight. I soon found sliding in a sitting posture the most convenient form of locomotion,
to which the stout fabric of my climbing breeches with their
double seat was admirably adapted. I even managed to glean
a few blaeberries in the passage. But the flies made this far from
enjoyable. The air was literally thick with them. They were
buzzing round my head, and kept getting behind my glasses.
Even the scientific anti-midge cream which was pinching and
burning my face did not seem to have much power over the
odious insects. The only way of keeping them at bay was by
lying quite still on your back. This outwitted their poor intelli-
gence, and they soon gave you up for a stone.

However, I was driven to the conclusion that July was no

month for mountaineering in these parts and, as it rained every single remaining day of it up to the very 31st, my conclusion was for this once given practical expression.

The road which crosses the pass of Ryvoan from Glen More to Abernethy is part of Rathad nam Mearlach, the Thieves' Road, and therefore a "right-of-way". A little north of the pass another track branches off eastwards to a footbridge on the Nethy, by means of which it connects with the Lairig an Lui path on the opposite side of the river. The latter threads its way from Nethybridge through what still stands of the great Abernethy Forest, then climbs gradually up to a featureless high moor at the foot of Bynack More, traverses the lower slopes of that hill towards Lochan a'Bhainne, and thence strikes for the fords of the Avon and Glen Derry.

Between the Lairig an Lui and the narrow glen of the Nethy the Bynacks heave up into the shapely summit of Bynack More (3,774 ft.), that is to say, the Great Bynack, so called to distinguish it from a lesser height on the west side, the Little Bynack—Bynack Beg, remarkable for its small rocky corrie which faces due west. Its existence, however, is often disregarded, as it is little more than a shoulder of the Great Bynack, which is then referred to simply as Bynack or Ben Bynack. South of Bynack More extend the already mentioned flatlands of A'Choinneach with an average elevation of 3,200 feet, a favourite grazing of deer, closely resembling the Great Moss of the Western Cairngorms. The Saddle links them up with Cairn Gorm, while the rapid stream of the Avon has severed them from Beinn Mheadhoin, of which the Bynacks are the logical and geological continuation.

Bynack More stands over 500 feet above the adjacent part of A'Choinneach and 1,200-1,400 feet above the Lairig an Lui path. It is a handsome steep hill of lenticular outline with a fairly narrow crest, divided into two summits by a grassy depression. Of these the higher, in the north, is traversed by an oblique system of rock ribs, which give it a corrugated appearance but present no climbing difficulty.

A little to the east and below the nick between the summits there is a remarkable constellation of three groups of dumpy tors, or outcrops of dark fine-grained granite which has resisted the weathering more successfully than the softer, coarse-grained pinkish variety. These are the Barns of Bynack, anything up to a hundred feet high on the valley side.

If you feel like adding a stiff pull to a thirty-mile trek from Nethybridge to Braemar, the traverse of Bynack More can be combined with the Lairig an Lui. Otherwise the hill is best reached from A'Choinneach or by the way of Ryvoan from Glen More.

South, across the Avon, Beinn Mheadhoin shows considerable resemblance to Bynack More in general structure, though it is much more bulky, heavier, and somewhat higher (3,883 ft.). As seen from Cairn Gorm, this peak displays a long whale-back of bleached khaki colour, studded with a row of four black tors, spaced along the crest with amazing regularity. It always reminds me of a buttoned-up greatcoat which has known no spit-and-polish for several generations of sergeant-majors. In reality the tors do not lie in a straight line: they are remnants of a rib stratification, similar to that of Bynack More, and much smaller than the Barns.

Beinn Mheadhoin rises fully 1,800 feet above the Lairig in massive steepness, showing here and there scattered outcrops of rock, and breaks off in precipitous cliffs and screes towards the deep green recess of Coire Etchachan which separates it from the outlying bluffs of Derry Cairngorm. It can be climbed at various points, but most easily from Loch Etchachan and the head of Glen Avon.

Coire Etchachan is in the process of transformation into a glen, and is vaguely suggestive of Glen Geusachan in the west. The burns have broken through its girdle of cliffs, and it ascends gently towards Loch Etchachan and the broad pass that divides Càrn Etchachan from Beinn Mheadhoin. In the south its abrupt scarp is formed by the edge of the spacious base which carries the graceful cone of Derry Cairngorm and links it up with the north-eastern shoulder of Ben Macdhui.

Derry Cairngorm is the most prominent feature of the Derry skyline, and credulous people often mistake it for Cairn Gorm, which it recalls in shape and configuration of slopes, whence the name. It also is the most elevated point (3,788 ft.) of the chain of heights which stretch from Coire Etchachan to Càrn Crom (2,847 ft.) at the confluence of Glen Luibeg and Glen Derry, where, according to a popular legend, some gold has been buried and never found, near an old solitary pine known as Craobh an Oir, the Tree of Gold. The legend gives some vague hints as to the site of the treasure that smack of Poe's tale of *The Gold Bug.*[1]

The strip of high ground south of Derry Cairngorm has been much worn by erosion, and its hummocky back whetted down so narrow as almost to deserve the name of ridge. Its average elevation above the adjacent valleys exceeds 1,000 feet, and its sides are steep, especially above Glen Derry, where live rock protrudes through the green mats of vegetation among scree-shoots and trickling rills. Just below the summit of Derry Cairngorm, on the Derry side, lies a small corrie which cradles a tiny sheet of water, fed by a burn cascading down the northern scarp. This is Lochan Uaine, the smallest of the breed of Green Tarns, a pale shadow of those of Cairn Toul and Ben Macdhui, but it has a special claim to fame as the theme of a Gaelic poem composed in the late eighteenth century by one William Smith which, put to music, ranks among the finest Highland songs. You would hardly expect a man of that appellation to indulge in Gaelic verse, but he was obviously one of those who transcend the limitations of day-to-day existence. A renowned deer stalker and a professional poacher who, with the connivance of the Laird of Rothiemurchus, made a practice of raiding the adjacent Forest of Mar, he was something of a philosopher and nature-lover withal.

It is by this Lochan Uaine that he built himself the " shiel " which was so " wondrous warm " when the hills were " cauld-rife " (this Caledonian adjective is grimly suggestive of ill-weather) and, last but not least, commanded a wide view of the

[1] See Seton Gordon: *The Cairngorm Hills of Scotland.*

ground that hostile gamekeepers had to cover in approaching his haunts. His "shiel" was eventually pulled down by his enemies, which fairly broke his heart but did not affect his habits.

Aye, those were the days. . . .

v. a. g.　　　Cantharellus cibarius

VI

EAST OF THE LAIRIG AN LUI

1. *The Eastern Cairngorms*

IF we look east from the summit of Ben Macdhui the real mountains appear to end with the cone of Derry Cairngorm; beyond extend featureless brown moors, streaked with the Indian ink of peat-hags and touched up thinly with the green crayon of grass and sedge. It is difficult to credit that this view can conceal mountains almost equal in height and visual grandeur to Braeriach or Cairn Gorm, and yet it does.

The Eastern Cairngorms stand a little apart from the rest of the system. As though jealous of their loftier brethren, they seem to have turned their backs on them, barricaded themselves off with a wide belt of lower ground which is yet sufficiently high to disguise them. No corries fringe their western flank and, except from Bynack More, we do not see much of their more rugged features until we are nearly on top of them.

Their individuality is due precisely to the existence of that stretch of high moorland which looks so uninviting from Ben Macdhui. It is Moine Bhealaidh and more popularly, in English, the Broom or Yellow Moss. In some ways a counterpart of the Great Moss of the Western Cairngorms, the Broom Moss is only about one-third of its area and fully a thousand feet lower. It does not really belong to the High Tops and corresponds to the so-called High Plateau.

Here let me explain that if we overlook from a superior height the hills and summits of the Scottish Highlands we will soon notice that they all approximate to two distinct planes or levels: the one of 4,000 feet or so, the other between 2,500 and 3,000 feet, known after Sir Archibald Geikie as the Highland Table-land and the High Plateau respectively. The first represents the ancient near-plain, that is to say the then ground-level, to which the once mighty Caledonian Mountains had been reduced by millions of years of wear and tear. When, at a later geological date, the land had been uplifted by about a thousand feet the old peneplain was parwashed away and broken up into isolated hill systems, while the same process of denudation set in at a lower level, producing there a new near-plain. Once more up went the ground and with it the new peneplain and the remnants of the High Table-land, which now became the High Tops, whereas the former was transformed into the High Plateau. Criss-crossed with water-courses and chivvied by the glaciers of the Ice Age, the High Plateau in turn fell apart into congeries of lower hills, which by reason of their younger age are less differentiated than the High Tops.

From this it follows at once that the Table-land and its descendants, the High Tops, are something altogether more distinguished than the mere High Plateau and confusing the two might give rise to a blood feud.

What then is the Broom Moss, Table-land or Plateau? Its average height of 2,800 feet above sea-level would indicate the latter; but it is a solid part of the Cairngorm " boss " and the tops of its upraised rim overstep the 3,000-foot mark. This does not fit together and, to reconcile the facts, it is usually assumed that the relatively low altitude of the Moss is the result of intensive glacier erosion at the confluence of the great ice-streams which used to descend from Ben Macdhui and Ben a'Bhùird.[1]

Thus it happened that the Eastern Cairngorms became separated from the compact mass of the Central and Western. They are formed by the tapering wing which the granite boss throws out to the east. In the west, the group is well marked off by the Lairig an Lui track from the Linn of Dee to the fords of Avon. The course of the Avon makes an even clearer boundary in the north. Glen Builg and the loch of the same name, straddling the watershed between the Avon and the Gairn, bring the Cairngorm granites to an abrupt end on the east side. But the southern boundary of the Eastern Cairngorms is somewhat

---

[1] See Alexander Bremner: " The Story of the Cairngorms," *The Cairngorm Club Journal*, 1940.

Mullach Lochan nan Gabhar in the massif of Ben Avon

arbitrary from the geological point of view. It follows the Dee down from the Linn to Gleann an t'Slugain, runs up that glen to Glen Quoich and thence along the Gairn to Loch Builg, taking in on the way a group of non-granitic hills between Braemar and Glen Quoich.

Our impression of the Eastern Cairngorms gained from Ben Macdhui is inaccurate in many respects. Even the Broom Moss is far more differentiated than it at first appears. A pair of " opposing streams "[1] has encroached deeply upon it and produced a wide pass which, together with Dubh Ghleann in the south, separates the massif of Beinn a'Bhùird from its sprawling flat-lands. In the northernmost corner of the Moss, Beinn a'Chaoruinn rises into a quite shapely cone of 3,553 feet, over 500 feet above it. This eastern sentinel of the Lairig an Lui forms an imperfect match for the far mightier Beinn Mheadhoin facing it across the pass. The north face of Beinn a'Chaoruinn is scooped out into a bouldery corrie and a constellation of small tarns nestles in the neck of ground between it and a subsidiary summit to the east. This peak, as well as the lower Craig Derry south of it, are chiefly remarkable as viewpoints from which to admire the cliffs and bluffs of Ben Macdhui, Corrie Etchachan and Derry Cairngorm, and, together with the Broom Moss, belong to the least visited parts of the Cairngorms, where deer, ptarmigan and blue hares can enjoy life unmolested by humans through most of the year and fatten for the delight of those who will come to slaughter them in the autumn.

Southwards from Craig Derry, which is not much of a hill but just a corner of the Moss plateau, the latter has been ground down between Glen Derry and Glen Lui on the west and Dubh Ghleann and Glen Quoich on the east side to a long tongue, curving at the tip and pointing towards Braemar. The burns flowing into the bordering valleys have shaped this tongue of high ground into a succession of cake-like hills, Beinn Bhreac (3,051 ft.), Meall an Lundain (2,550 ft.) and Creag Bhalg (2,190 ft.). Narrow passes, or rather defiles, divide them from one

---

[1] A pair of streams facing one another across the watershed.

H

Dubh Lochan from Beinn a'Bhùird

another. The two upper passes contain small tarns and display low, fragmentary rock scarps on the higher, north-west side.

This feature is connected with the local climatic conditions, which differ in many respects from those of the other parts of the mountains described in the preceding chapters.

The Sou'Wester, that roaring lion of Speyside, exhausts most of its fury and its moisture on the western and northern heights and reaches the Eastern Cairngorms in a chastened mood. Their climate is correspondingly the drier, as it also is the colder, for the Sou'Wester's every loss is a gain to the chilly Nor'Easter which ranges, supreme, over the easternmost tops. These, however, check it on the approaches to Glen Dee and its tributary valleys. Accordingly, it is the east wind that blows hardest at Braemar and Inverey; while the north-western gales break through the Lairig an Lui and the defenceless northern rim of the Broom Moss, to torment the pinewoods below and, in winter, pack snow-drifts into the passes of its southward heights where, in consequence, the rocky scarps referred to above have developed on the windward sides. Simultaneously, the debris sliding out on the snow, which must have accumulated there much more copiously in the past when the climate was colder, have dammed the outflowing streams, producing tarns. Such, at least, is my reading of the Book of Nature.

Yet the Broom Moss and its hills are no more than a prelude to the Eastern Cairngorms, which heave up beyond it in two powerful massifs, both touching on the 4,000-foot contour, Beinn a'Bhùird and Ben Avon.

Having a smaller bulk of granite to deal with, circumdenudation has progressed farther in this part of the mountains than in either the Western or the Central Cairngorms. Dubh Ghleann in its headward advance has almost severed Beinn a'Bhùird from the matrix of the Broom Moss. On the east side the Quoich Water has joined forces with Allt an t'Sluichd, its " opposing stream " in the north, to reduce the link between this peak and Ben Avon to the fairly narrow isthmus of The Sneck, some 700 feet below the level of the Highland Table-land as represented here by the North Top of Beinn a'Bhùird (3,924 ft.)

and by Ben Avon (3,843 ft.). Beinn a'Bhùird itself, for all the flatness of its outline to which it owes its name—the Table Mountain[1]—has been squeezed into a steep mound by its eastern corries, while ice and water have driven deep glens, gullies and corries into the massive sides of Ben Avon.

Ben Avon is, in fact, something more than a single mountain; it is a whole range of hills. A considerable stretch of the Table-land is still preserved about the main summit and the whale-back is uniform enough as far east as Mullach Lochan nan Gabhar; but beyond that point it breaks up into a succession of well-defined summits, diminishing in height as we approach the critical line of Glen Builg. The numerous tors of hard granite which crown these summits and are scattered over the sides and shoulders of Ben Avon form the most outstanding feature of its views.

To the south, between Glen Quoich and Gleann an t'Slugain, lies a group of lesser heights which attain in Càrn na Drochaide (Castle Hill) 2,681 feet above sea-level and conceal the view of the Eastern Cairngorms from Braemar and Deeside. Being of schistose formation, with some dykes of felspar porphyry and quartzites, these hills do not properly belong to the granite system of the Cairngorms.

2. *The Flat-topped Hill of Fierce Corries*

The configuration of Beinn a'Bhùird is determined by the fork of Glen Quoich and its subsidiary, Dubh Ghleann, or Black Glen, which embrace it from the south, while in the north the wide scoop of Muckle Slock (Slòchd Mòr) enters deep into the mountains mass. From the Broom Moss in the west Beinn a'Bhùird rises in a billow well over a thousand feet above it. The billow is moderately steep half-way up, but almost level on the top, where it culminates in two indistinct prominences known as the North and South Top, nearly two miles apart. The first is the higher (3,924 ft.) of the two, but the difference between them does not exceed 60 feet. The lowest point of

---

[1] Beinn a'Bhùird (pronounced Ben a'Boord): Mountain of the Table. Bùird: table (board).

the " Table " is only about 100 feet below it. Here, in a green
hollow where snow often lies in early summer, is the source of
the copious stream which, flowing south parallel to the summit
ridge, has separated from the hill a fold of lower ground known
as An Diollad.   Yet another stream rises a little below the North
Top and, having gathered on the way the waters of some minor
rills, runs down into the Black Glen with its ancient pines.

The North Top is mainly a surveyor's affair and would have
passed unnoticed save for the cairn with which it is marked, so
completely is it lost among the square mile or more of the surrounding " peneplain " where an aircraft crash-landed during
the war.   Eastwards the " peneplain " swells up into an obtuse
height known as Cnap a'Chlèirich, that is to say the Cleric's
Knoll, which owing to its height (3,811 ft.) is often described as
" the third Eastern Cairngorm ", though the neighbouring Ben
Avon could produce a number of shapelier summits for this
purpose.   Beyond the Knoll the ground breaks away in a
steepish gravelly slope towards The Sneck.

The " peneplain " of the North Top is hemmed in between
two rocky corries, the Stony Corrie (Coire nan Clach) in the
south and the Rough Corrie (Garbh Choire), part of Muckle
Slock, in the north, of which particularly the latter frowns with
a row of formidable granite buttresses.   Northwards to the
Avon, the hill projects in a rapidly narrowing shoulder which
carries a stalking path from Glen Avon.   The whole eastern
flank of Beinn a'Bhùird is occupied by a succession of corries,
with the 800-foot high black buttresses of A'Chioch as a prominent landmark.   The South Top (3,860 ft.) is not nearly so flat
as the North: it has been undermined by the eastern corries
and forms a visible rise even on the " Table " side, while in the
south it drops to the glen below in a massive and rapid sweep
known as Bruach Mhòr, or " Great Steep ".

The best approach to the hill from Tomintoul is by way of
Glen Avon and the stalking path up the northern shoulder,
flanking Muckle Slock.   Alternatively, one can follow the path
into the latter, whence a deer track leads up the screes and
between bands of rock to The Sneck.   This pass gives an equally

easy access to Ben Avon and is connected with Gleann an t'Slugain and Braemar by a path which forms the usual way from that side. The Slugan path forks a little short of the Quoich Water, over which a footbridge carries one " prong " up Bruach Mhòr and so to the South Top.

Beinn a'Bhùird can also be tackled from the Linn of Dee, best by way of Glen Lui and Clais Fhearnaig, connected by a good clear path with Glen Quoich where one can pick up either an old overgrown cart-track or any of the deer tracks leading to An Diollad and the Black Glen, which offer two variants of approach to the summit.

In every case a circuit of over twenty miles is involved.

So much for topography.

I left the Linn of Dee at quarter to ten D.S.T. in the morning of 8th July, 1947, making for Clais Fhearnaig. The weather was uncertain, the scattered cumuli expressive of meteorological instability. The sun smiled on the coils of the Dee, locked in frenzied combat with the narrow cleft. My eyes and ears took in the wet turmoil beneath the heavy masonry of the bridge; the green coolness of trees lay softly on my sunburnt face; the road felt hard underfoot. I scanned the blue-and-white pattern of the sky, decided that it was going to rain and took the short-cut through the felled forest to avoid the tiresome detour towards the Mar Lodge. This short-cut, incidentally, is a " right-of-way ", even though there is no gate at its other end, where I had to clamber over the deer fence. A young stag stood still, watching my progress up and down the wires with curiosity and —perhaps—a touch of envy. Beyond, pines grew in groups among picturesquely scattered boulders, each tree leaning south-east with hardly any branches on the opposite side as a silent testimony to the power of the winter gales rushing down the glen. Flies buzzed round my head as I was nearing the oblong of young pines, at whose farther end, by the ruin of a croft and a small bridge, I would catch the Clais Fhearnaig path.

Here a burn flows down a deep, twisting ravine, in which some trees have survived the heather-burnings of the past.

A tiny bunny was sitting motionless, outlined clearly against the sky, its ears blood-pink in the sunshine. It was 10.30 a.m.

Clais Fhearnaig (pronounced Clash Ernag) is the strange defile, hemmed in between miniature hills, with miniature scree-fields and rock outcrops on the north-west side, which separates the shapeless Meall an Lundain from the equally shapeless Creag Bhalg. It is probably the work of opposing streams, with some contribution made by the snow packed in by the north-western gales. The name commemorates a long-extinct alder wood. The eastward burn has been artificially dammed to form a long straggling *lochan*, rather like a toy fiord, where ghostly-green water-weeds soar up in clumps from the muddy bottom. There is also a small round natural pool a little above it, almost in the middle of the pass.

The defile is sheltered from the winds, warm and well-watered, and it makes a fine show of the heather-zone flora.

Tall foxgloves were rearing their magenta heads. Bell-heather was in flower, mingling with thyme, dark-blue milkworts, frail yellow rock-roses and fragrant Gymnadenia orchids. Among the scree I could discern the trailing shoots of wild strawberry and the dark crumpled leaves of cloudberry.

A duck rose from the artificial *lochan*.

Somehow the place "felt" like the site of a prehistoric settlement from the dim B.C. era of small tribal godlings. There was no evidence to support this "feeling", but it mounted in me to the pitch of unreasoned certainty.

Beyond the nameless reservoir was the promise of a new country, for every pass is a frontier, though it may have no customs inspection and no foreign speech may rise round us in a drowsy tide when we have crossed it. There on the other side another clan might have lived, at war with the inhabitants of that long-ago Clais Fhearnaig, who might have been killed or enslaved if they had carelessly pushed on too far. I felt a little thrill in the pit of my stomach when I saw before me the scattered pines of Glen Quoich, the distant Ben Avon and the sombre "Great Steep" of Beinn a'Bhùird rising above the forest —quite a mountain!

The path ended in a downward meadow but, after some fumbling in the heather, I struck a good deer-track, apparently widened by human agency, which led me across the long slopes towards Dubh Ghleann and Beinn a'Bhùird.

Much sense and nonsense has been said and written against solitary climbing and rambling. I have climbed and walked in company and alone and enjoyed both. On a rock climb, when it is a matter of hard struggle with the elements, company adds to physical security as well as to mental balance, but as for exchanging impressions—I often find that as soon as there are other people about the crystal of my perception is chipped; my mind is no longer a keen seismograph recording every ripple of the tidal world; the hills cease to be alive with vague secret meanings, fleeting terrors and timid joys, and sink down to the commonplace of mileages, lunch-rests and weather prospects. In company social considerations cast their hum-drum net on one's thoughts and feelings, and how often a companion is like a neighbour's wireless, which one may enjoy but cannot switch off at will! There are, of course, perfect companions. Yet, like perfect neighbours, they are rare, more often dogs than men.

There were some deer along the Duke of Fife's old cart-road to the Mar Lodge. At the foot of An Diollad the forest crowded, dark, into the fastness of Dubh Ghleann.

I crossed the stream over stepping-stones and found myself among some big bushy heather, where the couching deer had worn out deep hollows in the peaty soil—the kind of erosion overlooked by geology. Up the slope, pines in open canopy, almost black against the light, were standing in pools of green fire, kindled by the morning sun on the young blaeberry shoots. An eagle rose heavily from a clump of old trees—there must have been an eyrie somewhere about. A roe-deer streaked, rusty-red, across the green hill. From the forest on my left came the thin persistent yapping of fox cubs.

Each time a dry twig snapped under my foot my pulse quickened, my hearing sharpened to catch the tiniest buzz in the surrounding hush and small haunting smells invaded my nostrils. That was how the deer felt up above as they pricked their ears to catch my approaching footfalls. It was a feeling of honey-scented awe, part-fear, part-rapture, a blend of apprehension and beauty, fighting readiness and idle contemplation, as though an echo of ancestral past were secreted at the back of my mind.

The ground was firm and dry. It was a delight, walking over the soft, short-clipped carpets of the berry growth, and I was quickly gaining height.

At midday the shepherding sun had gathered in his aerial flock. Cool cloud-shadows fell across the sultry heat and now and then a few drops of rain. At half-past one I was on An Diollad, where the path, having begun nowhere, petered out in moss and heather a little below the gravelly ridge. Across the green gully of Alltan na Beinne, the South Top rose, huge, streaked with grass and pink scree. Small, wary herds of deer were making off up the green watercourses among the khaki lavas of heather.

Having reached the head of the gully, I crossed the stream and struck for the South Top. Creeping azalea was in crimson bud in the lower reaches of its zone, but already bursting into bloom higher up the hill. Moss campion, on the contrary, was over, with livid withered petals, and only above 3,500 feet were its cushions still sprinkled with pink. I followed the gritty wind-terraces which ran upwards across the slope, at right angles to the south-west: they must be accounted for, I suspect, by the fact that the wind, on contact with the hillside, is thrown into evenly spaced gusts. This, incidentally, is also responsible for the wailing noise it makes. Thin smurrs alternated with bursts of blazing sunshine, which passed like sand-paper over my scorched and moistened forehead. The incline was steep and tiring, but at least one could make visible vertical progress. A heap of grey boulders above seemed to promise the summit. This, as usual, was a deception, but not quite; for there the gradient of the slope broke and flattened down and a cool breeze came sweeping from the north. Soon after the cairn appeared, and at 2.15 p.m. I reached the South Top.

Bynack was a graceful cone on the north-western skyline,

under piled creamy cumuli. To the north-east spread what seemed to be level ground, though I knew that it concealed the deep chasm of Beinn a'Bhùird's eastern corries and the whole of Glen Quoich. The black summit rocks of A'Chioch protruded above the level in the middle distance; farther away were the shadow-darkened heights of Ben Avon, all of about the same altitude. The dun expanse of wind-blown, barren plateaux, scattered with dark tors, made a perfect desert scene, "asking" for a camel caravan and a few dust-devils spiralling into the clouds.

Who knows but the Cairngorm Table-land might have been a desert at one time, before it was finally broken up by the Ice Age into fragmentary hills. Enclosed in a vaster land-mass, it would have had a much drier climate, untempered by the vicinity of the sea. At any rate, the tors and some of the pillowy head-rocks wear a strangely Egyptian or Mexican look and seem to have been modelled by a desert climate, where the heat of the sun, black frost and sand-blast were the determining factors. They may be taken to have extruded above the ice-sheet and thus been able to preserve their pre-glacial character; while the corries bear the mark of the different conditions obtaining at a later date. Official geology is silent about that, but then discretion is the main virtue of officialdom.

From the Top I walked down the wide "promontory" to A'Chioch (the Breast), to have a peep into the corries. Of these, Beinn a'Bhùird has three on the east side: south of the "promontory" the small Coire na Ciche, flanked by the buttress of A'Chioch, with a partial rock-frieze but mainly scree-bound; north of the "promontory" two large rocky corries, Coire an Dubh Lochain, sheltering the Black Tarn (Dubh Lochan), and Coire nan Clach (the Stony Corrie) divided by a nameless but quite impressive *fiacail*.[1] The tarn lay below, very dark beneath the sunlit screes at the plateau's edge, changing to a rich green and blue-black ink again as sun and shade wandered leisurely up and down the slopes. The pile of cumuli above Bynack More grew and shifted. More clouds were spilling over Ben Avon.

---

[1] *Fiacail*—a spur between corries.

The rocks of A'Chioch are of the "Egyptian" type and so, too, is the rather formidable flight of cliffs rising in huge, featureless and holdless slabs and pillars at the south-west edge of Coire an Dubh Lochain. The north side of the corrie is scarred with screes and largely grass-grown, while the *fiacail*, though steep, does not look difficult to a climber's eye. This situation is reproduced in the rather more spacious Stony Corrie. Also here the rocks gather massively in the south-west, while on the other side, which faces south and thus does not present conditions favourable to the accumulation of snow, the rock-frieze is low and much broken up with grass and scree. There are two small *lochans* at the bottom of that corrie, one of them an appendage of the Black Tarn.

I was piped back to the "Table" by the plaintive whistling of plover. Thrift and moss campion were in bloom, making broad splashes of pink on the gentle hillside. There was considerable variation in the intensity of colour from cushion to cushion of moss campion: some were deep carmine and others nearly white as though bleached by the sun, which, I think, they literally were, as it was always the older flowers that were the paler.

A menacing peal of thunder sent me down into the Stony Corrie over steep screes, grown with black-moss, which might be tricky in wet weather, some slabby rocks and intricacies of knolls and boulders. The *fiacail* had a fine face on this side, with rock of later, glacial or post-glacial, character, showing several plausible climbing routes. As I hesitated whether or not to take a photograph of these cliffs, the sun was gone and it began to rain. Fortunately, the rock outcrops provided some shelter and the shower did not last long. Yet the sky remained dark and there was more rumbling among the hills.

High, high up among the storm clouds an eagle was drifting, a barely perceptible dot a good thousand feet above the "Table" of Beinn a'Bhùird.

At 4.30 I reached the bottom of the corrie, where azalea and the bright green parsley fern draped the heaped stones. My eyes, however, intent on the big boulders, wandered over the scree-fields in search of shelter. I soon noticed a large inclined slab of pink granite resting on some smaller blocks a little way below the second *lochan,* and I hurried on towards it in the rapidly thickening rain. The second instalment of the storm was a real downpour, but I was quite proof against it under my "shelter stone", which offered enough room to stand upright. The rain diluted the distances and magnified the corries. The *fiacail* and the buttresses on its sides made a rugged skyline that would have befitted the Cuillins rather than the Cairngorms, though it shrank to more modest dimensions once clearer visibility reduced the optical scale of things.

There was a fascination in watching the spray beating off the cliffs in white fleecy sheets and the pale green lights creeping through the murk of clouds and the dull scintillation of the falling rain.

I munched my prunes contentedly, soaking them in the rainwater which was dripping off the eaves of my shelter, until, about five o'clock, the worst was over and I could resume my descent. Fifteen minutes later I caught the Slugan path some way below Clach a'Chlèirich (the Cleric's Stone). A small lizard, apparently numbed by the rain, was sitting limply in the heather. It made no attempt to escape when I took it in my hand, and coiled up snugly in the hollow of my palm, flicking in and out its forked tongue. Eventually, it walked leisurely off my fingers and disappeared under the roots.

I had a damp, uneventful walk down the muddy path, where dwarf cornel grew in profusion. Its fruit is said to stimulate appetite, whence its Gaelic name *Lus a'chraois*—plant of gluttony. Lack of restraint in food must have been a great offence in the poverty-stricken past, devoid of "tartan novelties" and other amenities of civilization. . . .

A few deer grazing in the glen gave me a casual stare.

My difficulties began when I had lightheartedly crossed the foot-bridge on the path to the "Great Steep". My intention, of course, was not to remount the hill but to find some way down Glen Quoich. I knew there was no path along the central part of the glen, but I felt confident of being able to find a practicable deer track. And it was this confidence that cost me much trouble and delay for, now on the one, now on the other side of the water I seemed to discern a path. The stream was deep and I had to take off my boots in order to cross it. I waded it twice and each time my "path" proved an illusion. The third time I was so thoroughly soaked and tired that I no longer cared if I fell into the water, and in this mood I managed to get across it over the thin and slippery, barkless stem of a fallen tree.

The forest around was wild and beautiful. The skeletons of huge pines lay strewn on the ground where they had been up-rooted by storms many years ago. Most of the damage was apparently due to the great storm which had struck these glens in the winter of 1893.[1] Yet the majority of trees must have died a natural death. Multitudes of withered pines, without bark or side-branches, were still standing upright like glistening tele-graph poles. So many of them were there, especially along the fringe of woodland half-way up Càrn Eilrig Mòr, that they gave the place an outlandish appearance, for the eye mistook them for the less conspicuous stems of the living trees.

The thunder-clouds were now dispersing and the sunshine re-turned, thin and watery, casting streaks of green glow on the undergrowth and sparkling on the raindrops which still lingered on the pine needles and heather sprays.

Alas, most of this beauty was lost to me. It was eight o'clock and I was far too tired and too hurried to savour aesthetic joys. Old bushy heather, almost waist-deep in places, squelching peat-bogs and overturned trees placed constant obstacles in my way, so that my progress was laborious and slow and I was glad finally to emerge on the green strath at the confluence of Glen Quoich and Dubh Ghleann, within sight of the now-abandoned stalking track to the Mar Lodge.

In the western sky clouds swelled up into castles of yellow cotton-wool and the declining sun threw into sombre promin-ence the livid mass of Bruach Mòr.

I was back at the Linn at 9.45.

[1] Seton Gordon: *The Cairngorm Hills of Scotland*, p. 49.

3. *Among Tors and Carpets*

Adjacent to Beinn a'Bhùird in the east is the massif of Ben Avon, which is wellnigh cut off from it by the great cavity of Slochd Mòr, or Muckle Slock in Scots,[1] and the head declivities of Glen Quoich, the two meeting in The Sneck, a pass gentle on the south side but undercut in the north by a step of broken rock and scree.

The main summit of Ben Avon is only about a mile from The Sneck and 600-700 feet above it, but the hill extends for six miles beyond it. The shape of the massif is not unlike a spruce branch, small twigs radiating from it on both sides and growing progressively thinner and thinner towards the end. Most of the streams encroaching upon Ben Avon's portion of the Highland Table-land face one another across the ridge, to which their efficacy in reducing it must be largely ascribed. Indeed, save for its highest part, Ben Avon forms, on Cairngorm standards, a narrow ridge with a number of clearly marked subsidiary summits. Almost all of them carry excrescences of dark granite of varying height and other tors are scattered broadcast over the plateaux, shoulders and spurs of the massif, giving it a distinctive and peculiar appearance. This is rather bewildering in mist, as it is difficult to tell at a glance which tor is which and whether one is moving in the right direction. The south-eastern hillsides, where a number of burns flow into the Gairn through short subsequent glens, are gentle, grass-and-heather-grown and, on the whole, of little interest except to a skier in winter time.

In the west the hill-faces steepen and assume a barren, gravelly character. Here two fairly distinct hills, the Great and the Little Càrn Eas (3,556 ft. and 3,189 ft. respectively), the latter of conical outline, have been separated from the massif by the action of the burns descending into the Gairn on the one and into the Quoich Water on the other side. Eastwards, above Loch Builg, the glen of Fèith Laoigh (The Calf's Burn) splits the mountain into two chains of small heights. The steep Big Brae,

---

[1]*Slochd, slock*—etymologically identical with the English *slough,* but nearer in meaning to the German *Schluchte*—chasm or gap.

rising into a cone of 3,354 feet, dominates the Builg prospects which, owing to the high position of Loch Builg itself (1,568 ft.), are subdued and rather uninspiring, particularly so as the higher summits remain invisible.

The most interesting part of Ben Avon is in the north, along Glen Avon. Slochd Mòr (Muckle Slock) between it and Beinn a'Bhùird is the nearest thing to the Rough Corrie of Braeriach the Cairngorms have to offer. On its east side, the north shoulder of Ben Avon, known as Stob Bac an Fhurain, contains a small rocky corrie, Slochd Beag or Little Slock, and carries on its back a remarkable group of tors (Clach Bun Rudhtar), the highest of which measures some 80 feet from base to top. Farther east, a morain tarn, Lochan nan Gabhar (the Goats' Tarn), occupies the concavity of another rocky corrie and Big Brae sends down two spurs, the East and the West Green Finger, crowned with combs of dumpy rocks which range from large boulders to sizable crags. Meall Gaineimh (2,989 ft.), the last outpost of Ben Avon overlooking Inchrory, boasts Clach Bhan (the Women's Stone), a large tor with a number of roomy potholes, "chairing" in which was supposed to assure easy child labour. The tradition had apparently been started by the "Very Fair One", Lady of Fingal, who, before she was carried to her death by the raging waters of the Avon, used to bathe in the rainwater that gathered in the potholes of Clach Bhan. Having regard for such a distinguished example, numerous pilgrims, until well after the middle of the last century, thought little of crossing the hills to perform the strange rite; and, if the accounts are to be believed, it worked, such is the power of faith, however preposterous. It may, of course, be argued that being chaired in a pothole is a harmless and possibly wholesome tonic as compared with the various modern specifics obtainable from the chemists.

Other potholes, the result of rotation by the wind of gritty water, are of more modest dimensions. Sometimes they have been worn so deep as completely to tunnel the rock, or else the side of the tor that once contained them has weathered away and only a long groove, resembling the mark of a gigantic claw, remains to show where the pothole used to be. Three such " claw marks " can be admired on the summit tor of Ben Avon.

From Inchrory a path climbs up some way towards Clach Bhan and makes a good start for those who want to traverse the whole length of the massif. Otherwise, any of the shoulders of the hill above Glen Avon will make a practicable route of ascent or descent. The Sneck can be reached through Muckle Slock, which does not present at this point any serious difficulty. A number of deer tracks lead through the fragmentary rocks of the frieze onto the pass.

Half-way up Glen Avon two stalking paths give access to Stob an t'Sluicht of Beinn a'Bhùird, which can likewise be used to climb Ben Avon, especially by those returning to Tomintoul. This is, however, rather a stiff pull, though the views of the corries, gleaned on the way, will repay the trouble.

Proceeding from Loch Builg, one has the choice of two paths running up Càrn Drochaid (yet another Castle Hill). Once there, one is more or less above the heather, which makes climbing on the lower slopes so tiring, and within an easy distance of the " leaning tower " of Coutts' Stone (Clach Choutsach), whence the main summit can be gained in half an hour.

The usual way from Braemar is by the Slugan Glen and The Sneck, which is quite an expedition, as most Cairngorm tours are. The route is identical with the approach to Beinn a'Bhùird's North Top, so that most collectors of " Munroes "[1] combine the ascent of the two in one fell swoop.

After some hesitation, the midsummer of 1947 composed itself into a curious pattern in which each hot sunny day was followed by a dull one, with often a thunderstorm interposed between them.

The best part of July 25th fell into the first category, the few clouds wandering like lost sheep about the horizon although, apparently, it rained at Nairn. Tomintoul had had no rain that

---

[1] *The Munro Tables* are a list of all Scottish peaks of and exceeding 3,000 feet above sea-level, whence these are known as *Munroes*. The ascent of thirty *Munroes* is the qualification required for admission to the Scottish Mountaineering Club.

day and its high, windswept moors were dry to walk on. Sitting
by the fence on Tom na Bat, a small height south of the village,
I looked at the tor-studded outline of Ben Avon, slate-blue and
wistful in the distance of 10-12 miles, and played with the notion
of a scorching day on the Tops. But the next day broke grey,
though there was promise in the sky as I was leaving for Inchrory sharp at 8.50 a.m. D.S.T. It was the early hour of loud
footfalls on the flags, when the morning has not yet shaken the
dew off its eyelashes and the last cobwebs of vapour linger on
the meadows.

The glen of the Avon was richly green and somnolent below
the dull magenta of the hillsides covered with massed bell-
heather in bloom. Kine lowed pacing towards their pastures.
Grey mists were trailing over the northern hilltops.

I hurried on to "Birchfield", three miles up river, where John
Wilson, the Inchrory head keeper, had promised me a lift to the
Lodge at 9.30. This was going to shorten my itinerary by six
miles of road-walking, and I had a long trek to the Derry ahead
of me as well as a heavy rucksack on my back.

I arrived punctually and, having put our heads together, we
decided that Caol Ghleann, or Sma' Glen as it is locally called,
and the West Green Finger would be the most economic way
to the High Tops taking in Lochan nan Gabhar, on which I had
photographic designs. I said good-bye to John Wilson at 10.15
at Inchrory, crossed the foot-bridge on the Builg Burn and proceeded up the Avon along the rock trough of the Linn, enclosed
in a spinney of birch and pine, to the uneventful heathlands of
its upper glen. The tors showed dark on the foreshortened hillsides and the mist-line was still low. I did not hurry, giving
the clouds time to lift and, I hoped, disperse before I had reached
the *lochan*.

After negotiating some moderately boggy ground at the entrance to Sma' Glen, I caught the deer track above the burn.
Thousands of deer must have passed this way at various times,
for the track was wide and so well trodden as to give the impression of an artificial footpath. On my left was a steep rise;
ahead the glen opened into a wide hollow and divided into three

The Caledonian pines of Glen Quoich
Glen Avon and the Cairngorms from Tomintoul

branches. The easternmost of these was bounded by the rocky crest of the East Green Finger; the West Finger was straight in front of me, its rocks telescoped into a knob. Above it, Big Brae stood out in a massive cone against the lightening clouds, through which some sunshine was seeping indeterminately. The view gave no indication of the corrie containing Lochan nan Gabhar, which lay just a little west and behind the West Finger, anything but green from this side. The top of Ben Avon was swallowd up in the shifting mists, in which Clach Bun Rudthar rose in dim outline like a couple of ruined towers.

Two roe-deer appeared. First a doe came leaping along the ravine of the burn; then a buck crossed the track some twenty yards away in long easy sweeps, like a well-trained race-horse on the turf, without taking any notice of my neatly camouflaged self. As soon, however, as I removed my off-white wind-jacket, disclosing the light-blue shirt and the salmon-coloured jersey under it, he became greatly alarmed and slowly retreated up the hill with an angry bark. He was obviously in rut, which with roe-deer sets in about a month earlier than with red deer, and very excitable. About half an hour later, when I was a good mile up the glen, I could still hear his husky barking coming from a commanding knoll on the left skyline.

Walking now on the one, now on the other side of the burn, which were both rather wet, I found myself at twenty-past noon in the elbow of the glen at the foot of the West Green Finger. The hill began steeply but comfortably, with a stretch of burned heather followed by a lace of gritty channels dredged by the spring melt-waters and affecting a kind of zigzagging pathway. A good deer track ran across the lower slopes towards the *lochan*, but I spurned it for the crest of the hill with its maze of rocks, gravelly corridors and blaeberry-grown hollows.

On the way I started a few grouse and a blue hare. Another roe-deer barked somewhere among the tors. Multitudes of ash-grey Geometer moths were fluttering up at my every step, their wings imitating the grey patterns of weathered granite so as to make them indistinguishable from the stones on which they alighted.

I

The Ben Avon heights from A'Chioch, Beinn a'Bhùird
" *The Goats' Lochan is cradled in a deep secluded hollow* " (p. 130)

It was sultry, which made climbing with a heavy pack tiring, and I was glad to take it off and sit down for a long rest in a rock passage overlooking the tarn. A juvenile wheatear, looking big and fluffy as is the way of young birds, watched me impassively for a long while from the distance of a few yards, as I unpacked my lunch and camera and made myself comfortable on a patch of soft turf among the boulders. The rocks felt cold and the sky chilly in its indeterminate greyness. The mists had risen somewhat and the towers of Bun Rudhtar were now clear, though the tops above them remained shrouded in sluggish cloud. A herd of deer was outlined on the green skyline where Big Brae and Mullach Lochan nan Gabhar met in a shallow pass.

The Goats' Lochan is cradled in a deep, secluded hollow, enclosed by steep and even precipitous grass-slopes and in the south by an abrupt hill-face, built-up with three tiers of cliff-friezes, none of them particularly high or difficult, but the whole making an impressive sight. Between the crags crescents of grey snow were still defying the hot summer and white rills were trickling in silky threads down to the waters of the tarn, pine-green under the frowning sky.

I enjoyed a few scrambles on the tors of the "coxcomb", which abounded in short chimneys and somewhat holdless slabs, and, at half-past one, my hopes for better lighting having proved vain, gathered my belongings, crossed to the east of the ridge and made up towards the summit cone of Big Brae. This, however, I did not feel like climbing and instead cut across the steep incline towards the shallow pass where some deer were grazing. The angle increased as I drew nearer to the *lochan*, which showed finely at my feet between outcrops of dark granite, heaving up from scree-shoots and grassy hillsides. In places the grass was rather uncomfortably steep, giving scant purchase to the foot, and the rucksack was a little awkward to balance. Dangerous this was not, but after a heavy rain one might risk a nasty slip on such ground. Anyway, being in no mood for climbing gambols, I was pleased to strike a reasonably wide deer track which did not require so much attention in negotiating.

At the top was a broad, flat concavity, where deer lay in juicy peat-hags. The view was after the style of the Great Moss, but, unlike it, the rise of the Mullach on the south-west was over-spread with a thick, soft and springy carpet of crowberry, azalea, dwarfish bilberry, ochre-tipped sedge and false reindeer moss, which completely hushed up my footfalls. I was now walking into the mists, where some tors loomed up darkly—the phantom castles of the heights.

For half an hour or so I steered south-west by compass, though the mist was never so thick as to make orientation really difficult. Then the cloud ceiling lifted, disclosing Coutts' Stone on my left, the tors of Stob Bac an Fhurain on my right and the Couch of the Yellow Stag, that is to say the highest summit of Ben Avon, about a mile ahead. Beinn a'Bhùird remained immersed, but there seemed to be sunshine in the Braemar glens, which were swathed in a milky-blue radiance, and the distant Ben y Ghloe showed clear. On the gentle green slopes beneath the bearded fringe of cloud, some deer clustered round the snow-wreath where Allt an Eàs Mhòr had its source.

I peeped down into Slochd Mòr, but it was like a boiling cauldron from which shaggy mists came spiralling upwards and spread over The Sneck.

Without undue hurry I reached the summit tors of Ben Avon at 3 p.m., just as the cloud curtain went up from the North Top of Beinn a'Bhùird. There I was greeted by a strangely human call, but nobody answered my enquiring exclamation and when I looked round the edge of the rocks I could see only a covey of ptarmigan taking wing.

The summit cairn is perched at the top of the largest tor, which can be climbed along the ridge without much difficulty, though surely no stag, yellow, grey or red, could ever have couched there. The granite is weathered and inclined to hold-less rotundity, assuming shapes reminiscent of Aztec sculptures, not malevolent like some of the sharper rocks but rather por-tentously childish and naïve. There is quite a good face—of some stylized Central American Blimp—half-way below the cairn on the east side.

I attempted the summit from the nick in the middle of the

big tor but, although, I think, feasible, it involved an awkward inverted grip on a block of quilt-like formation with a nasty drop as penalty for failure—so I desisted. Frankly, I was feeling rather tired and unenterprising. The weather, albeit not unpleasant for hill-walking, was of the heavy unnerving kind. I tried some scree-running down the steep barren slopes in which Ben Avon falls away to The Sneck, but my effort was equally unconvincing and it took me, all in all, over half an hour to get there.

A little sunshine filtered down from the hesitant sky, fingering the rock outcrops, the scree and the green grass-shelf that ran oddly parallel to and a few yards below the pass on the Slochd side, and filling the Rough Corrie of Beinn a'Bhùird with the gloom of shadow, above which clouds piled, lurid blue.

Slochd Mòr is a little over a mile across at the head and nearly two miles deep. It is not particularly steep on the side of Ben Avon, whose cliffs are much broken up with scree and vegetation and nowhere form a continuous rock face. What is left of them looks uninviting to a cragsman's eye, though perhaps of no great technical difficulty; just piles of precarious debris, rotten to the core. The pass itself is easily negotiable. Yet, if the Slochd face of Ben Avon has more height than grandeur, the Rough Corrie of Beinn a'Bhùird, looking north-east and therefore subject to a more intensive operation of the cliff-producing factors, throws up a row of forbidding buttresses. Among these the Mitre Ridge catches the eye about half-way between Cnap a'Chlèirich and the North Top. Hardly a ridge, not even a *fiacail*, it is rather a tower in the process of separation from the main mass of the plateau behind it, which it slightly excels in height. The rocks of the Mitre are nearly perpendicular, little differentiated, except round the edge to the west where the ascents have been made.

Leaden weariness was upon me and very slowly I made my way up the sharp rise of Cnap a'Chlèirich.

The wind had left curious ripple marks on the grit, spaced with mathematical precision, as though a harrow had passed over it.

When I had reached the top of the Knoll I felt that I could not possibly walk another mile without a good rest and a drink of water. Fortunately, two burns rise on the edges of the plateau a little way beyond it and flow in the opposite directions, one into the Stony Corrie and the other into the Rough Corrie. It was the latter that I chose. The pink jewels of moss campion were still there to greet me—late in the year—and the mossy banks were dry. I filled my mug and lay down on my back, gazing into the clouds, sipping water and chewing chocolate. As is usual, the great stillness around me seemed full of strange noises, light footfalls and whispers. The gold wrapping of Cadbury's " Mild Dessert " was a gaudy intrusion into the chaste colour scheme of rock, moss and sedge—a pathetic speck of human comfort in a vast, stern world. The clouds gathered into a dense canopy and the corries turned to sinister ink. A curtain of mist obscured the summit of Ben Avon and cool moisture suffused the air. Yet it refused to rain.

The long rest, the chocolate and the water had refreshed me, and when, at 5 p.m., I resumed my climb my legs carried me swiftly up the gentle grey incline. In fifteen minutes I was by the cairn of the North Top, to which, obeying a childish impulse, I added three small stones. I did not linger there. The sky looked threatening and I was anxious to slip away from under the descending mists. So, briskly, I strode down in the direction of the Broom Moss. Knob-tipped stag's antlers, still in velvet, bobbed out suddenly in front of me, disappeared and bobbed out again a little farther off, as he reared up on his hind legs the better to see what tricks I was up to.

At that moment I could well participate in the mystic awe that the sight of man inspires in wild creatures: he must appear to them what a walking robot would to us. It is the upright posture that has something uncanny about it to a quadruped eye. Here was I, striding in a jerky, mechanical way—with none of the fluency of movement of four legs working in unison—in blue, dun and white, with an uncouth grey hump on my back, a horrifically plucked head with just a little fur on the top, and huge glassy eyes (I wear spectacles at most times), like those of an enormous owl, embedded in a piece of apparently raw flesh: enough to strike terror into the heart of the pluckiest denizen of the wilds! No knowing what a creature like that might do —spit fire, belch smoke, pour forth thunder or flash sudden cold lights in the dark. . . .

So, in terror, the deer herds moved away from me. The wind was on my back, bringing me their pungent feral smell from the high ground of Beinn a'Bhùird, while my own scent—that mixture of sweat, leather, boot-polish, chocolate and anti-midge cream—was spreading alarm along my path.

The Broom Moss lay at my feet, a humble moth-eaten rug of dusty-green, pale sienna and peaty-black. Beyond, the High Tops of the Central and Western Cairngorms rose in a majestic crowd of peaks, cliffs and corries, among which clouds swelled and subsided, broke up and re-gathered in slow unceasing unrest; and now and then a shaft of sunlight would cast sudden gold on summit or face.

Breathing in the great freedom of the moors, I walked into the western light, which grew redder and redder as I approached the Derry woods. I reached Luibeg at 8.45. Not so much my legs as my arms were tired and a strange loquacity came over me.

Highland rush

VII

THE BURN'S WAY

1. On Streams and "Mounths"

IN mountains of circumdenudation, carved out of plateau blocks by erosion, the peaks and ridges are subsidiary to the valleys. Other mountains are affected by the action of water, ice and snow and eventually destroyed by it: but the hills of the Cairngorm type owe to it their very existence. The enlargement of the glens, the deepening of the stream gorges, the "shattering" effect of the snow on the hill-faces and, in the past, the friction of the flowing ice, have moulded them into their present likeness, imbued them with majesty, fear and beauty—in brief, given them their life.

At the present time there are no glaciers, not much snow, and the future of the hills is in the hands of the burns.

Owing to the irregular shape of the granite boss of the Cairngorms, they are said to possess what is known as a radial drainage system; that is to say, their waters flow outwards in every direction. Yet, as has been noted elsewhere, the whole mass is tilted to the south-east, and for this reason most streams show preference for this "airt". Nor is the matter altogether as simple as this. The two Lairigs have split the Cairngorms into three sections which may be approximated to three equal contiguous squares forming an L-figure. Within each of these the drainage is more rigorously radial; but, since some parts of the Table-land have been reduced to ridges, their drainage has assumed forms resembling those found in the mountains produced by the folding of the earth-crust. Here the secondary, subsequent streams flow down the opposite hillsides at regular intervals into the main, consequent valleys, each stream of the left side fitting in between the two of the right. The Cairn

Gorm massif forms the best example of this arrangement, which can also be traced on Ben Avon and the Sgorans.

Even this, however, is only approximately correct: the situation is rather chaotic, conforming to no definite text-book pattern, and one can seldom find so many opposing streams, i.e. streams facing one another across the watershed, as one does in the Cairngorms. In consequence the Cairngorm glens may follow almost any course, with a tendency to intersect each other at right angles in the chessboard fashion. The big trunk valleys that date back to the old Caledonian Mountains of which all trace has long been effaced perpetuate the off-latitudinal and off-longitudinal directions of their subsequent and consequent streams. Glen Feshie, Gleann Einich, the Lairig Ghru, the upper Glen Dee, as well as the glens composing the Lairig an Lui " pass ", all run more or less from south to north with a westerly deviation; Glen Geldie, Glen Avon and Glen Geusachan have an off-latitudinal lie. The distribution of the minor valleys and gullies, formed at a later stage after the levelling of the ancient mountain system, reflects the radial drainage that came into being with the uplift and partial destruction of the Highland Table-land and in the main persists to this day. Thus we really have two distinct drainage systems superimposed in an inextricable tangle, on top of which comes the local subsequent drainage of the post-glacial period.

The chains of trunk valleys form the arterial highways of the hills, the immemorial "mounths", or public over-hill paths leading from one locality to another. Drovers used them to bring cattle herds across the hills, to which the Lairig an Lui, i.e. the Calves' Pass, owes its name, as possibly does the Lairig Ghru, though experts differ as to the derivation of this name. The caterans, or robbers, sneaked across them on their forays and clans marched over them in their ceaseless wars. The caterans are commemorated by such names at Allt Preas nam Meirleach—the Stream of the Thieves' Bush—in the Lairig Ghru, or Cnapan a'Mheirlich—the Thieves' Little Knoll—in Glen Avon. When the "sma' stills" were still smoking in secluded places, brewing illicit drink, one might have surprised on one or another of these tracks a convoy of shaggy ponies, tied head to tail, with "ankers", "carrochs" and "panniers" slung over their backs and "a contingent of Highlanders armed with bludgeons" in attendance.

Aye, the arrival of such a convoy was an occasion for great jollification, as will be readily gathered from the fact that an "anker" was a wooden keg containing twenty pints of whisky. Yet the real thing was the gang's return from the "run", when "pipers and fiddlers were brought into action; and dancing and scenes of wild hilarity, mingled with Gaelic shrieks, hoochs, leaps and bounds ensued". The Gael regarded the distilling of whisky as his birthright and nothing would inflame his feelings against the *Sassenach* more than any interference with it. Accordingly, the authorities took a mild view of such activities, partly not to compromise their position by attempting the impossible, partly for more hedonistic considerations; but the improvement of communication strengthened the hand of the law and by 1850 the trade in illicit liquor had been stamped out in the district.[1]

The caterans had been dealt with vigorously after 1745, when the Inverness hangman was concerned more with common robbery than with loyalty to the House of Hanover. Anyway, they had been but a memory long before the last " sma' still " was put out of action.

2. *The Long Trek*

The Lairig an Lui, connecting Abernethy with Braemar, is the longest of the Cairngorm "mounths", involving a total distance of thirty-seven miles, much of which is pretty rough going, though this " pass " was considered more suitable for the tender calves' feet than the shorter way over the boulders of the Lairig Ghru used by the mature herds. The passage was usually done in stages.

The Lairig an Lui track runs from Nethybridge through what remains of the great Abernethy Forest to the Forest Lodge or

[1] Rev. John Stirton: *Crathie and Braemar* (Aberdeen, 1925), pp. 362-4.

Rynettin, and thence on the right (true) side of the Nethy, a country of bogs and scattered pinewoods which presents exceptional opportunities for losing one's way, to the foot-bridge and bothy at the foot of Màm Suim, where it joins up with the path from Ryvoan and turns east to climb the crest of Bynack More. In its lower part the track has many variants, and it is simpler to follow the cart-road to Rynettin and on to the Ryvoan bothy and catch the comfortable foot-path which branches off to the east about half a mile short of the Green Lochan. This path brings us to the Nethy foot-bridge referred to above and so to the Lairig an Lui proper; and, though it adds a " crooked mile " to our trek, this is more than made up for by the certainty of being on the right way.

On 7th July, 1947, starting from Aviemore, I chose a somewhat different route—by Loch Morlich to Ryvoan, where I caught the path to the Nethy foot-bridge.

The expected lift to Loch Morlich did not materialize, which meant some seven miles of hard macadam over and above the scheduled distance, and it was not until one o'clock that I reached the Green Lochan.

We had an optimistic barometer which persisted in oscillating between "fair" and "very dry", without any visible reference to the actual atmospheric conditions. This time, however, I had taken its word, and it turned out to be not a bad day. Light intermittent showers alternated with spells of moderate sunshine and clouds provided enough shade to temper the moist July heat.

The sun smiled on the Ryvoan bothy as I struck the Bynack path.

The bothy, three-quarters of a mile beyond the tarn, is in a state of progressive disintegration, but about one third of the building is still roofed and in relatively good condition. The winter before some people stayed there for ski-ing in very severe weather and found it habitable. The other bothy, by the foot-bridge, is new, clean and sound.

From the foot-bridge one could walk up the Nethy glen to The Saddle and rejoin the Lairig track by the fords of the

Avon, which made a more interesting variant; but, being familiar with the surroundings of Loch Avon, I chose the usual route, which climbed in a long curve up the gentle heather-slopes of Bynack More.

Some sheep were scattered along the bare strath of the glen, down which the young river glittered in a weary meander. Despite the boisterous shape of the Bynacks and the steep scarp of Stac na h'Iolaire, the scene wore a wistful, sub-arctic look, with a suggestion of lassitude about it, and the long path, with its cairns and white grit, held little to cheer the eye.

The summit of Bynack More is within easy reach of the path, above which it rises in a low green cone divided by a grassy repression from Bynack Beag, which appears from here as a distinct peak half a mile to the north-west. But, having a strenuous programme before me, I resigned myself to the Lairig " mounth ", which was threading its thin gritty way through a doleful desert of stunted heather towards a group of rocks resembling a ruin. More dark ruins crowned the crest of Bynack More on my right. To the north-east all was high heaths, so high as to reduce the adjacent Cairngorm peaks to the size of uninspiring downs.

It was drizzling. A shepherd was gathering sheep somewhere about the Barns of Bynack and frantic barking and bleating spread out remotely in the grey pool of silence. The upper hillsides were green after the warm weather and prolonged rains this spring and offered good pasture.

I passed the small lonely water of Lochan a'Bhainne, about which spotted orchids grew in considerable numbers, and plunged down the incline of Allt Learig to the crossroads of the Avon, where two glens and two " mounths " intersect at right angles. At 4.15 p.m. I took off my boots and waded the full river over slippery stones, remembering the fate of the unlucky Lady of Fingal, after whom, some maintain, the A'an (Avon) is named: for this was Ath nam Fionn—the Fingalians' Ford—and, presumably, the place where she had been swept off her feet and drowned. To-day the water was only up to my knees in the deepest place, but it had a good punch behind it and I had to help keep my balance with my ski-stick to escape a ducking.

In sunnier weather there might have been more interest in the place, but the day had made up its mind to mourn the good Lady of Fingal. There was little colour in the scene. Clouds were spilling over the tops, releasing passing smurrs.

I lay down on the bank and watched the water slide away in thick transparent sheets, like huge panes of wavering plate-glass.

The defile between Beinn a'Chaoruinn and Beinn Mheadhoin, my next stage, is like a deep trough, where straggling *lochans* sit in stone-studded flats. The eye does not range above the lower slopes and the hills on the sides appear as low, even-topped mounds. Beinn Mheadhoin throws up some slabby rocks, lined with dark rills but nothing much to speak of, and the views are dull and restricted. The bottom of the trough rises slowly to 2,446 feet and then breaks off in steep slopes towards Glen Derry. The late Sir Henry Alexander describes that glen as "rather dreary", but when approached from the desolation of the Lairig track it comes like a revelation of beauty.

It was green, intensely green after the grey drabness of the defile. The eastward hillsides, which are mostly grass-grown, were green too: while in the west the scarps and crags of Coire Etchachan and Ben Macdhui fanned out in an Alpine panorama. Far below, in the middle of the glen, was a vast level meadow, free from stones, which looked like a lake and must have been one at some distant date before it had been silted up and become forest. Now the forest likewise had gone, save a few straggling pines round the edges, leaving the flat a preserve of grass and field flowers. It was pale phantom green in the evening light and the pines crowded in a dark mass at its farther end; beyond was amber brightness and Glen Lui.

I ran quickly down the stony path, but it was not until six o'clock that I trod the green flats of Glen Derry. The sky had brightened up and diffuse sunshine had gilt the cliffs of Derry Cairngorm, Coire Etchachan and the triangular rock face of Beinn Mheadhoin, rising above it like a dark steeple; still higher up, the summit of the peak formed a green dome, crowned with a symmetrical black tor—a tower and two wings on the sides, as though it were a castle of evil robbers guarding the entrance to the High Tops.

Hundreds, if not thousands, of deer were spread along the green grazings, the fawns bleating anxiously at my passage. Here the Derry Burn flowed in a clear steady stream over an even bed of pink sand until it reached the dam, used to pond up its waters in the old timber-floating days but long since derelict, at the step of the valley and tumbled down it into the white turbulence of the falls and the brief repose of the glaucous rock pools. On the step the scattered trees of the upper glen gathered into a sparse stunted pine-stand that took the brunt of the upper and lower winds. Farther down, the firs grew in girth and height. The Derry woods were unspoiled—no fellings, no rifle targets. The cool calm of the evening was upon them and blue smoke was rising from a bonfire lit in a small township of tents by the empty lodge.

After a dense plantation of pine and spruce, some thirty to fifty years old, came the green flats of Glen Lui with scattered foundations of demolished crofts, whose inhabitants had been evicted after the first Jacobite rising of 1715, in which the Earl of Mar had lost his earldom and very nearly his head. It had begun with a bad omen, for the gold knob had fallen off the Stuart standard just as it had been unfurled as the signal of rebellion. Or had the fabulous whisky punch the Earl had mixed in the rock bowl of the Quoich for the success of the enterprise aroused the envy of the gods? However this may be, his brother and successor had not taken kindly to the faithful clansmen of Glen Lui, which must have sustained quite a crofting township at the time, as witnessed the low stone dykes grown with foxgloves among the grass. Even no rowans were left to mark the vanished homesteads. . . .

The last four miles of the road were weary. It was darkening. Flies swarmed obnoxiously round my head. A thin veil of haze rose from the Dee and the Lui Water.

At a quarter past nine I crossed the bridge spanning the Linn of Dee with the consoling thought that never again need I " do " the Lairig an Lui.

3. *Storm in the Lairig Ghru*

The Lairig Ghru is the shorter route from Strathspey to Deeside and said to be the rougher of the two Lairigs, though I suspect that the "roughness" is optical rather than tactile. There are certainly more rocks about but, not being a calf, I see little difference in the texture of the ground underfoot. Possibly the pass itself between the Pools of Dee and the highest point (2,733 ft.) is something more of a scree-field than most of the Lairig an Lui, but I have seen people pushing their bicycles over it, so that it cannot be too bad on commando reckoning. . . . Far be it from me to advise anybody to cycle over the Lairig Ghru, or for that matter the Lairig an Lui! "Wish me luck as you wave me good-bye . . ."

The distance between Aviemore and Braemar is estimated at twenty-seven miles either way, though I am not too sure that this figure will be obtained on every occasion if the guide-book mileages are added up in detail, and there may be a difference depending on whether we start at the one or the other end of the " mounth ". The sad fact is that, however scrupulously we apply a string or thread to a map of mountain country, the map is flat and the ground is not, so that our reading is bound to fall short of the reality. Moreover, the surveyors justifiably dislike the zigzags of minor pathways and are inclined to represent them by arbitrarily straight " dotted lines " on which the walker would be foolish to sign. Thus it happens that the late Sir Henry Alexander gives the total length of the Lairig an Lui as thirty miles and Seton Gordon as thirty-seven miles. From the preceding pages it will be seen that I hold with the latter, on optical evidence.

Yet whatever the number of hair-pins, literal or metaphorical —and both will be found in the Lairig Ghru—it is a remarkable example of mountain architecture. It is a straight gash, without any glens or even corries on its sides, splitting in twain the

main granite mass of the Cairngorm boss, not unlike the Trans-
versal Valley of the Lunar Alps—the Cairngorms generally
have a somewhat "moony" look. The effect has been achieved
through millions of years of concerted erosion by two opposing
streams: the Dee in the south and the Druie in the north. Ice
has effectively intervened in clearing up the protruding rocks
and spurs and produced the long cliffy scarps of the Lurcher's
Crag and Sròn na Lairig. On the south side the simplicity of
the design has been marred by the intrusion of the streams and
glaciers pouring down the Rough Corrie of Braeriach and Glen
Geusachan, which have given the upper Glen Dee a wide and
open look, making it into what I have described elsewhere as
"the Hall of the Cairngorms".

On the Dee side the Lairig path has two variants: the one
making from the Linn of Dee straight up the glen, either by the
main road to the White Bridge and the Chest of Dee or by a
foot-path that skirts it to the north; the other following the Lui
Water up to the Derry Lodge and the bottom of Glen Lui Beag,
where it crosses the stream by a rickety foot-bridge and contours
the base of Càrn a'Mhaim, to catch up with the first variant
opposite the Corrour Bothy. Thereafter no skill in pathfinding
is required until Rothiemurchus is reached, where trouble begins.
The first uncertainty is by the big cairn in the forest at the
meeting of three roads, of which the left—west—is the right one.
Then we have to withstand the temptation of crossing either of
the two attractive timber bridges in a forest clearing which lead
nowhere in particular and to proceed, instead, along the churning rivulet to an iron-and-cement contraption erected in 1912 by
the Cairngorm Club. There, a tablet has been provided with
useful information about the times and distances to various
places, among which Coylum Bridge is two miles and Aviemore
four miles away. Few, if any, walkers cross this bridge, as there
is in close vicinity another timber bridge more conveniently
situated. In vain has it been barricaded with a piece of wire
netting to stop the rabbits—hikers and rodents disregard it in
unison.

Those coming from Braemar may now compose their

anxieties, but whoever is walking in the opposite direction must keep his eyes skinned once he has shut behind him, as I hope he will have, the fatal gate at Coylum Bridge, for the right path is not always easy to trace and various traps await the unwary. If in doubt, he will be well advised to follow the road to Tullochgrue which eventually brings him to the same place as the walking path.

In the past, as elsewhere intimated, the Lairig Ghru "mounth" was much in use for bringing the Speyside cattle herds over the hills to Aberdeenshire markets, and the rocky defile resounded with the lowing of winding kine. The caterans, prudently, preferred to keep their movements dark and kept mum, and the whisky-smugglers must in the main have followed suit. But on some other occasions the pipes and the bugle have sought the warlike echoes of the Lairig crags. The Lairig Ghru was the main thoroughfare of the warring clans and of the Shaws and the Grants in particular in their protracted feud. Thus in 1527 the Grants raided the Deeside Shaws, wreaking great havoc and slaughter and leaving a multitude of orphaned children, who were afterwards brought by the Earl of Huntly to his castle and fed there like swine from a trough. Half of them were subsequently adopted, kindly, by the Clan Grant and nicknamed, unkindly, "the Race of the Trough". This affair was the subject of one or two "compositions" in which "notarial instruments" were drawn up and signed by the contending parties, but more than that was required before the last of it had been heard.[1]

During the Civil War Montrose marched his army across the pass against Argyll's Covenanters, having taken the wise precaution of dumping his cannon in a bog on the way up.

And I, having taken the unwise step of sending by post from Braemar everything I could, or thought I could, dispense with, including my oilskin cape (so tired was I of carrying a heavy pack), left Luibeg on July 28th, 1947, in the company of a Manchester schoolmaster.

The day before had been brimful with sunshine, painting

[1] Rev. John Stirton: *Crathie and Braemar* (Aberdeen, 1925).

" . . . the water had folded small, like translucent silk, in the burn's elbow by the bridge" (p. 145)

streaks of glowing verdure among the pines of Fèith na Sgòr above the keeper's cottage. The smoke had risen from the "lum" in a straight blue column and the water had folded small, like translucent silk, in the burn's elbow by the bridge. But the next morning—we left at 8.45 D.S.T.—did not fulfil its promise. Grey downy clouds were obscuring the hills and the air was sultry, though cool.

My companion was wearing grey flannels and ordinary "walking shoes"—an attire not to be recommended for this crossing—and the size of his rucksack was an undisclosed multiple of mine. Accordingly, I offered to have as many rests on the way as he deemed proper and the first of these took place soon after we had surmounted the initial rise of Càrn a'Mhaim. The path along Allt Preas nam Mearleach was somewhat peaty, but mercifully still dry. Beinn Bhrottain showed ahead as a low grey wall, decapitated by cloud.

Some twenty minutes later we were in Glen Dee, where a group of walkers, overtaken by the night, were just beginning to stir in an overcrowded tent. There was some exchange of opinions regarding the exact position of the Corrour Bothy, which was very difficult to spot—a large grey boulder among a number of smaller grey boulders. And the sun was not shining on the heap of rusty tins that might have added colour to the scene! In my superior wisdom I poked a finger at a belt of peat-hags and, as I later had occasion to discover, missed the bothy by some fifty yards.

A few blaeberries, gleaned on the way, had further delayed us. Nevertheless we were making good progress and this part of the path was comfortable enough. Above, on our right, battalions of mists were retreating in fleecy curls into the black rocks of Càrn a'Mhaim. The Geusachan heights, the Devil's Point and Cairn Toul were pale slate in the uncertain light. Thunder was growling distantly among the hills, but there seemed to be no direct imminence of a storm and for all one could see it might yet clear up.

At 11.30 we passed the stone by which, according to tradition, the three luckless tailors had died one Hogmanay night on their

K

The Lairig Ghru

way to a dance in Braemar, and an hour later we sat down to lunch above the first step of the Lairig Pass, roughly half a mile short of the Pools of Dee.

Thrown into relief by the mistiness of the background, the Angel's Peak displayed to advantage the steep angle of its north face. Cairn Toul was clear. Above the swish of falling waters, great stillness reigned among the hazy bens. Grey clouds were creeping sluggishly over the western summits. A few desultory drops of moisture fell from the sky. Then, suddenly, without any apparent reason, lead-blue dusk overflowed the corries. The sky above Cairn Toul darkened, a red lightning wreathed its top and a peal of rasping thunder rolled from rock to rock. I looked up: steely phantoms were spilling over Braeriach in rapid lasso loops. Darker and darker it grew, as though it were a solar eclipse. The path showed dimly, the stones glinting, pale, in the twilight. A ghostly whiteness bulged over the cliff-sweep of the Rough Corrie, toppled over and began to advance, quickly obliterating the view.

The storm seemed to be moving at a tangent and we ran fast up the path in the hope of getting out of its way; but we had made little headway before lightning came splashing and crackling on the brows of Braeriach and Ben Macdhui, which hemmed in, lowly, the broad pass, and a straight heavy rain rushed upon us down the westward hillsides. I thought it prudent to retreat into the deep ravine of the Dee and await developments there; so there we huddled, with rucksacks on our heads, against the streaming bank as hail and water enclosed us with a white impenetrable wall and thunder roared, crashed and hissed on all sides. Soon the stream at our feet swelled into a raging torrent, rocking the ground with its pulse.

In a few minutes I was soaked to the skin, my only protection being the thinness of my parachute-silk windjacket and my sleeveless tennis shirt, which were glued tight to my body. My companion did not fare much better despite his raincoat.

After a quarter of an hour or so the downpour had slightly eased off and, having little to lose, we decided to go on. We passed the first, larger Pool of Dee, and then the second, a mere puddle amidst a scree-field. To me it was like a mildly nightmare Regent Street during the blitz before the all-clear had gone —a mixture of magnificence, make-believe and vaguely apprehended danger. I could hear the wicked hissing on the boulders of the "silent" electric discharge and left and right the wavering fiery threads connected to the rock outcrops. I instinctively accelerated my pace on the high open stretches of the path, to slow down again in the harmless hollows. In his townee shoes and awkward coat, my companion was bravely keeping up with me as I danced over the heaped boulders in the mood of battle hilarity.

We passed several false summits, produced by moraines and scree slides, under which the Lairig streams often disappear, giving one the impression of flowing uphill, and, amid a new onslaught of the storm, we reached the two large cairns of the topmost point. Four men who had been coming up from the other side had turned back and were now leading the way, a few hundred yards in front of us. There were more people farther down the glen.

Our hair was pasted to our heads in thin wet wisps and water was streaming down the tips of our noses. I kept blowing at mine, to head the stream off my open neck, with moderate success. My thick climbing breeches weighed like a suit of armour.

As we emerged from the defile on to the wider, lower terrace of the Lairig glen, a hoary tumult broke loose above the cone of Càrn Eilrig and dispersed in flocks of cotton-wool over the blue Strathspey. The sky brightened up behind the Sgorans and gradually a white ragged veil displaced the massed nimbus and the sun came seeping through. Soon after the rain stopped, so that we were able to take off and wring out some of our clothes and spread our shirts and jackets on a large cairn, where they dried quickly in the brisk breeze and sunshine, while we munched our "pieces". There was literally not a dry patch left on me and I squeezed pints of water out of my luckless breeches, but, fortunately, the depths of my rucksack contained a dry sweater and a scarf with which to cover up my chilly nakedness.

At 3 p.m. we gathered our belongings and hurried on to Coylum Bridge to catch the 'bus to Aviemore, which we did easily enough. Two more showers passed over us on our way and, while sheltering during one of them under the pines of Blackpark, we heard a short sharp report as though of a field-gun fired, as a tree was struck by lightning somewhere in the neighbourhood.

At Aviemore I said good-bye to my companion and ducked into "Pot Luck" for a high tea. White cloudlets spread a fleecy mantle over the round shoulders of Braeriach and mist again filled the V-gap of the Lairig Ghru.

This was a considerable rain and thunderstorm and, I believe, caused some flooding of the Dee, to which this river is prone, but not nearly so catastrophic as that of August, 1829, of which Sir Dick Lauder has left us an eyewitness account.

He writes:

"During the afternoon the wind and rain gradually increased, and about 5 o'clock it blew a perfect hurricane, driving clouds of rain before it, somewhat resembling snow-drift. It was during one of these violent gusts of wind that the first flash of lightning occurred. It was intensely vivid, and then followed peal after peal of thunder, not of the rolling kind, but 'as if whole batteries of the pieces of Heaven's ordnance had been discharged in rapid succession'. About 7 o'clock in the evening the thunder ceased, but the wind and rain continued, and many of the smaller streams, already swollen, commenced their havoc. Shocks of earthquake were felt at Allanquoich, and at Crathie, three of Dr. Robertson's men-servants, who were sleeping in a loft, started from their beds, felt the house shake, and heard a noise as if the slates were falling off the roof. The combined horrors of this dreadful night led many people in Braemar to imagine that the end of the world was approaching.

"The Dee reached its height at different places in Braemar

between the hours of 8 and 10 in the morning of the 4th. By correct measurements by Dr. Robertson, at six different points of the river, the average breadth of which was 130 feet, the mean rise of the whole was 15 to 16 feet."[1]

In the age of atomic bombs it would take a lot to make people imagine that the end of the world was approaching. Still, it must have been quite a storm, and it is left to us to picture what it was like at the time in the Lairig Ghru.

In more recent times serious floods of the Dee occurred in 1914 and 1920.

4. *The " Mounths " and Glens of the Eastern Cairngorms*

Glen Dee forms the natural continuation of the Lairig Pass, which may be said to come to an end at the White Bridge, where the Dee receives the waters of the Geldie Burn and reorients its course from south-south-east to east with a slight northward deviation.

Less than half a mile above the bridge is the Chest of Dee, where the river pours down in a twisting cataract into a wide square pool, hemmed in by rough-hewn granite rocks and fringed with some birches and aspens. The bottom of the pool, which is quite deep, is formed by smooth slabs traversed by a vein of quartz which is clearly visible through the clear aquamarine-tinted water. It is well worth while taking the somewhat longer branch of the Lairig Ghru path by way of the White Bridge to see the Chest.

The oft-referred-to Linn of Dee is a popular beauty-spot and on a sunny summer day the bridge which spans it is thronged with cars, loving couples and photographers, but early in the morning or out of season you will have the place to yourself and may be able to forget the masonry that overhangs the narrow channel the river has worn out for itself in the swell of hard schistose rock barring its way. Compressed in places to a width not exceeding three feet, the water is pumped through the

[1] Quoted after *Crathie and Braemar,* by Rev. John Stirton, p. 372.

snaky cleft with tremendous force, and when the river is in spate its clamour will be heard for a mile or more in the valley and farther on the heights. The bed of the Linn is still well above the level of the river below it, though it has already dredged a passage many yards deep in the obdurate rock. Despite the orange peel and warning notices, the Linn, with its seething rock cauldrons and sinuous dark gaps filled with pulsing foam, is a thing of beauty. Having broken out of its restraining grip, the Dee spreads out, wide and placid. Here the unhurried swells and small glittering ripples mark the shallow current, plashing on the sand and grit that border its banks below the dark canopy of conifer forest.

The Lui Water, which falls into the Dee half a mile or so farther down, flows through a stretch of fine old pine-stand, foaming on pink granites and green-blue schists, and breaking into angry falls. It is a powerful stream, fed by the waters of Lock Etchachan and the burns of the Derry and the Lui Beag.

The centre of Inverey, a small village of no great interest in itself, save as a very convenient starting-point for the Cairngorms with a tradition of hospitality and understanding of the needs of climbers and walkers, is two miles below the Linn by the road on the right (south) side of the river. The Victoria Bridge spans the Dee between the Linn and Inverey and gives access to the Mar Lodge, which was during the war used as a commando training centre and now wears a sad and derelict look, though it will presumably be done-up in the near future.

Braemar is a fashionable tourist centre five miles by road from the Linn. Its fame is wide, but its permanent population is small and it has only a few shops, apart from a very snappy affair with antiques, some hotels and a youth hostel. There is also a castle with a mildly varied history and, of course, on the first Thursday each September there are the Braemar Highland Games, graced by royal attendance, with massed pipe-bands, march past of the clans, pibrochs, neat pedibars, the tense balancing of the caber by wide-stepping kilted legs, the concentric muscle-play when the long-handled hammer is swung round the head, and all that, irrespective of weather, which is apt to be unkind to human gatherings.

Glen Quoich and Gleann an t'Slugain are the two valleys of the Eastern Cairngorms facing Braemar. Both are wooded in their lower parts, and the former almost through its entire length. The Quoich Water forms some interesting falls and gorges, as well as the famous Earl of Mar's Punch-bowl, after which the glen is named—*quoich* (caweekh) meaning " bowl ".

Gleann an t'Slugain is the best approach to the Sneck and the Eastern Cairngorms; through it, too, runs the " mounth " to Tomintoul, up to the small abandoned lodge at the head of the glen and over a low watershed to Glen Quoich where the path divides. Its left branch leads to Beinn a'Bhùird and is, on this occasion, no business of ours. We follow the right branch as far as the heathery base of Càrn Eas Beag, where a clearly marked pass indicates the position of the Gairn headwaters. This is our goal and we must not let the apparent absence of a path disconcert us unduly: it does materialize a little higher up, and it would be pure waste of time trying to find it too soon— just head for the pass!

There is nothing of great interest in Glen Gairn, though we may use it to climb Ben Avon if we feel tired of other routes; it is as plain as any glen can be until we reach Loch Builg and the sad remains of a shooting lodge above it (5 miles). The " mounth " continues along the east bank of the lake, down Glen Builg to Inchrory and thence to Tomintoul through the green valley of the Avon.

Glen Builg can also be reached by road from Balmoral or Ballater, and it was at the latter place that after lunch, one day of mixed sunshine and cloud, I hired a taxi to convey me to the Corndavon Lodge, three miles short of the loch. The driver swore that it was impossible to get any farther, though if my opinion is to be trusted the road before the lodge is in a far worse condition than beyond it. However this may be, I entrusted my body to an aged but still powerful Rolls Royce which whisked me up and down the steep inclines of narrow roads while my eye roamed idly over the views. The latter were some-

what indifferent, as the upper Gairn flows through a monotonous, treeless country of empty sheep-runs, with here and there
a lonely stone cottage and an occasional glimpse of Ben Avon
with its "pimples". It did not take long to cover the intervening twelve miles, and at half-past one I was again on my
light and ready feet by the small grove sheltering the Corndavon
Lodge. My head required a few minutes to get used to the
ambient of pedestrian locomotion and continued to swim buoy-
antly through the regions of second gear as I quickly trod the
deserted road; for the walker's world is essentially different from
the tyre-grinder's and like East and West they find it hard to
meet.

In a half-hour I was by the group of tarns introductory to
Loch Builg. The sun came out scorching hot as I was passing
the gate that gave admittance to the "mounth" skirting the
eastern side of the lake. Though by itself a fine sheet of water,
Loch Builg has little distinction: the surrounding hillsides are
low and formless, and only the flowering of the heather or the
play of the sky can redeem the insignificance of its views. I did
not pause long to admire it but, when at the other end, yielded
to the warmth of the sun and the glitter of the water and subsided into the heather at its edge to drowse and watch the bright
and dark ripples crowd upon each other. Now the dark would
gain most of the offshore mirror, now the bright silver bring the
whole loch under its sway, driving the murky tremors into the
shelter of little bays and stones. There was rest in water,
mother of all life, freedom from strife and self-assertion, and I
closed my eyes against the bright sunshine which filled them
with the scarlet glare of blood. The tinkle of wavelets entered
my ears and my weariness, and my awareness sank into the
subconscious world of scattered images. Unwillingly, I roused
myself from my stupor and slipped my arms under the straps
of my rucksack.

In a few minutes I felt under my feet the light clanking limestone scree and the sudden abundance of small flowers marked
the richer soil. Milkworts, daisies, thyme, clover and multitudes of nodding yellow rock-roses were scattered broadcast

along the path winding down into Glen Builg. The sterile granite had retreated up the western hillsides, grown solid with ling, which to the east had given way to pale limestone grass. Outcrops of pigeon-blue and ash-grey rock had replaced the pink and black boulders. Some junipers and birches, spared by the heather conflagrations, were still lining the gullies and the water-courses where fire had been checked. Farther down the glen, sadly singed trees were making a brave effort to revive here and there among the charred, branchless trunks of their less lucky fellows.

Higher up the eastern slopes red scree and soil were intruding upon the white limestone grit, thus disclosing the presence of the overlying red sandstone which became more prominent on the way to Tomintoul.

In a green depression I tasted of the soft limestone water, so different from the harsher drink of granite burns, and mounted the path that cut across a steep grassy slope winking in the breeze with the yellow of innumerable rock-roses, which seemed to grow here to an exceptionally large size. The white-washed Inchrory Lodge was now in sight behind a pleasant birch grove. Meanwhile the clouds had gathered over the hills into a thick lowering canopy which presently released a sharp shower.

At Inchrory the Avon forms another " crossroads ". Having emerged from Loch Avon, twelve miles to the west, it follows an easterly course but, upon taking in the Builg Burn, swings sharply north towards Tomintoul at an angle of rather more than ninety degrees. This, however, has not always been so. At one time the Avon used to continue eastwards and fall into the Don, or what has since become the Don; and the low pass facing Glen Avon above the lodge is neither more nor less than part of its old bed. The headwaters of the Don are barely half a mile from the elbow of the Avon, and the Don valley is the geological continuation of Glen Avon. The Inchrory Pass is low, only about a hundred feet above the Avon's present bed, and a cart track crosses it to the Dalnadamph Lodge.

It is usually said that the Avon, which originally flowed into the Don, has found a band of soft limestone in the north and opened for itself a way through it to Tomintoul and the Spey, thus leaving the Don in the lurch. Yet, if we examine the evidence on which this " accusation " is based, we will soon see that it does not stand close scrutiny by a geological Sherlock Holmes.

In the first place, had the Avon continued faithful to its old bed it would have been a river so much more important than the thin upper Don that the latter would have been lost in it and simply would not exist as a separate entity. In other words, its alleged " desertion " by the Avon was, in reality, the beginning of its independent existence.

In the second place, the Inchrory Pass consists of the selfsame limestone for the sake of which the Avon is said to have abandoned its old association. Had the pass been of igneous formation this might conceivably have been the case; but it is hard to imagine why one lot of limestone facing the current and, therefore, exposed to its maximum erosive force should have been abandoned for another lot of identical rock on the side where the current's erosive action was weak and ineffective. Clearly, some other factors have intervened.

As I see the situation, a long time ago the pre-glacial Avon flowed in a deep gorge or canyon, in much the same way as the Water of Ailnack, six miles to the north, still does to-day. This gorge traversed the site of the present-day Inchrory, where it received the tributary gorge of the ancestral Builg Burn and, without any trouble, continued into the valley of the Don which was but its further extension. Came the Big Ice and glaciers began to slide down the gentle slopes of the ancient Ben Avon. One of these was nursed into strength in the northern corries and gullies of the peak and descended into the Avon gorge, jammed it, shattered and tore its sides, until they were widened into the glen that we know to-day. But at Inchrory it found its further progress barred by another glacier which had sneaked round the corner and got in first down Glen Builg, impinging with great force upon the putative pass which divided the Avon from the valley of the pre-Water of Ailnack and the stream that must have flowed into it down this pass. In consequence there was a terrific " traffic jam ", intensified by the fact that at the foot of Glen Avon lay a band of hard granite which slowed down the glacier of the Avon.

The two glaciers met and wrestled, crushed and cracked one another, and " trampled down " the soft limestone ground on which they fought into a deep cavity. The sun looked on and bided his time, until he got tired of this show and dismissed the glaciers. Powerful streams gushed out of the receding ice. The Avon rushed gleefully down the brand-new wide glen but, when nearing Inchrory, he found that a neatly polished granite hump had been put in his way. He flung himself at it with fury and, in due course, wore out in it a trough-like channel which, once English mixed with Gaelic became the language of the place, was to be known as the Linn of Avon. Meanwhile the Builg Burn had been hurrying to meet his old friend, but when he arrived at the tryst he did not recognize the place. It had become a deep hollow into which the Avon was spilling thinly over the granite step in the east. Jointly they filled it with their waters, till these overflowed the pass to the north, much worn down as it had been by the ice. The Avon being checked in its progress, it was now the Builg that had most of the say and most of the punch and, coming from the south, he punched north. While the Avon was busy wearing down the obstreperous granite band, the Builg reduced the pass and they both hurried onwards in a new bed to overwhelm the Ailnack at Delnabo.

In Glen Avon the ice wrought the magnificent recess of Loch Avon; farther downstream it was, however, given inferior material in the shape of the flat-topped High Plateau closing in on both sides and, strive as it might, the result was not very exciting. With the old forest gone, the glen is monotonous and drab. You can have a peep on the way into the Great Slochd and the Sma' Glen, but there are not many points where this can be done and the average pictorial interest of Glen Avon's middle part is small. It shelters the Faindouran Lodge which, lying as it does at 1,920 feet above sea-level, is supposed to be the highest shooting lodge in Scotland. Above half a mile downwater from it there is a rock called Cnapan a'Mheirlich (the Thieves' Knoll), to testify that the "infamous bykes of lawless lymmars" used to pass this way. The glen has also many associations with the Fingalian legends, some of which have been touched on lightly on other pages.

Such and other thoughts were filling my mind as, many thousands of years after the disappearance of the glaciers, I was nearing the Inchrory Lodge with its pleasant rockery. Colonel Haig, proprietor of the Inchrory Estate, was in residence and the chimneys were smoking. John Wilson, the head keeper, was there too and, luckily for me, on the point of driving back to "Birchfield". A lift was welcome, as the rain showed no intention of stopping and six miles are six miles, geology or no geology.

The Avon flows to Tomintoul in a deep, green, tree-lined glen of fertile rural appearance, whose greenery seems exuberant by contrast with the rueful barrenness of the neighbouring high moors.

I walked the last three miles over a derelict road, swarming with rabbits, where wild strawberry was spreading its trailing shoots over the red sandstone gravel, and entered the streaming Tomintoul in a brisk shower of sunlit rain.

5. *The Valley of the Fairy Stream and the Marsh Glen*

Glen Feshie and Glen Geldie, which between them form the western and south-western boundaries of the Cairngorm Mountains, are another natural "mounth" connecting Speyside with Braemar. The total distance involved is about thirty-two miles, whether we start from (or end at) Kingussie or Kincraig, which are roughly equidistant from Braemar.

From Kingussie the route runs by road over the Spey Bridge at Ruthven to the Tromie Bridge, a little way beyond which a forest track climbs the steep rise to Drumguish, a hamlet hidden behind a pinewood. From Drumguish a rough road, passable for cycles, crosses a wide open moor with scattered pines, rising gently on the way to a low scarp below which a small river, sparsely lined with trees, is spanned by a foot-bridge. The foot-bridge is somewhat off the main track, which leads to a ford; both give access to the green flats of Balguish with a lonely shepherd's cottage. An old sheep-fank across the flats is our next landmark, whence a clear moorland track brings us to Glen Feshie, half a mile below Stronetoper.

At Kincraig, which is a more interesting approach, we have the choice of two routes: one by way of the little village of Insh, on the other side of Loch Insh and two miles from Kincraig, whence by a metalled road along the left (west) bank of the Feshie; the other by way of Feshiebridge, whence over the bridge and to the right past a group of cottages, into the open moors on the right side of the glen, until Achlean is reached. There, we pass the croft, cross the swaying foot-bridge by the school-house and regain the main road.

Up Glen Feshie the way is clear and, despite the dreadful devastation wrought by war-time fellings, never lacking in interest: we recross the river by the bridge below the head keeper's cottage and, having done this, keep to the east side of the glen. A scree-and-rock-rimmed defile admits us to the unspoiled and most beautiful part of Glen Feshie but, once we have left behind the last birch orchards and Landseer's bothy at its head, the scenery subsides and flattens down like an unsuccessful cake. This is a prelude to the mournful moorland, where the Feshie has by headward erosion undercut the watershed and thus deflected into itself the course of the Eidart, until then a tributary of the Geldie. Up this moorland goes the path, becoming less and less distinct, to a foot-bridge on the Eidart, on which it would be rash to count as more often than not it is not there. The Eidart, fed by the burns of the Great Moss, flows in a rapid and abundant stream; in dry weather it can be waded without much difficulty, but not so after a wet spell or when the snows are melting on the High Tops. A long detour upstream may then be necessary and the country is generally boggy, which does not make it any more pleasant. The Eidart crossed, we have some two miles of moors to the upper Glen Geldie and the Geldie Lodge, where we are once more on firm ground.

Just as Glen Feshie, which, incidentally, is a corruption of the

Gaelic Gleann Fèisidh—the Valley of the Fairy Stream—is one of the most beautiful and, considering its length, most uniformly interesting glens in the Cairngorms, so is Glen Geldie unquestionably the dreariest of them all. Yet down it we must go, past Glen Tilt and the Bynack Lodge, a couple of unoccupied cottages, a bridge resting quietly on the river's bank and up northwards to the White Bridge, where we can leave the Geldie with a sigh of relief and follow the Dee to whichever place we choose.

The "mounth", except for the watershed, is negotiable by bicycle and even the crossing of the latter is not so heroic an effort as trundling one's hapless mount over the boulders of the Lairig Ghru, though tastes may and do differ.

I have spent much time in Glen Feshie and given it much space, so that I dare not, and probably need not, add to its descriptions; but one clear day of the early September 1943 comes back to me with vivid insistence.

Marjorie and I had arrived from London about a fortnight before, but the weather and other circumstances had supervened, so that it was our first day in the Cairngorms. We left Achlean early in the morning under a pale blue, cloudless sky, the air still cool after the lengthening night. There was no wind, but even when it grew hot later in the day the heat was already tempered by the declining diurnal arc of the sun and never oppressive.

The river stood fairly high but ran clear, splashing down over grey and pink stones, dipping into glimmering pools and filing endlessly away towards the grey-blue Monadhliath beyond Kincraig. We followed the left bank all the way, past the lodge with its old firs, to the wide strath in the middle of the glen where it divides into three branches, the westernmost of these carrying a path to Glen Tromie and the easternmost being the main "stem". In the fork Creag na Caillich (Old Woman's Crag) squats—a steep, blunt hill, fringed with rocks on two sides. We made for the central glen, where Highland rush grew in profusion, dangling its dainty little tufts at the tip of long arching stalks, and then up the grassy sides of a small water-course to the top of the Creag.

The hillside was abrupt and tiring, but we were in no hurry, the air was dry and light to breathe and the sun lay kindly on our backs. The top was covered with a thick carpet of golden-moss, small heather and blaeberry, already turning crimson, with some club-mosses raising their silver-green brushes from the tangle. It was warm and herb-scented and we lay down on it, watching the small pearly clouds sail slowly up from the wide blue horizon, puff out as they approached and pass behind the sun. A light breeze was gently stroking the lowly growth and hurrying russet waves over the sedges above the source of the burn.

The eastward scarp of the hill is over a thousand feet high. The summit terrace of damp heather moor breaks off abruptly towards it, bulging over rock pillars, immersed in rapid screes which sweep down the face to the slabby rocks with spinneys of birch and young pine. Down below, in the narrow defile of the Feshie, pines are like dark moss-cushions and the transparent stream is a line of small stone and gravel over which straggle white cobwebs of foam. Opposite—another scarp and a flight of grey screes. . . .

We adventured some way down the steep face, but found it rather uncomfortable for our present liking and withdrew. Instead, we followed the glen along the summit terrace up to a gully, down which a sizeable stream was dropping in steps towards the Feshie. Alongside it a deer-track zigzagged through the heather and over hummocky rocks, but we preferred the gully where we had some easy, cool scrambles over slabs and boulders at the side of thin, narrow waterfalls. This brought us to a stretch of even sward, screened by birches and solitary pines, above a river pool of fairy clearness. Through it and up the step of rock at its upper end salmon were making their way up against the stream. Every few minutes a graceful silver shape would rise into the air with a powerful flip of the tail, plunge into the foam, flutter in the quick, shallow water on the step, gather itself into another, lower leap and clear the obstacle.

Down in the defile the river widened and grew shallow, but the current was heavy and the water biting-cold, with no stones to give one a rest on the way across. We did not succeed in wading it and had to follow the foot of the rocks to where the Feshie, having burst through the narrow bottleneck, broke into several channels divided by gravelly shoals.

Next day the weather held, though there was more cloud in the forenoon and it looked at one time as though it was going to rain.

We took the stalking path to Ciste Mearaid and crossed the broad shoulder of the Great Moss towards Coire Odhar. The wind on the top was strong and contrary, but in a matter of fifteen minutes we stood on the high step above Loch Einich, which lay below, dark and restless, the wind scattering flurries round its peacock edges. The shadow-darkened cliffs of the Sgorans flanked the wide view. A small herd of deer was grazing in a green hollow on our left.

An indistinct path or deer-track threaded its way through the broken rocks, over the steep stone-shoots and grassy ledges at our feet. In following this we found a small flare parachute and two unexploded ten-pounder shells embedded in the scree, which we skirted over a rocky shoulder to avoid sending stones down upon them. The detour involved us in some complications, but the rock-frieze of the corrie was low and much broken up, so that we were soon clear of it and walking quickly down the long and steepish hillsides, grown with grass and all manner of mountain plant and generously strewn with boulders. The total drop was over 1,500 feet, so that the descent was quite a strain on our pavement-weary legs and we were glad to find ourselves on the path running along the west shore of Loch Einich. The clouds had gone and the sun glittered on the banks of gritty sand and the dark depths. The shadows were waxing in the buttresses and gullies of the Black Sgoran. It was about four o'clock when we squeezed our way across the sluice gate at the foot of the lake opposite the melancholy chimney-stack, the sole remnant of John of Corrour's bothy.

Gleann Einich, which is in English the Marsh Valley, lay open against the western sun and it was sweltering-hot on the broad sheltered strath where the Beanaidh river had cut out for

Glen Lui with Càrn a'Mhaim in the distance

itself a meandering ravine through the thick layer of glacial drift. Stretch of brown **moor** succeeded stretch of brown moor, on which the last of the ling was still glimmering in thin lilac patches, as the mass of Braeriach and the dark outline of the Sgorans were sinking lower behind the horizon at our back. The Tree of the Return was indeed a relief; then the green pines of Rothiemurchus came into view inside the deep ravine.

The forest was still unspoiled.

Troops were camped in the clearings and military vehicles dispersed under the trees for protection against enemy aircraft. We were shy of asking for lifts and arrived at Aviemore, dead-tired, with the best part of twenty miles behind us, at 7.15 in the evening, five minutes too late for the last train to Kingussie, where we were staying. The problem of accommodation loomed large for a while, but was soon solved by an obliging friend who put us up for the night.

Am Beanaidh, Rothiemurchus

L

Loch Einich from the edge of the Great Moss

VIII

ON THE LOCHS AND LOCHANS

1. *Waters, Blue, Green and Brown*

IT was a soaking midsummer with the rain pouring down for days from the overcast skies. The streams were in spate, foaming and roaring down the hillsides. Huddled up in my waterproof coat, I was crossing a rocking foot-bridge slung over a narrow gorge with a raging torrent below. The water was dark and menacing, the colour of black coffee, with bluish glints on its trembling coils. Laces of brown spume were rushing past underneath my feet to be engulfed in cavernous pools, seething and bubbling in clammy rock chambers. One could hear big stones being washed downstream as they went by knocking on the bed and leaping the falls.

The sight held in it a grim fascination, the sound of the endlessly spilling waters acting as a kind of mental lullaby, and an old man had obviously abandoned himself to it, for he was standing half-way up the bridge, his eyes intent on the water, sucking thoughtfully at his pipe.

At my approach he made a faint movement with his head, took the pipe out of his mouth, and said gravely:

"Aye, it's from the peat," whereupon he relapsed into silent contemplation.

The purport of his cryptic greeting was instantly clear to me: it referred to the colour of the water.

A Highland burn may gleam dark cobalt against the sky, or streak raven-black across the snow-covered countryside, but its usual colouring is amber, like whisky or the eyes of a blackface sheep. This is due to peat or, technically speaking, to a solution of organic acids derived from the decay of vegetation in the peat bogs. The intensity of the brown tint varies greatly from day to day. On calm sunny days the water will be almost colourless to a downward gaze, with just a suggestion of brown over the greater depths; but during the spring thaw and in rainy weather it may darken to the shade of sepia.

On the other hand, the natural hue of distilled water is blue and, if clear of organic impurities, it appears as such once a sufficient volume is present to bring out its faint coloration. As we ascend towards the heights, above the region of peaty moors, the quick-flowing waters of the burns and rivers lose their brown tinge. The Feshie and the Dee are pale green. The Avon is usually described as "white", that is to say colourless, which may be due to the presence of iron oxide neutralizing the green colouring caused by an admixture of humic acid.[1] Most running water with sources among the screes and rocks of the Cairngorms, as well as the high-lying lakes and tarns, is very nearly pure, with just enough mineral and organic matter in solution to modify the blue to that lovely shade of sparkling aquamarine found in mountain pools. Only in the lower course do the streams and rivers become polluted by peat, turning at first green, then yellow and amber-brown. If there is much iron oxide about, the water may acquire a reddish colouring, further intensified by a red deposit on the submerged stones; but this is rare in the Cairngorms, and such "Red Burns" as there are owe their designation to the colour of the granite screes among which they rise rather than to that of their waters.

The lakes of the Cairngorms are not among the largest nor the deepest in the country. The most extensive of them, Loch Morlich, occupies the relatively modest area of 300 acres, and its greatest depth does not exceed 50 feet. Others are somewhat deeper, but none of them can even remotely approach Loch Morar's 1,017 feet.[2]

Broadly speaking, the Cairngorm lakes fall into three groups. The lochs and lochans of the approaches sit in the hollows formed by the uneven accumulation of glacial drift, sometimes described as "kettle-holes", at the foot of the high hills or on

---

[1] J. E. Marr: *The Scientific Study of Scenery*, p. 201.
[2] The depths and dimensions of the lochs are given, whenever possible, after Sir John Murray's and Laurence Pullar's *Bathymetrical Survey of the Scottish Fresh-Water Lochs* (Edinburgh, 1910).

the wide plateaux of undulating moorland. Some of these water-basins have been more or less silted up and reduced both in depth and extension to mere pools that may occasionally dry up in prolonged drought exposing a surface of cracked peat mud. Higher up the glens, valley lakes occupy true rock basins eroded by the ice and dammed by terminal moraines or deposits of drift, and some smaller sheets of water fill the glacial rock cavities at higher levels. Finally, the corries contain moraine tarns of various size, most of which, however, are only negligible pools. The lochs deposited in the passes by the receding glaciers form a link between these three groups, as in their case glacial erosion, uneven distribution of drift deposits and terminal or lateral moraines have all combined to secure the water. The Green Lochan of Ryvoan, Loch Builg and Loch Pityoulish may serve as examples of this type of lake.

Most of the larger lochs are found on the northern side of the hills, where these attain the greatest altitudes and where the glaciers had maintained themselves longer. The irregularities in the deposition of glacial drift along the wide valley of the Spey have given rise to a whole cluster of water-basins. Only Loch Morlich, Loch an Eilein, Loch Gamhna and Loch Pityoulish, not counting a few minor pools, lie within the Cairngorm district as defined by the Rivers Spey and Feshie and the Craiggowrie-Meall a'Bhuachaille ridge. Loch Pityoulish marks the utmost reach on the hills in the north-west. Yet Loch Insh and Loch Alvie are just across this, in any case somewhat arbitrary, boundary and form prominent features of the Cairngorm landscape. Other large lakes and tarns are scattered over the glens, plateaux and corries of the Central and Western Cairngorms. The Eastern subdivision of the hills contains but two small moraine tarns: Dubh Lochan, or the Black Tarn, in an eastern corrie of Beinn a'Bhùird, and Lochan nan Gabhar under a rocky spur of Ben Avon; while at the foot of the latter peak the bleak waters of Loch Builg with their attendant pools spread as an eastern counterpart of Loch Pityoulish, setting a limit to the farthest eastward stretch of the Cairngorm Mountains.

The lochs of Strathspey belong to the drift class, which is

characterized by an oval or irregular outline, and, not resting in true rock basins, seldom attain great depth. Their waters, owing to the low situation, are not particularly pure, and their general aspect, apart from accidental reflections from the sky and the surrounding scenery, is some stage in the scale of grey tints, from silver and pearl to black lead. They all lie within the wooded area north of the main Cairngorm massif, where the dusky greens of pinewoods mingle with the lighter foliage of birches and occasional oaks, beeches, rowans, bird cherries and larches (the latter incomers in Britain, first introduced into Scotland towards the end of the eighteenth century), grasslands, cultivated fields, and brown or purple heaths. Autumn is the time when the russets, browns and yellows of the deciduous trees, bracken and grasses transmute their cold steely mirrors into deep glittering blue. Late in October or early in November the hills assume that peculiar damson colouring above the faded ochre and umber of the grass and the dark, gold-sprinkled madder of birchwoods, and the waters respond to their mood, combining to scenes of stern and cruel grandeur, a fitting background for some tale of bravery, endurance, sacrifice, troth or treachery, ruthlessness and hatred.

It was on a wild November night, lashed with sleet and snow, in the old timber-floating days that young Allan Grant went up the long glen to open the sluices of Loch Einich and release its ponded waters for the morning "run". He completed his task but was found dead next day not far from the sluice gate, where he had succumbed to exhaustion with an uneaten half of the bannock his mother had given to her only son.[1] I fancy the rocks of the Sgorans were glowing damson-black that day, as they were on many another day when darker deeds were done.

2. *The Lochs of Speyside*

The picturesque Loch Alvie, with its wooded peninsula, church and cluster of houses half-way between Kincraig and Aviemore, lying as it does north of the Spey, properly belongs

[1] Elizabeth Smith of Baltiboys: *Memoirs of a Highland Lady* (London, 1898).

to the Monadhliath—the Grey Mountains—but the foothills of the " blue " Cairngorms are just across the river, so that the lake comes within the compass of their views.

Loch Insh near Kincraig is formed by the spreading waters of the Spey above the confluence of this river and the Feshie, which constitutes the technical boundary of the Cairngorms. To-day the greatest length of the loch is a little over a mile, and its greatest breadth some two-thirds of a mile, but at one time it used to extend as far as Kingussie in the south-west, where it has left a legacy of half-drained marshland which is periodically invaded by its waters during the spring floods.

Loch Insh is not properly a drift lake, though its existence is partly due to the distribution of glacial deposits on the sides of the Spey valley. In fact, its position gives it partly the character of a valley lake, thanks to which its waters, ponded back by the moraines of the old Glenfeshie glacier, attain the depth of one hundred feet. Situated in the midst of the broad strath, it feels the full fury of the western winds and will often run considerable breakers, which may make a boat excursion a dangerous venture in uncertain weather. The loch is pleasantly framed with birch and oak woods; an old church is tucked up among the pines overgrowing a small hillock near the Kincraig bridge over the Spey (itself a rather flimsy affair); and the wooded island of Tom Dhu adds a further touch of variety to its views. Loch Insh affords good fishing, and in the early spring and late winter the adjacent marshes swarm with water fowl, whooper-swans hooting at one another across the thawing ice.

Although divided by the Feshie and a stretch of forest and moor from the main hills, the loch is a conspicuous feature of the Western Cairngorms. Creag Mhigeachaidh falls towards it in an abrupt triangular scarp scarred with scree-shoots, up which some pines and rowans climb among the rocks. Above, Geal-chàrn and the western spurs of the Sgorans swell up in steep, billowy ridges, and Braeriach displays the rocky rim of its northern corries. To the south, the wide Glen Feshie opens up with birch groves and streaks of pinewood still spared by the axe.

Late in August, the flaming summer of 1945, I walked from
Kincraig over Feshiebridge to the Moor of Feshie and Allt
a'Mharcaidh, a stream that rises high on Sgòran Dubh Mòr
and turns sharply west on reaching the low ground. Here its
course is regulated to prevent damage to the tree plantations
which are protected by a high deer fence running parallel with
the north bank of the burn.

The woodlands at the foot of the hills were a jumble of stony
roads, decaying branches and stumps, with solitary trees still
rearing up here and there on the war-time principle of the survival of the unfittest. But farther east, towards the bend of the
burn, the forest closed its ranks. Stillness reigned there, with
the buzz of bees on the heather and the tinkling of water winding down the maze of ravines and fairy " knowes ". Old pines
and birches were spaced sparsely among the heather and juniper
bushes. Luscious green grass covered the damp hollows of the
ravines, and isolated islands of heather sat in it like soft purple
pouffes. Aloft, the hills rose in serried slopes towards the high
crown of the Black Sgoran.

The water of the burn was no longer brownish but clear white,
washing away like liquid glass over pebbles of pink granite, and
Highland rushes bowed their graceful heads towards the shimmering pools. I felt a keen, almost painful, joy as my bare feet
plunged into the cold stream and sought the rounded surfaces
of the smooth underwater stones. I was in no hurry to reach
the other bank and, when there, collapsed into the deep heather,
abandoning myself to idleness and lunch.

From a small bothy a few stone throws from that place, an
indistinct path leads through a parkland forest to Loch Gamhna
(pronounced like Gown), a small lake fringed with reeds and
water-lilies which, lying at the neat height of 888 feet, feeds with
its waters the somewhat shopworn beauty spot of Loch an Eilein,
48 feet below it in the north-east.

As I struck Loch Gamhna about 2 p.m. a heron rose from the
reeds and circled heavily awhile on its widespread wings. Then
a flock of graylag geese took wing at my approach, and passed
curiously some fifty yards above my head with the sound of

telegraph wires in the wind. Old tree trunks embedded in the
mud of the shore shallows resembled aged slumbering crocodiles.
Trout were playing in the loch and leaping out of the water in
pursuit of insects. Now here now there concentric ripples would
spring up, widening and widening, until they flattened out completely in the smooth mirror, darkened by the shadow of a
passing cloud.

In a few minutes I reached the circuit road of Loch an
Eilein.

I had tea in the cottage standing in the green glade at the foot

of Ord Ban, where some tourists burst in noisily, asking me
various questions to which I mumbled awkward replies, shrinking within the shell of my sunlit solitude.

Loch an Eilein lies in a sheltered hollow beneath the bulky
shape of Creag Dubh which rises from the dark forests in
shelved steps towards the ridge of the Sgorans. In the north,
Ord Ban, a wooded hill of small elevation (1,450 ft.) which throws
up some rocky ribs and hummocks, separates the hollow from
Strathspey. In the east spreads the vast sea of pine, badly mauled

by the war-time fellings, all the way to the wavy outline of the
Craiggowrie-Meall a'Bhuachaille ridge which encloses the horizon.   Of the big hills Cairn Gorm and Cairn Lochan belong to
the Loch-an-Eilein prospects, but one gets of them only an
oblique view with a foreshortened perspective.

Thus the outlook is somewhat restricted and dominated by the
graceless slopes of Inchriach, stripped of their forest mantle.
Yet the surroundings of the lake, and particularly Ord Ban and
the lower Kennapole Hill between it and Loch Gamhna, offer
many enticing nooks and tree-framed views.   Old knobby pines
still spread the snaky tumult of their branches above hazel and
birch, and great boulders, clad in moss and lichen, heave up
from the green grass slopes where in springtime violets and primroses come out in abundance and where rabbits hold their evening revels.

The loch's chief title to fame is the castle built on piles on an
islet near its northern shore.

It is from this islet that the loch takes its name—the Lake
of the Island.

The castle dates from the thirteenth century and used to be
a stronghold of the mighty Norman family of the Comyns,
Lords of Badenoch, whose name is prominent in the early annals
of Scotland and who had held sway over these lands until they
were waylaid by Farquhar Shaw and foully slain on Calart Hill
near Pityoulish.   What happened after this is not quite clear,
but it seems that the Shaws followed up this deed with some
territorial annexation.   Sometime in the sixteenth century the
Shaws, having incurred royal displeasure, were in turn evicted
from Rothiemurchus by the Clan Grant, who established themselves there after a protracted feud.   With the abolition of the
clan system of communal property, their possessions became a
personal estate of the Grants of Rothiemurchus, who still own
them to-day.[1]

The castle is in ruins.   Grown with ivy and flanked with trees,
it presents to the north a fragment of a tower with a hole of a

---

[1] See Sir Henry Alexander: *The Cairngorms*, and Elizabeth Smith of Baltiboys: *Memoirs of a Highland Lady.*

window and a long blank wall pierced by a single doorway leading straight into the water. The whole makes a somewhat
shapeless pile, which causes much worry to the numerous artists
and photographers seeking novel compositions. The castle is
said to be connected with the shore by a subterranean passage
whose whereabouts, however, have been lost to tradition.

At one time an osprey used to nest on the ruin and fish in the
waters of the loch but it, too, has been "evicted" by the zeal of
egg-collectors or perhaps by the unlovely habits of the tourists
who often indulge in putting the statement that the castle is
"only a stone's throw from the shore" to the practical test, and
will also stand and yell to hear the echo of their voices reflected
from its walls.[1] This is said to have a "weird" effect which,
not having gone deeper into the matter, I am unable either to
confirm or deny. . . . But oh!—how the Comyns must be turning in their sudden graves!

Opposite the islet, a cottage of respectable age and pleasant
appearance offers teas and light refreshments, and chickens walk
and peck about a fenced-in grass field containing a memorial
and a bird-cherry. In May the tree is a burst of white blossom,
in autumn of bright gamboge yellow, thrown into bold relief by
the dark forests and the grey-blue waters.

Loch an Eilein is quite deep, attaining 66 feet and, fed by
a number of springs at its bottom, long defies the most severe
frosts, though during the "Shinwell" winter of 1946-47 I crossed
it on ski on two occasions. Ski are a reasonably safe form of
locomotion for this purpose, but those intending to skate on the
lake ought to read the inscription on the memorial before they
commit themselves to this venture—it would be unkind to add
any more memorials to this one!

The loch is shaped like an irregular oblong which has been,
so to speak, simultaneously squeezed in on all four sides. Its
greatest length, taken diagonally, is about a mile, but it is less
than a quarter of a mile in the "waist".

It is, of course, a beautiful place, but I can never bring myself
openly to admit it. Somehow the castle, the tea-shop, the boat

[1] Alexander MacKenzie: *Trees in the Highlands* (Elgin, 1912).

and the two motor roads connecting it with Aviemore (four miles), over which summer visitors flock in on foot and wheel, make it too much of a post card.

A rough cart track rings the loch and another, known as the Thieves' Road, once used by the Lochaber cattle " rievers ", leads from it to Glen More and Loch Morlich through the devastated woodlands of Rothiemurchus, making a pleasant but longish and somewhat monotonous walk.

Some two miles south among the moors of Gleann Einich lies an inconspicuous lochan bearing the unexpected name Loch Mhic a'Ghille Chaoile, that is to say the Lake of the Thin Man's Son, whereby hangs a story. It is so named in honour of the local hero who intercepted and engaged single-handed a party of raiders until he was killed, thus giving the men of Rothiemurchus enough time to get ready and repulse the assailants. A rusty dirk, found in the peat bogs by the tarn, is said to corroborate the story, though it may have no connection whatever with the famous incident.

3. *Loch Morlich of the Wide Glen and the Green Tarn of the Fairies*

Loch Morlich sits among the drift flats of the wide Glen More which form a triangle between the massif of Cairn Gorm and the Craiggowrie-Meall a'Bhuachaille ridge towards the Pass of Ryvoan and its Green Lochan.

Although rather shallow (maximum depth 49 ft.), Loch Morlich is the largest of the Cairngorm lakes, over a mile in length and two-thirds of a mile across, with a superficial area of 300 acres. It is situated at 1,048 feet and the High Tops swell up immediately above it, attaining in the summit of Cairn Gorm the height of 4,084 feet. Little remains of the noble Glenmore Forest, while the new plantations are still too young to replace the veteran pines of the past. Enough of these, however, are left standing to give you an idea of what the place was like before the inroads of axe and tractor, and trees still ring the loch, although but thinly in the west. On the east side, where breakers are rushed inshore by the westerly gales, there is a wide beach of pink sand from which a detachment of sturdy, wind-worn firs rises above the tangle of snaky roots. Aloft, the rocky corries of Cairn Gorm and Cairn Lochan frown darkly under the canopy of boiling cloud or rear up, distant and placid, in the blue sun haze above a stretch of rolling high moors, scooped out into folds by meandering water-courses.

The loch is undoubtedly one of the most magnificent sights the Cairngorms have to offer but, unfortunately, the beach is spoiled by an ungainly boathouse, barbed wire and some other " souvenirs " left by the Glenmore Snow and Mountain Warfare Training Centre; nor have the " timber operations " improved its appearance. The township of wooden shacks clustering round the sawmill at its lower end makes you hurry past rather than pause to admire the wide mountain-scape. As at the time of writing the " operations " have been almost completed, it remains to be hoped that the timber camp will not fall into the hands of squatters and that the huts will be dismantled and removed by the Forestry Commission which is in charge of these matters.

Since the road from Coylum Bridge was repaired and titivated by the military the loch has been easily accessible from Aviemore by car and bicycle, and on a fine summer day it is apt to be overrun by picnickers and tourists who, apart from the temporary display of vehicles parked under the trees by the beach, leave there the inevitable permanent legacy of papers and bottle glass. It is a right-of-way road, but it would be a good thing if cars were not admitted beyond the forest gate at the lower end of the lake.

About two miles east of Loch Morlich by the Thieves' Road, in the deep pass of Ryvoan, flanked by steep, crag-rimmed screes, there is a moraine tarn of strikingly green colouring, to which it owes its name, Lochan Uaine.

It is one of the four Cairngorm tarns of this name, and the most accessible of them.

The Green Lochan nestles at the foot of the screes of Creag nan Gall, and probably owes its rise to a lateral moraine and the rock fragments that used in the past to slide down over the snow accumulating on this side of the pass until they formed a mound parallel to the foot of the screes. In fact, the level of the pass is considerably lower than that of the lochan and a quick stream, rising in the hill opposite, drains west into Loch Morlich. This stream flows alongside the tarn—a rather unusual situation—whereas the latter has no visible outlet, as its outflowing waters have been swallowed up by the loosely piled boulders at the base of the enclosing mound. It seems that there once was another tarn in the pass at a lower level, since silted-up and overgrown.

When seen from the surrounding heights, the lochan appears almost emerald-green. This is due partly to the factors mentioned at the beginning of the chapter, partly to the reflection from the pines which enter the pass in a long tongue and struggle up the screes on both sides above it, partly to the contrast with the pink-and-lilac-tinged screes which serve to underline its natural tint, partly to what I am personally inclined to believe is the most important single contribution to the combined effect, the " fact " that the fairies use it to do their washing in. The wee folk, as is well known, are clad exclusively in green and, being a trifle old-fashioned, do not go in for fast colours.

It would be a fine sight to surprise the tiny mantles, rinsed in the cold clearness of the tarn, fluttering in the breeze on a gossamer line; but a warning must be appended that those who look at such things run the risk of losing their eyesight altogether.

As for myself—alas, I have never seen that, but I have seen the lochan and it is a thing of beauty.

4. *Pityoulish, Sad and Fair*

Loch Pityoulish is the last of the large drift lakes on the Cairngorm side of the Spey. It lies near the Coylum Bridge-Grantown road, and the Newtonmore-Grantown 'bus will deposit you a stone throw from its shore; but it does not enjoy quite the same popularity as Loch Morlich and Loch an Eilein. Possibly because its setting is more modest. No great hills tower up immediately above it. It is only some two-thirds of a mile in length and less than a quarter of a mile across. The somewhat dubious remains of Pictish fortifications submerged under its waters[1] do not stand comparison with the very real ruins of Loch an Eilein. Thus the gregarian mind finds little about it to feed its imagination.

The loch is within easy walking distance of Coylum Bridge, and one dull November day I took this way of approach, following the tree fringe left when the forest had been felled as shelter for sheep and cattle from the bitter winter gales.

Grey clouds were trailing over the High Tops and rain came sparsely on the gusts of an icy east wind. The tree-grown bank was swarming with rabbits which scampered off at the sight of me into holes under the roots of the pines and dark douglas firs.

At one time Loch Pityoulish must have extended a good way towards Drumintoul Lodge and Coylum Bridge, and this bank was its shore. The old bed of the lake is still plainly traceable in the configuration of the ground, though it is now occupied by fields and pastures. But at the southern edge of the water you come upon a marshy stretch, criss-crossed with ditches, to which it has not yet abandoned its claim and which is periodically submerged during the spring floods. There the loch, squeezed in between the Calart Hill and Creag Chaisteal, the last outlier of the Cairngorms, begins in a straight line with shallows and mudflats where graylag geese and the wild duck folk wade and feed among the reeds. Farther north the loch deepens, attaining 74 feet, for here the head of the old glacier to which it owes its existence has scraped out a hollow by "bulldozer action". A shelf, clearly marked along the east shore, forms a natural road round that side of the water and gives a rough measure of the thickness of the ice during the last glaciation. At the north end the loch is shallow. Here it is typical drift country,

---

[1] "There is an island in the loch, which appears when the water is low. It is evidently artificial, and probably was used as a place of defence. Perhaps it had a crannoge as part of the structure, or it may have been connected with the Stone Fort on the hill above (*Creag Chaisteal*)." W. Forsyth, M.A., D.D.: *In the Shadow of Cairngorm* (Inverness, 1900), p. 58.

with ravines and fairy "knowes", grown with grass and bracken, open birch groves and solitary oaks.

All this, however, still lay ahead of me as I struck off right towards the hills, across the old bed of the lake. Black cattle of the hornless Aberdeen-Angus breed were dotting the fawn expanse at the end of which the water glittered in a thin steel edge. Chickens were pecking away at the oat seeds among the stubble left by the belated harvest, and the stacks at the field gate completed the rural scene. Up the slopes on the other side oaks were standing in small groups, robust and solid, spreading out the dark zigzags of their branches under their heavy capes of burnt-sienna foliage. Blue smoke was rising from the hillside above for a hundred yards or so, until it was caught by the wind and instantly obliterated.

The ubiquitous "timber operations" had brought here a touch of industrial squalor. The churned-up ground was strewn with reddish pine bark and studded with cow dung which, combined with the icy wind, made it savour of a Russian Five-Year Plan with the curves of "timber production" soaring to the delight of all statistical hearts. At this moment, however, mine was deaf to the call of "Progress" and I hastened on to where, entrenched behind a dyke, the forest still stood.

It was mainly birch, but pine showed dark at the rim of the fore-shortened skyline. The glacial shelf had petered out and the path narrowed down. It was damp and chilly among the trees. The birches had scattered most of their gold and up and down the hill tall, slender stems reflected my passage in a gentle, parallactic choreography of chalks, greys, subdued greens, madders and silvers above the tapering obelisks of junipers, some of which measured well over twenty feet in height. Below, the water gleamed blue among the branches against the yellow ochre of the west shore, with its pines and larches.

Trees of the same species show considerable differences in resistance to cold. Some birches were still nearly green, while others already bare, save for a few russet leaves that would stay till the next spring.

Farther on the wood opened out, with birches tripping down

Loch Pityoulish from Creag Chaisteal
The Comyns' castle on Loch an Eilein

to the loch over the rolling hillocks, pale yellow with the autumn grass. Among them a round dyke encloses a tiny graveyard where the Ogilvies of Elgin sleep. No tombstones mark the graves, which were on that day outlined in the blue of gentians.

The loch lies between two hills of very unequal stature, the Calart Hill a mere dwarf by comparison with Creag Chaisteal (the Castle Hill) on the east side. At one time the depression occupied by the waters of Pityoulish must have been a pass but, since the hills beyond the Calart have been utterly levelled down by the erosion of the Spey, this designation no longer fits. In the Calart there is a hollow where blae- and cowberries prosper on the mouldering bones of the Cummings (Comyns) who were treacherously slaughtered by the Shaws in 1396 (there being no guarantee that in favourable circumstances the relationship would not have been reversed, we must refrain from indignation). The other hill derives its name from the ruin of a Pictish fort that adorns its summit. No slaughter is associated with it, an omission which is probably due simply to the fact that its history is totally unknown.

Yet Creag Chaisteal, the last of the Cairngorms, is a remarkable hill. It contains, as it were, in a small area samples of every type of country you can find among them. Birchwoods come half-way up the slopes. Higher up, old pines stand spaced over a steep moss-grown incline and grassy hollows are contained by the slanting rock ribs that will yield good " bouldering " practice to the climber. Then it's heather and peat-hags, among which sit small sheets of water scattered with the white puffs of cotton-grass. In the summer, I think, one will find wild strawberries disputing possession of small patches of soil ensconced in the rocks with bell-heather, rock-rose, Alpine lady's smock, needle-whin, milkwort and, possibly, a cluster of tall purple foxgloves; this is as good a guess as I can make, for I have never been there at the right time of the year to see them for myself. It was always winter or autumn when weather was too bad for the High Tops.

And the day which I have chosen to introduce you to Pityou-

M

The bleak waters of Loch Builg
Loch Morlich, the largest of the Cairngorm lochs

lish was grey and chilly, with November smurrs rushing past on the gusts of an east wind. . . .

A fleeting sunbeam shimmered on the birch tresses. Graylag geese rose from the water and flew across it in an inverted V. Loch Pityoulish lay cold and quiet—a mirror of polished steel reflecting the fair sadness of autumn, and I felt loath to leave it.

5. *The Lochs of the High Hills*

On the other side of the Cairngorms, among the bleak treeless moors that stretch eastwards from the foot of Ben Avon, lies the long Loch Builg which, together with Glen Builg and the upper course of the Gairn, marks the eastern boundary of this mountain system. It is situated at 1,568 feet on a pass forming the watershed between the Avon and the Gairn, and thence the Spey and the Dee, and drains impartially both ways: in the north—openly by the Builg Burn that falls into the Avon at Inchrory; in the south—covertly by underground channels which bubble up into a group of lochans. Of these, one, Lochan Oir, that is to say the Tarn of the Gold, deserves special notice, for tradition would have it that gold lies hidden at its bottom and is guarded by a cunning kelpie, one of those supernatural creatures who may reveal themselves at will as handsome white horses or as fair ladies dressed in green and who are given to various naughty tricks.

The greatest length of Loch Builg, which is rich in char and trout, is just below a mile, and it is about a quarter of a mile wide. Yet, despite its considerable size, lying as it is in exceptionally bleak and featureless country, it is the least attractive of the large Cairngorm lakes; though it, too, has its fine moments and will sometimes glow at night with a weird phosphorescence, due to the presence of luminiferous infusoria.

Resting in a true rock basin, dammed at both ends by lateral moraines and 86 feet deep, it approaches in character the valley lakes. The latter are usually fairly deep, elongated in shape and tending towards a rectangular outline with a meadow occupying the silted-up ground at the top and a beach of coarse sand

the bottom end, and both running across from shore to shore
in a more or less straight line. The valley lakes are represented
in the Cairngorms by Loch Avon and Loch Einich, whose
scenery, with its rocky scarps, ice-worn inclines of terraced slabs,
screes and corries, has been described elsewhere in considerable
detail. Owing to their depth, they usually appear the colour of
lead or indigo when looked at from above, and darken to soot
when the surrounding hills are under snow. At close quarters,
however, their water is pellucid aquamarine, through which the
pinkish grit and the underwater stones show rust-red, thus in-
tensifying the complementary greenish tint of the lake which
gradually deepens to black towards the centre. Over it the
shimmering ripples dance and the reflected images of hill, sky
and cloud dip into it in phantom clearness. On a windy day,
which is frequent, the water is grey and angry, shot through
with gleams of electric-blue and silky green, and white horses
ride on the small rapid breakers. Sometimes, on the lee side,
one can feel the spray permeating the air hundreds of yards
before the loch is reached.

Loch Avon, lying at 2,377 feet as against Loch Einich's 1,650,
is much the higher of the two and a quarter of a mile longer
than the latter, which measures one-and-a-quarter miles in length.
On the other hand, Loch Einich's average width of 600 yards
exceeds the maximum width of Loch Avon, which is only 450
yards, and its total area is somewhat larger, while its lower
berth adds to the stature of the neighbouring heights. Loch
Einich must be described as open and windy, while Loch Avon
is shut-in and sheltered. Trout live in Loch Avon, and Loch
Einich contains both char and trout in great abundance. As far
as I have been able to ascertain, no soundings of these lochs have
ever been made, and their depths remain a matter of conjecture.

Loch Avon is difficult of access and has escaped human interference: no boat has ever been put on its waters nor bothy built
on its shores. Loch Einich, on the other hand, can be easily
reached from Aviemore along the glen of the same name, and
a rough cart-track leads up to its very bottom end where there
used to be two bothies, both burnt down during the war.

In the old times, before the Clearances had scattered the population of the Highlands through the Empire and the U.S.A., the grassy slopes of the Sgorans and particularly the meadow of Coire Odhar at the top of the loch were regularly used as summer grazings for cattle and horses. A shieling stood there, in which a Lady Grant of Rothiemurchus once gave birth to the son and heir, nicknamed John of Coire Odhar, who left money to build Coylum Bridge and a house at the foot of Loch Einich which was always to have meal in it. Lest the significance of this should escape the unenlightened, may I add that the hardy mountain folk of those days could subsist a whole day on a handful of meal, which they ate mixed with cold water, much in the same way as the Himalayan shepherds of our own times live on a bagful of *tsampa*? This ought to appeal to E. E. Shipton, who believes in travelling light. Of course, quite recently I have met a lady who thought nothing of crossing the hills in foul weather with heather tops and star-moss as her only food, but . . . she was English, a *Sassenach* that is to say. A Hielan' laddie would do nothing of the sort, unless perhaps he were a Commando. This, however, is already a different story.

Mrs. Smith of Baltiboys (née Elizabeth Grant) writes in *Memoirs of a Highland Lady*, p. 226:

" This (meal) they generally ate uncooked, mixed with either milk or water as happened to suit, the milk or water being mostly cold, few of these hardy mountaineers troubling to keep a fire lighted in fine weather. This simple food, called *brose*, is rather relished by the Highlanders; made with hot water or with good milk they think it excellent food; made with beef *broo*—the fat skimmings of the broth pot—it is considered quite a treat."[1]

---

[1] Brose is regaining favour with mountaineers, and certainly its food value is out of all proportion to its very small weight and the ease with which it can be prepared. I have never tried to make it with cold water which, I think, would need a tougher stomach than I possess; but oatmeal, well mixed with boiling water and properly seasoned (with sugar or salt), is quite palatable and easily digestible, though there definitely are people with whom it disagrees.

This was in the time of "that wicked man Bonaparte"; but even at a much later date, when brose had gone out of fashion, many old folk rested content with little in the way of food. I have heard tell of an old body whose lunch consisted invariably of a slab of cold porridge between two chunks of bread. He seems never to have eaten much else, and had saved enough money to buy himself a fine house, but was not destined to savour the fruit of his efforts, for soon after he died of malnutrition. Here is a story and a moral. On the whole, however, to judge from available testimony, the Highlanders of old used to be hale and strong and did not contract pneumonia after a night spent on a bare hillside with the tartan plaid as their only cover. Or is it that the medical standards of the time were not too exacting?

Yet all this—the shieling at Coire Odhar, the bothy with meal, and the hardy ways—belongs to the past. Coylum Bridge alone still stands and the sluice gate where the Beanaidh issues from Loch Einich, long disused save as a somewhat awkward bridge to avoid wading the stream below.

Loch Einich used to possess a varied, and chiefly malignant, supernatural population, while our old friends Am Bodach and A'Chailleach ruled the elements and harassed the fishermen engaged on its waters.

As for Loch Avon, a Tomintoul story goes—and I heard it, too, from a Roman Catholic priest (Tomintoul is a Catholic parish) who thought it prudent to add, "But you need not believe it", which advice you may or may not follow . . . well, the story goes that the loch was once haunted by a kelpie in the shape of an unusually beautiful horse. Many a rider was tempted to bestride it, to which the kelpie submitted meekly enough, but no sooner had he mounted it than the kelpie plunged into the loch's inky depths, where with time a substantial collection of riders must have accumulated. But there was a young man in Tomintoul who arrived at Loch Avon equipped with a silver bridle, which he surreptitiously slipped over the kelpie's head. This done, the kelpie was as powerless as hairless Samson, and he led it in triumph down to the village.

The story is silent about their later fate, but it must be presumed that they lived happily ever after and a finer horse there never was. Anyway, " the bridle still hangs there " though, as the Norse tales are wont to put it, " the more you look for it the less you can find it ".

To-day both Loch Einich and Loch Avon have secluded sandy beaches, those of Loch Avon the more alluring owing to its sheltered position and also of finer grain. At the right season blaeberries and cloudberries will be found round about; deer will file past over the corrie-tracks and eagles circle above the crags.

The rock tarns of the high plateaux, of which Loch nan Cnapan and Loch nan Stuirteag in the Great Moss are the best examples, rest in rock cavities dredged out by the differential pressure of the ice, and tend towards a circular or oval outline. The same applies to the moraine tarns of the corrie-land. These, too, are as a rule based on a rock basin produced by the friction of the glacier descending from the precipitous mountain-sides at the point where its movement was slowed up on meeting the level or gently inclined bottom of the corrie; but they are additionally contained by moraines deposited by the retreating ice at the last stage of the glaciation, or by mounds of debris sliding down over the winter snows.

Most of these tarns are small but Loch Etchachan, which must be classed as one of them, in Ben Macdhui, attains considerable dimensions. It is held in the giant cup of the corrie below the rocky bluffs facing Beinn Mheadhoin and sprawls right across the wide neck of ground between the two hills. Its inkspot contour has the maximum extension of about half a mile where the Derry Burn is gradually eating its way through the moraine barrier above Coire Etchachan, down which it flows towards the Lui Water and so to the Dee. Situated at 3,058 feet above the sea, the loch is frozen over for seven months or so in the year. Despite this, trout manage to survive there.

When seen from the Derry path to Ben Macdhui on the background of the drab and barren hilltops exposed to the prevailing westerly winds, the loch appears bleak and desolate. But if you venture over the heaped boulders and the rock ribs of its north-western edge a different sight will meet your eyes. Protected from the bite of the west and north by the mountain mass above it, and getting a full share of morning and midday sunshine, this side harbours quiet places with quick, foaming waters and luscious green sward clinging to the base of the rocks and the abrupt hillsides plunging into the dark deep. It will be gloriously hot there on a warm sunny day and, if you have time to spare, you may linger on some terraced slabs and watch the trout play and the reflections of clouds glide over the blue mirror at your feet or be tempted for a swim.

Loch Etchachan is often described as the highest lake in Britain, but there are several considerable Cairngorm lochans which exceed it in elevation, and the pride of place properly belongs to the tiny sheet of Lochan Buidhe lying at 3,683 feet in the nick of the Ben Macdhui-Cairn Lochan table-land. Among the larger corrie tarns mention must be made of Loch Coire an Lochain of Braeriach and the three Green Lochans (Lochan Uaine) of Ben Macdhui, Cairn Toul and Derry Cairngorm. Strictly speaking, all corrie lochans could be justifiably called "Green", as their waters, framed by the reddish scree, display to advantage the green-blue colouring characteristic of the high mountain pools. All of them remain locked under ice for the best part of the year and when, in May or June, frost at last loses its grip on the windy heights, miniature icebergs will be seen floating over the dark glaucous depths. The streaks and cornices of snow above cast dazzling-white reflexes, and the grim rock bastions dip their murky shadows into the pellucid crystal of the sleeping tarn. Or else, when a breeze awakens the ripples, they will dance and glitter with fairy lights. For a tarn is like a living thing, and as the ice first begins to move it will moan and sigh and whisper, stretching its weary limbs.

Yet, at any time of the year when a corrie lochan is free from its icy lid, the restful peace of still water contrasting with the strife and menace of the cliffs and the wistful barrenness of the scree holds in it a fascination that may date back to the remote aquatic past, shared by the human kind with the other species of the animal kingdom, or else arise from the aesthetic enjoyment of a balanced composition—I cannot tell which and, in truth, does it really matter?

A Glen Feshie pine

IX

THE PASSING GIANTS OF THE GLENS

1. *Speaking of Deer*

DEER, as is well known, possess those soulful woodland eyes under long eyelashes which the less fortunate Hollywoodians would fain give their ears to acquire. Otherwise, however, their ways do not always conform to the standards set by Walt Disney and the ladies of the passing age who, having themselves been brought up in ignorance and deportment to be pieces of ornamental uselessness, incline to view the world in similar light.

A blue storm was gathering over Glen Feshie. Faint thunder growled menacingly behind the hills and a chilly breath came down the defile, spreading gooseflesh over the river where, having burst a way through the rocks and screes crowding upon it on both sides, it ran into wide, placid shallows, as though taking a rest after the strain of its upper course. The first drops of falling moisture were settling on my face as I hurried down the glen to the shelter of the lower woods.

I glanced back.

Dark and sturdy, like a detachment of grim Pictish warriors, the ancient Caledonian firs stood against the fading light, ready to face the onslaught of yet another gale . . . the passing giants of the glens.

In a clearing by the lodge a detachment of soldiers in khaki battledress were receiving instruction in "snow and mountain warfare". Pieces of petrol cans, perforated with bullets, were nailed here and there on to the tree branches, where they were made to deputize for the human targets to come. This was the wake of the mightier man-made storm that had just passed. . . .

However, speaking of deer. . . . Red deer, somewhat smaller than their Continental kin, and roe-deer are the only two kinds of deer at present found in the Cairngorms. Originally reindeer were common on the Highland hills, but they became extinct sometime about the thirteenth century, while the red deer which used to be, like the roe-deer of our days, forest animals, adopted the habitat and to a great extent the ways of their vanished predecessors. This, incidentally, together with the unfavourable shooting selection which tends to eliminate the best specimens, may have been responsible for the decrease in their size (assuming that at one time they did not differ much from the Central European race). In any case, the open rough grazings of the contemporary " deer forests ", which are forests only in name with hardly any trees left, do not seem to satisfy their natural requirements in full and they often supplement their diet with various unorthodox tit-bits.

Red deer have been known to gobble up trapped rabbits,[1] and I suspect that the recent scarcity of grouse need not be wholly attributed to foxes, worm infection or unfavourable weather conditions; for, after all, there is not a great deal of difference in taste between a rabbit and a fledgeling, though this is only a guess and possibly a mistaken one. On the other hand, it is well established that deer act as hill scavengers and display tastes usually associated with hyenas. I have never heard of their eating carrion, though they may do this as well, but they show a marked liking for a tasty skeleton. Deer have been found dead, choked with bones and even with a calf's skull[2]— pretty tough fare for a gentle herbivore! The habit of eating bones has apparently developed from the practice of gnawing cast antlers, in which both stags and hinds indulge. They also consume paper, handkerchiefs, socks and other articles of wear-and-tear, and on one occasion I saw an Alpine waterproof jacket half-eaten by deer, though they must have found the fabric somewhat unpalatable as they could not get through all of it in the three years it had lain abandoned (according to the date on the paper in one of its pockets). Ant's eggs and slugs are other items of the deer's bill of fare.

Slugs are, of course, " vermin " from the gardener's point of

---

[1] Seton Gordon: *The Cairngorm Hills of Scotland.*
[2] A. M. T.: *Diets of Deer*—" Nature Notes ", *The Scotsman*, Nov. 9, 1946.

view and are not to be encouraged in proximity to lettuce. A warning, however, must be added that there is no general agreement as to what constitutes "vermin" and each of the "country interests" has its own ideas on the subject. Thus, to a game-keeper all small carnivores—foxes, polecats, badgers, wild cats, owls, etc.—are unquestionably "vermin", while he will take a mild view of rabbits, though he may not regard them as "game". But all of the animals listed above are the forester's and most of them also the farmer's friends, as they help to keep down the numbers of their natural enemy, the rodent. Pheasants are certainly "game", but an agriculturalist feels no enthusiasm for their presence in a cornfield. And, sad as this may seem, deer are definitely "vermin" from the forester's angle and, though he may not desire their total extermination, he would like to keep them in check and is particularly anxious to exclude them from newly planted areas. The reason is not far to seek: red deer eat every seedling tree, coniferous and deciduous alike, they come across, so that it is unusual to find a young tree in a deer forest save in most inhospitable places or near much-used roads and human habitations.

In the olden days the Highlands were up to some 2,500 feet a sea of pine forest, mingled with birch and in the lower reaches with oak, from which the higher hill massifs reared up like islands. On these the reindeer roamed, while the red deer shared the forests with the wild cattle and the beasts of prey, most of which have been totally exterminated. Through thousands of years of mutual adjustment a fine equilibrium had been achieved. The deer ate the saplings and nibbled at the resinous bark of pine then as they do to-day, helping in this way in the task of thinning-out the stand, which is now performed by axe and saw. Yet the bears and wolves saw to it that there should not be too many deer, and thus preserved the young pines from total disappearance, similarly the foxes kept down the hares (rabbits were introduced into this country from France at a later date), pine martens the squirrels, etc. etc., in the natural community of animal and plant, until in came Man, like a bull into a china shop, and upset it all.

Tracts of forest were burnt down or felled to clear the ground
for arable and pasture, and in some cases the felled trees were
never removed, as seems to have happened on the site of the
present Moss of Kincardine.[1]   Yet far more forest was burnt in
warlike operations as a means of defence or offence, especially
during the Viking raids.   Thereafter, man made war upon the
woods, as they provided hiding-places for caterans and wolves,
and with the advent of large sheep flocks much fine pine went
up in smoke to open up new grazings.   The last large area of
pinewood was deliberately burnt for this purpose as late as 1813.

Some three hundred years have elapsed since the last Cairngorm wolf was killed in Glen Derry; and, although the sportsman's gun served to keep the deer in check, they were multiply-
ing far more rapidly than was good for the trees, with the effect
that the remnants of the Caledonian Forest still surviving in the
recesses of the Cairngorm glens continued to retreat.   The tree line
was creeping lower and lower.   Simultaneously, the sheep all but
exterminated the birch and by eating the softer grasses and herbs
laid the hill pastures open to the coarser growth that was not spared
by the cattle which had preceded them.   In this way the uplands
of Northern Scotland have for the most part become the econo-
mically useless wastes of heather and bracken we know to-day.

In almost any Cairngorm glen one comes upon evidence of
vanished forests.   Old, bleached skeletons of pines lie buried
under the peat and heather, and are occasionally uncovered by
floods miles above the nearest living tree.   Glen Geusachan, the
Mar deer sanctuary, is completely treeless.   Yet its Gaelic name,
the Valley of Pines, is well justified by the ancient tree stumps,
trunks and roots upon which one stumbles over its entire length.

---

[1] " The Moss of Kincardine, in the upper part of the valley of the Forth,
appears to owe its existence, at least in one place, to the fact that the thick
oak forest which once covered its side was felled by man.   Below the moss the
stumps and trunks of large trees were found crowded as thickly upon the clay
as they could be supposed to have grown there . . .   Here we see how a district
of fair woodland . . . has been turned by man into a waste of barren morass
and mire—a place of shaking bog and stunted heath, where he cannot build
his dwelling nor plant his crops, and from which he can extract nothing save
fuel for his hearth . . . so long as the conditions of growth remain favourable
for the marshy vegetation." A. Geikie: *The Scenery of Scotland*, p. 421.   Some
of the Cairngorm moors show considerable resemblance to the Moss of Kincardine.

In fact, the place must have been densely wooded some centuries ago up to about 2,500 feet. To-day the nearest living tree at an altitude not exceeding 1,600 feet is in Glen Lui Beg, some three miles as the crow flies from the confluence of Glen Geusachan and Glen Dee, though straggling pines ascend above 2,000 feet a little farther east in Glen Derry. The first trees encountered on the way down Glen Dee are a group of birches and aspens at the Chest of Dee, four miles below Glen Geusachan, but there are ample remains of pines along the course of the Dee to show that the forest used to extend a good way beyond that glen towards the Lairig Ghru Pass.

In Glen Derry, Dubh Ghleann and Glen Quoich the scattered rearguards of the retreating forest are still resisting the march of desolation up to somewhere between the 1,800 and the 2,000-foot contours. But on the colder northern slopes the present tree line drops below 1,700 feet, and only seldom attains this height.

All these high-growing trees are weathered veterans, stocky, gnarled and rugged, counting many narrow rings of annual growth under their bark. When they die of old age or are uprooted by some storm of exceptional severity, they will leave no offspring and the forest will have receded by another mile or two. Thus the deer gradually squeeze out the pines. The only and obvious remedy, long mooted but as far as I know never put into practice, is to fence off parts of the old stand to allow young trees to spring up and mature.

When in Glen Feshie, during the war, military practice shooting had kept the deer away for two or three years, little pines began to come up everywhere upon the hitherto treeless hillsides, and I found some seedlings as high up as 3,000 feet. But when I was last there, late in 1946, most of them had already gone. In the upper part of the glen, where distance and bad roads have conspired to preserve a patch of Caledonian Forest, young trees climb up high over precipitous rocks and steep screes as though in conscious search of most unfavourable conditions, but seem studiously to avoid the richer and less exposed soil of the more accessible places.

Many trees, young and old alike, perish during the spring

heather burnings, when the fire often gets out of control, especially if a sudden wind springs up after it has been started; and crofters and sheep farmers have as a rule little respect for trees, though they may value a belt of older stand as winter shelter. I have seen whole areas of fine forest badly singed and even totally destroyed through negligent heather burning. There is, in fact, an old feud between the forester and the agriculturist, which is based largely on misconceptions. Agricultural communities form the most conservative section of mankind, and even in our enlightened times will often hearken to the traditions and superstitions of the hoary past. In the remote pioneering days forest was as cheap as dirt and arable and pasture most precious possessions; trees had to be cleared laboriously to open up the land and gave shelter to the wild beasts that attacked man's flocks and crops. It would seem that the ancestral memory of those days lingers on. In any case, plans for reafforestation have always excited vehement resentment among country folk.

The average Highlander, especially of the older generation, is no tree lover and generally prefers the country "open", where the biting gale, unchecked by woodlands, drives over the " bonnie heather ", desolate peat-hags and shaking bogs to rattle the windows of his home and push the smoke down his chimney. It is rare to see anything except the traditional rowan, once meant to keep away the evil spirits, by a Highland homestead which will stand more likely than not in the least sheltered spot the locality has to offer. This appears foolish enough to-day, wise precaution though it used to be, for it was important to be able to spot the approaching enemy in good time, nor was a clear field of fire an amenity to be despised.[1] The conditions of the country were unsettled and, quite apart from the Sassenach on whom the Scottish nationalists blame all the woes of the world, there were robbers and private illwishers in plenty to whom murder came easily and who usually got away with it, as the king's writ did not run in the Hielan' hills and the law was administered spasmodically and haphazardly. The necessity has long passed but the habit has been slow to die.

[1] Henry Grey Graham: *The Social Life in Scotland in the 18th Century.*

Owing to constant wars and internecine strife, Scotland was by the end of the seventeenth century badly denuded of trees, and when the first attempts at reafforestation were made they met with embittered opposition.

To quote from Henry Grey Graham's *The Social Life in Scotland in the 18th Century*, pp. 198-9:

". . . up to 1750 attempts at planting were hesitating and limited, partly from lack of money, partly from opposition of the farmers and country-people. Hedges and trees were regarded as their natural enemies, and they bitterly complained that the roots spoiled the ground, the shade killed the grain, and the branches fostered the birds that devoured the crops. In vehement dislike and aggressive resistance to this new and dangerous innovation of planting, the people did everything they could to hinder it. Under cover of the night they pulled up the saplings, tore down the branches, and maimed the trunks, and often in the morning the dismayed laird saw that in the darkness the labours and pride of years had been ruthlessly ruined."

Nowadays, of course, such excesses are unlikely, and the opponents of reafforestation put forward more reasonable objections. But there has been no great change in the fundamental attitude, and trees are often wantonly destroyed; although in the Highlands the slow-witted deity of public opinion is beginning to incline towards the understanding that in forestry lies the natural economic future of this part of the country. In the Cairngorms in particular the timber trade used to be the main source of the population's wealth before the boom in sheep farming and deer shooting, which has now come to its historical end, and the rather modest development of the tourist trade.

2. *Forests and Foresters*

The north-eastern foothills of the Cairngorms get all of the cold winds and none of the warm, so that the surrounding country belongs to the coldest and bleakest parts of Scotland.

There are some clumps of birches about Inchrory, along the Builg Burn, and a few trees grace the lower part of the long Glen Avon, but otherwise the "Forest of Glen Avon" is completely treeless, although there must have been something in the name at one time, as is shown by the numerous remains of trees along the upper course of the Avon.

On the other hand, the deer forests of Mar, Rothiemurchus, Glen More and Glen Feshie, even if they, too, consist largely of high ground above the tree line and the glens already abandoned by the retreating trees, are forests in more than a metaphorical sense. All of them contain considerable areas of woodland which pleasantly relieve the Arctic melancholy of the hills.

The narrow Glen Dee cannot produce such a splash of greenery as the wide flats of Rothiemurchus but its lower reaches, beginning with a point some two miles above Inverey, are densely wooded and forest enters deep into the northern glens. These, open to the warm breath of the south winds and protected by the massifs of Beinn a'Bhùird and Ben Avon against the withering fury of the north-eastern gales, offer conditions favourable to the growth of trees. Most of the forest about Inverey and Braemar dates back to the beginning of the nineteenth century, but it contains some firs of much hoarier age, measuring up to thirty feet in circumference. Higher up the glens, the trees are self-sown. The glens Lui, Derry and Quoich are wooded along almost their entire length, and nowhere else in the Cairngorms does the forest penetrate so near to the main peaks or reach such altitudes. Dubh Ghleann and parts of Glen Quoich at the foot of Beinn a'Bhùird shelter some compact areas of Old Caledonian pines, which can be rivalled only by the woods of the upper Glen Feshie. Also where the Derry Burn flows into Lui Water there is a fine stretch of pinewood. Sparse forest and isolated clumps of pines ascend up Glen Lui to the very mouth of Glen Lui Beag, but at one time even that glen must have been wooded all the way up to the Corrie of Red Spouts, and I have seen some decaying wood of considerable thickness only a hundred yards below the pass that divides Ben Macdhui from Càrn a'Mhaim.

"Evensong." The Derry
The Woods of Strathspey in winter garb

In the past the Derry Forest extended all the way to the head of the glen and well up into Coire Etchachan. Some of the small burns flowing into the Derry from Beinn a'Chaorruin are solidly roofed over with tree roots and stumps. These are now buried under two or three feet of peat, and if one knew the speed with which peat accumulates in these conditions one could easily calculate the time when this dense forest perished. It looks as though it was either felled or destroyed by fire, for the remaining stumps are upright and of relatively small cross-section. On the other hand, trees at that height would never have achieved full stature and would have been stunted in their growth, so that it is impossible to say how long they had lived without counting the annual rings, which I have not attempted to do.

To-day one must walk about two miles down the glen before coming on the first tree. Glen Quoich has not been affected to the same extent, but the upper halves of both these glens are only thinly held by trees and provide striking examples of the unfavourable balance between the deer and the pine. Not a young tree is to be seen. Solitary old pines cling to the bare hillsides, some dying, many already dead, a few still of lustrous green, powerful in limb and girth.

Deprived of the support of the forest community in the age-long struggle with the wind, these firs do not shoot up tall and straight, with high symmetrical crowns, like the lowland kind. Their forms have been adapted to local needs. The stems, short and stumpy, often grow twisted like corkscrews the better to resist the storms. They begin branching almost at the base and, instead of spreading upwards, their branches tend to hang low, almost trailing on the ground; while those at the summit are short and closely packed, forming a thick brushy dome which, if cut off and flung over the hills by a giant hand, would bounce off like a ball without breaking. The wood of these trees is exceptionally rich in resin, so that any scar left where a branch has been torn off or broken by the wind will soon be plastered over and healed.

At the edge of the tree line the pines are stunted in their growth and what we may at first take for a young tree is in

N

Kennapole Hill in May
Glenmore with Meall a'Bhuachaille in the background

reality a dwarf of venerable age. There is something uncouth about their rugged outlines and when the first fall of snow spreads its ashen hue over the lifeless brown moors, where sheets of ice glisten dully in the wintry light, some of them have struck me as almost ugly.

The barkless bodies of the dead trees, overturned by forgotten storms, add a further touch of melancholy to the scene.

Yet a high-growing Scots fir in its prime is a beautiful tree, perfectly harmonized with the surroundings in which it lives. It is a distinct regional variety of the Forest Pine, evolved through thousands of years of natural selection and climatic adaptation. If the race were allowed to perish, no other tree would thrive there. Should an attempt be made to reclaim for the forest the glens where trees used to grow in the past, this can be done only by self-seeding from the surviving specimens which, in fact, is the usual procedure in reafforestation at the higher altitudes (though Nature requires much helping to expedite matters).

The experiments made with the creeping Mountain Pine have not proved successful, while the five-needled Stone and Weymouth Pines, also adapted to mountain habitats, are not in favour with the foresters in view of their susceptibility to the pine blister disease. Even with the Highland Scots Firs it has been found that the pines from the regions of low rainfall in the east and centre do not do so well in the wet Western Highlands, and *vice versa*.[1] On the other hand, the Canadian Sitka Spruce and Douglas Fir grow well in the Cairngorms and have been used to a varying extent in the old and new plantings; while the Larch has become completely acclimatized at the lower levels since it was first introduced towards the end of the eighteenth century, and there are many fine specimens of this tree to be found about Braemar and Invercauld.

The high-lying woods of the Braemar glens escaped the axe during the war-time fellings, but considerable areas in Glen Lui and farther down the water have been cut or thinned out.

Yet the main forest country lies north and west of the hills,

---

[1] I am indebted for some of these details to Mr. James Fraser, Conservator of the Inverness Division of the Forestry Commission.

where the broad flats and undulations of glacial drift, sheltered by the rampart of the Monadhliath in the north-west and by the Cairngorms in the east and north, contain (or should I rather say, *used* to contain?) some of the finest timbers of the district.

The stretch of land between the heights of Loch an Eilein in the south-west and Craiggowrie in the north-east, the Spey and the massifs of Cairn Gorm and Braeriach, some eight by six miles in all, is divided into Rothiemurchus and the Glenmore or Queen's Forest. The division, however, reflects the difference of ownership rather than that of geography. Rothiemurchus is the property of the Grants of Rothiemurchus, and Queen's Forest, conceived as a reserve commemorating the Silver Jubilee of King George V, is in the hands of the Forestry Commission. Also Inchriach, between Loch an Eilein and Feshiebridge, is the Commission's holding, while the Glen Feshie woods belong to the Kincraig laird, Sir George MacPherson Grant. All this does not affect the appearance of the trees, except for the fact that there has been little planting of recent date on private land.

When I first saw Rothiemurchus a few years ago it was a huge expanse of sombre green, interrupted only by the fields of Tullochgrue, stretches of moorland and a handful of farmsteads ensconced among the tongues and oblongs of woodland between Coylum Bridge and Queen's Forest. Here and there birches showed light or a patch of sward with the ruin of an abandoned croft and the inevitable rowan would come into view by the winding stream.

After crossing the bridge over the Spey at Aviemore one entered the precincts of the forest. Enormous, dark Douglas firs flanked the road, almost awe-inspiring with their skeleton-like lower branches stifled by the heavy shade of their dense crowns. The trees were like a rough Gothic cathedral, whose portals and pinnacles had been blackened by age. In the gateway of the lofty firs Braeriach heaved up ponderously with the sockets of its corries—a giant reclining on a carpet of pinewoods.

Beyond the village of Rothiemurchus, where the road ramified, pines, sitkas, Douglas firs and larches crowded tumultuously on all sides. Higher up, the native pine gradually swamped the foreign conifers. The rusty pink and orange branches stretched up like sun-tanned powerful arms supporting the green, billowy domes. Beneath, the junipers stood sentinel over the mystery of the forest, where the cushioned tangle of blaeberry, cowberry and heather overspread the ground, fungi reared their coloured heads and the gorgeous plumes of ferns spurted from the soil in scattered sunshine. Suddenly a rustle would come from the thicket, which might be a roe deer, perhaps a wild cat or a badger. . . .

To-day most of this magnificence is no more. A large area of fine pine stand from about Polchar and Loch an Eilein to the Loch Einich road has been felled. Gone, too, are the old Douglas firs, a loss apparently appreciated by some motorists— possibly the silent majesty of the trees threw into unwelcome relief the unimportance of their fretful selves, though more prosaically they blamed the shade for icing. Much of the forest between Aviemore and Coylum Bridge and along the road from the latter to Pityoulish has likewise been cut or thinned practically out of existence. Yet Black Park with its old pines in open canopy continues to reflect its former glory and, generally speaking, along the right-of-way path to Braemar one escapes most of the devastation. A considerable area of forest at the foot of the conical Càrn Eilrig and the mouth of the Lairig Ghru is still intact, though it can boast few trees of any great size or age. The trees climb the steep scree slopes of Càrn Eilrig but do not penetrate far either into the Lairig or Gleann Einich, which are both exposed to the chilly northern winds and get a good taste of the westerly gales as well.

As we move north-east we come to a kind of no-man's-land, a battlefield of trees, dividing Rothiemurchus from the Glenmore Forest. Wind-worried pines rise sparsely among a multitude of stumps. The ground shows traces of fire. Here and there, among the maze of tracks and bridges, splinters of bark and wood mark the sites of "timber operations". Only along the Luineag, issuing from Loch Morlich in Glen More, is there a denser growth which coalesces with the main body of the forest at the approaches to Coylum Bridge. Profiting by a respite from the depredations of deer which have been kept away by the increased military and timber traffic on the Glenmore road, self-sown sapling pines have come up in abundance, dotting the heath with glaucous green. Nature has spaced them so evenly as often to give the illusion of an artificial plantation. How long they will be able to survive there no one can tell.

Rothiemurchus is for the most part self-sown and is descended, so to speak, in a straight line from the Old Caledonian Forest. It has, however, been repeatedly felled during the last three centuries and suffered much damage from fires, so that it does not contain a great many big old trees, the best of which are found in the neighbourhood of Loch an Eilein.

In fact, as already intimated, the timber industry used to flourish on Speyside in the old days, providing the means of livelihood for a considerable part of the population. There was some local demand for wood for iron smelting in Abernethy, but most of it was floated down the Spey and shipped by sea to other parts of Britain. Haulage was difficult, roads were poor, and the transportation of timber had to rely chiefly on water. For this purpose the large streams were dammed at some suitable point, usually near where they issued from a loch, and their ponded waters kept in readiness by a sluice. The felled and lopped trees were drawn by horses to the assembly places lower down along the water-course in preparation for the " run ", when the sluice gates were opened and a sudden rush of water was released to convey the timber to the Spey.

This was no mere " business ", but a romantic traditional occasion. The handling of the wood in the swollen torrent demanded considerable skill and gave the lads an opportunity to display their manly prowess before the admiring eyes of the weaker sex. To recapture something of the atmosphere of the time I will quote from Mrs. Smith of Baltiboys' *Memoirs of a Highland Lady* (London, 1898), p. 220:

" The night before the run, the man in charge of that particular sluice set off up the hill, and reaching the spot long before daylight opened the heavy gates; out rushed the torrent, travelling so quickly as to reach the deposit of timber in time for the meeting of the woodmen . . . The duty of some was to roll the logs into the water; this was effected by the help of levers . . . The next party shoved them off with long poles into the current, dashing in often up to the middle in water when any case of obstruction occurred. They were then taken in charge by the most picturesque group of all, the youngest and most active, each supplied with a *clip*, a very long pole thin and flexible at one end, generally a young tall tree; a sharp hook was fixed to the bending point, and with this, skipping from rock to stump, over brooks and through briers, this agile band followed the log-laden current, ready to pounce on any stray lumbering victim that was in any manner checked in its progress. There was something graceful in the action of throwing forth the stout yet yielding clip, an exciting satisfaction as the sharp hook fixed the obstreperous log. The many light forms springing about among the trees, along banks that were sometimes high, and always rocky, the shouts, the laughter, the Gaelic exclamations, and above all, the roar of the water, made the whole scene one of the most inspiriting that either actors or spectators could be engaged in."

Once the load reached the Spey, it passed into the hands of the Spey floaters, a race apart who concentrated about Ballindaloch. They were sturdy lads and knew the cunning ways of the river, the profession being passed down from father to son for many generations with a compound interest of cumulative experience. The tree trunks were tied up in rafts, which were handled by means of long poles, in much the same way as they still are in Sweden, Canada, or the Carpathians.

All this show of activity was sustained largely by whisky. The day's work began with a dram, followed by a larger potion at midday to which a bannock and some cheese were added; another dram closed the daily round. As for Spey floaters, " a large bothy was built for them at the mouth of the Druie in a fashion that suited themselves; a fire on a stone hearth in the middle of the floor, a hole in the very centre of the roof just over it where some of the smoke got out, heather spread on the ground, no window, and there, after their hard days' work, they lay down for the night, in their wet clothes—for they had been perhaps hours in the river—each man's feet to the fire, each man's plaid round his chest, a circle of weary bodies half-stupefied by whisky, enveloped in a cloud of steam and smoke, and sleeping soundly till the morning."[1]

The Balkan and Carpathian shepherds still flourish on similar ways; yet, though it is true that man's fibre is much tougher than many townspeople suppose, such a life is not quite so healthy as we are often led to believe, and rheumatism and tuberculosis collect a heavy toll. Here, however, the old ways have long fallen into oblivion and the loch sluices have not been in use for nearly a hundred years. Nowadays tractors bounce about the woods, churning black humus and rust-brown bark pulp; then canter-hooks come into play as lorries are loaded and unloaded, and screaming sawmills make short shrift of the seasoned veterans of the forest. Only the taste for whisky has not changed and the "woodman" of to-day still enjoys his "dram"; in many cases this taste accounts for half his weekly pay-packet.

The old ways were comparatively slow, so that the forest had a chance by and by to heal its scars. But already during the Napoleonic wars, when Rothiemurchus is said to have yielded between £10,000 and £20,000 a year, it was despoiled of all its best timber and it needed about a century to return to form. Then the Kaiser brought a new calamity on the world and the Cairngorm forests were again called upon to make good the shortage of imported timber; lastly the Führer has left on them his mark of devastation. And, as though to emphasize the connection, much of the felling has on both occasions been done by German prisoners.

Glen More did not fare any better.

In 1786 the Duke of Richmond and Gordon, whose property it then was, sold the Glenmore timber for £10,000[2] to the Hull

[1] Elizabeth Smith of Baltiboys: *Memoirs of a Highland Lady*, p. 220.
[2] The Rev. John Marius Wilson (Ed.): *The Imperial Gazeteer of Scotland* (London and Edinburgh, 18??), pp. 807-8. The Rev. William Forsyth gives the sum as £20,000 in his work, *In the Shadow of Cairngorm*.

firm of Osbourne and Dodsworth, who made a thorough job of it and departed with £70,000, leaving behind a dubious reputation for morals and the sobriety of their employees and a sight of desolation.[1] "At that time," writes Sir Thomas Dick Lauder, "many gigantic skeletons of trees above twenty feet in circumference, but which had been so far decayed at the time the forest was felled as to be unfit for timber, had been left standing, most of them in prominent situations, their bark in a great measure gone—many of them without leaves, and catching a pale unearthly looking light upon their grey trunks and bare arms, which were stretched forth towards the sky like those of wizards, as if in the act of conjuring up the storm which was gathering in the bosom of the mountains, and was about to burst forth at their call."[2]

Again the forest recovered to be despoiled during the First World War, when the Canadian foresters who were working there cut most of the finest trees, many of which were abandoned rotting on the ground. Since the woods passed into the hands of the Forestry Commission—which holds there 12,500 acres, 4,000 acres being classed as plantable—a considerable replanting programme has been carried out. Most of the young trees are Scots firs, many of them self-sown, but sitka spruces and some Douglas firs have also been planted, while occasional birches add another element of variety to the scene. As yet, however, these plantations are young and stretch in bluish rectangles up the brown slopes of the Craggowrie-Meall a'Bhua-chaille ridge and the outliers of Cairn Gorm. Time will, no doubt, temper their present regimented regularity, and once the protective fences have been removed, the new plantations will merge with the remnants of the old forest, the more readily so as many mature pines have been left for seed among the former and self-seeding will blur the boundaries between the different species.

During and after the recent war most of the best pinewood around Loch Morlich was felled, where only a few selected trees

---

[1] Alexander MacKenzie: *Trees in the Highlands* (Elgin, 1912), p. 23. Also Wm. Forsyth: *In the Shadow of Cairngorm*.
[2] Sir Dick Lauder: *Gilpin's Forest Scenery*, quoted after *The Imperial Gazetteer of Scotland*, p. 808.

remain and, what with the large area above the loch destroyed by fire, not much is left of the famous forest. Yet a fringe of pines still surrounds the loch, and along its east bank their dark shades mingle with the light, ash-green crowns of old birches, while some mighty tercentenarians rise at the approaches to the lodge and, sparsely, along the Cairn Gorm path. Northward, towards the Sluggan Pass over which a road runs to Kincardine and Boat of Garten, the forest closes its ranks, composed in the main of young trees. On the Sluggan Pass itself, however, both inside and outside the Commission land with its usual warning of forest fires, there is a stretch of beautiful old pine stand which spills over the steep slopes of Creag Chaisteal and the hummocky back of Creag Ghreusache to the lower-lying birch groves.

When I was last there the ground was sodden after weeks of rain, sleet and snow, so that my nailed boots made in it deep ruts at each step. Grey easterly clouds floated overhead, releasing upon the forests swarms of heavy snow-flakes, which fluttered down like white downy moths. The scene was transformed into a Chinese drawing, with only the edges of the phantom pines outlined, darkling, step after step, row after row, below the ribs of broken rock, heath, withered grass and scree. Beyond, the big hills stood, clad in milky whiteness, and a patch of yellow sunshine rested diffusely upon the summit of Cairn Gorm. The cold air in my nostrils had about it the quality of whetted steel, the air of the northern seas over which sped the Viking longboats.

Yet another occasion is engraved even deeper upon my memory.

It was at dayspring, in early autumn, when the moors were silver with dewy cobwebs and white mists were trailing along the heather-grown hillsides that had, among the silky blue of young pines, the gloss of hammer-wrought copper. The invisible burns, reeking with steam, raised diaphanous veils which multiplied the distances and exaggerated the gradients.

Then the sun came through, pink and fresh, and dipped its shining fingers into the coolness of the awakening day. The white curtains of mist were drawn aside and the Cairngorms appeared, far, flushed and airy.

In the west, the woods of Inchriach are chiefly old birch in open canopy with juniper coppice, but there is some pine at Feshiebridge and considerable areas have been recently planted with pine and Douglas fir. Birch and oak groves crowd round Loch Insh and birches and alders line the course of the Feshie; but the lower part of its glen has been badly denuded of pine-woods, with only small patches left here and there and a fringe lining the steep *craigs* of the east side. Here scraggy thickets clamber over the boulder screes, the favourite haunts of wild cats and foxes, secure alike from the deer's teeth and the lumber-man's axe, and spill over into the short glens rising towards the Sgorans.

The fine old woods of mixed pine and birch along the rapid stream of Allt a'Mharcaidh are unspoiled, and so is Badan Mosach—the "Wee Woodie"; but the ancient and proud pine forest about the middle of the glen has been laid low by the Canadian Foresters, who have left much wood lying about. Some of the felled pines were of the "cabbage" formation, all branch and hardly any stem, beautiful to look at but econo-mically useless, as no sawmill could get through the intricacies of their timber. They are still there, unclaimed for the pro-hibitive cost of labour and transportation. However, despite this senseless waste, a sufficient tree screen remains to dissimulate the extent of the devastation, and with time the forest should re-cover. The Duchess of Bedford's tree, seventeen feet in girth at the cutting line, the twenty-foot fir by the lodge and many other gnarled giants have been spared. Woods still clothe the west side of the glen and scattered pines and birches ascend the billowing hillsides of the east. Yet various military installations rob this part of Glen Feshie, where Landseer did much of his work, of its pristine glory, giving it a somewhat suburban appearance. In order to escape from the sight of hutments, rusty barbed wire, rifle targets and practice trenches, we must follow the Feshie into the narrow defile guarded by escarpments of rock and scree. Along the stream powerful Caledonion firs share with birches and alders the strip of level alluvial ground, and pine and birch push high up the moss-grown, rocky watercourses, rapid scree-fields and gullies on both sides.

Beyond the defile the glen takes on a milder, bucolic look. Green flats studded with grey boulders spread between the heathy slopes of the hills which steadily diminish in height, eventually to subside into the dismal bogs of the upper Glen Geldie. Small groves of birch and pine hug the west side of the valley above the clear shimmering pools. As Glen Feshie makes a sharp turn to the east, the scene changes once more. The trees disappear and we have to walk several miles along Glen Geldie before we come on a few isolated birches.

Nevertheless, barren as it is to-day, Glen Geldie, too, used to be forest-grown in the dim past and pinewoods climbed high up the slopes of Monadh Mòr and Beinn Bhrottain. Here and there the peat-hags disclose the remnants of stumps, trunks and branches, and perhaps one day new trees will spring up in their place.

Douglas Firs
Quiemore

X

IN THE WORLD
OF PERPENDICULAR VALUES

1. *The Walker's and the Climber's Optics*

MOUNTAINS seldom, if ever, perpend, much less over-hang, for the simple reason that such architecture defies the law of gravitation and could not maintain itself for long. The most fearsome precipices have an average inclination of seventy, perhaps eighty, degrees, though in parts, where rock stratification allows, they may approach and exceed the perpendicular.

In the Cairngorms the High Tops belong to the horizontal rather than the vertical scheme of things, while on most sides the hills slope gently, giving the walker a wide choice of routes by which to evade the more difficult features. They are essentially the walker's and not the climber's mountains, and their peculiar problems of distance and climate have produced a breed of indefatigable ramblers who would think little of doing forty miles in a day with a heavy pack but shrink in terror at the very thought of going up or down a slope that falls away at more than half a right angle. To them a steep scree-field where small stones have an alarming way of slipping from under one's feet belongs to the realm of the inaccessible and the corries are to be admired from a respectful distance as places appropriate to eagles and " She Devils ". This, too, has been the stalker's and the holiday " sportsman's " attitude, and has in the eyes of Colonel Thornton endowed the cliffs of the Sgorans with Himalayan proportions (the sporting old colonel was given to exaggerration).[1]

Yet it is not only that the people who have for so long regarded these hills as their rightful preserve had little or no

[1] *Sporting Tour* (1804).

interest in rock climbing as such, viewing it as a crazy pastime; the structure of the Cairngorms itself offered no natural inducement to cragsmanship. In other, more rugged, mountain systems a modicum of climbing experience and general ability of dealing with "perpendicular problems" are necessities of communication: however easy the route we may choose, there will always be rocks and precipices near at hand, so that both our eye and our foot gradually get used to them. In the Cairngorms, on the other hand, where rocks are confined to corries and the glacier-worn sidings of some glens, there is no gradual transition from the level to the perpendicular: the latter comes up against our senses with a bang. The cliffs and buttresses of the corries appear stupendous and terrifying and our natural impulse is to leave them alone. Even, optical and psychological factors apart, the contrast could hardly have been greater, as in any hills the corrie formation is responsible for the most nearly vertical rock-faces.

In the Cairngorms the cragsman sets himself a somewhat unnatural problem: he deliberately goes out in search of difficulties. To pass from the general to the personal, I have done a fair amount of climbing in other hills, including some pretty tough routes that it would be difficult, nay impossible, to match in the Cairngorms; yet, however difficult the mountain feature we chose, we did not strive to complicate our route in "doing" it. There were difficulties enough and to spare, and our task was to find the reasonably easiest line of ascent or descent within the limits of the chosen objective. Not so with your Cairngorm climber: he rushes at any difficulty that he can see in or about his way, regardless of whether or not his meanderings combine into a logical whole. This is, no doubt, a sporting attitude, by comparison with which the ways of me and my like are rather tame; but as a relative newcomer to Cairngorm rock-craft I find it slightly bewildering and am inclined to doubt if I would fancy a companion with this mental twist on a really big mountain. I suspect that he might find it just as difficult to be rid of his habit as I do of mine.

This, however, is a recent development which has as yet had

too little time to leave a perceptible mark on the catalogued routes. In the past the scales were tilted the other way, and for the reasons described above the Cairngorms were seen through the hill-walker's rather than the climber's optics, with the result that most of the early ascents were more timid than the contemporary routes in other hills. The shooting season and game preservation used considerably to interfere with all forms of mountaineering, favouring winter climbing, which was conveniently explained away by the desire of adding snow and ice to the difficulties of the route as compensation for the lack of height. Thus, it was argued, one could enjoy Alpine conditions where in summer one would find but an indifferent rock climb, which is sound truth but not the whole truth. Apart from the preponderance of shooting, a very important reason for the development of winter climbing was the general rottenness of Cairngorm rock and the frequent association of mountain with bog which made many routes relatively the safer and the more accessible in winter. Difficulty of access to the main corries imposed further limitations on climbing activities, though by no stretch of imagination can it be held to account for the relative neglect of summer cragsmanship.

The upshot of it all is that most ascents have been made on the snow by steep gullies and chimneys of low technical difficulty, but very dangerous in summer-time owing to frequently wet and rotten rock and the amount of loose debris which the leader simply cannot help dislodging on his followers, strung out in a vertical line below, without any shelter against this friendly bombardment.

The general situation is reflected in the fact that there is no adequate climbing guide-book to the Cairngorms and those who want to study their climbs in detail have to peruse the articles and notes in *The Cairngorm Club Journal* and *The Scottish Mountaineering Club Journal*, whose standard of accuracy varies greatly from case to case. Sir Henry Alexander's *The Cairngorms* contains brief descriptions of the earlier climbing routes but, quite apart from being out of date, the descriptions are mostly very sketchy, barely allowing one to identify the climbs and giving next to no indication of their difficulty. This, undoubtedly, adds to the pleasures of exploration, as one can never know quite what to expect, but it also leaves the door ajar for perplexity and disappointment. Thus, for instance, having read in the *Guide* that the north-east ridge of the Angel's Peak was a rock climb, I hopefully started out with a party to see what it was like. We had a pleasant airy walk with a little scrambling but found the rope we had taken with us a perfectly useless encumbrance, while the " mere wall " to which the ridge was said to narrow proved to be a figment of somebody's imagination. It seems incredible that so obvious a route should never have been attempted before 1926, but there is no previous record of its having been climbed.

As a rule I have found the guide-book routes much easier than I have expected from their descriptions, but the reverse is not impossible and allowance must always be made for weather changes which in the Cairngorms affect the scale of difficulty to an even greater extent than in many other hills.

2. Rocks and Climbs

There are few ridges in the Cairngorms and still fewer aretes. Càrn a'Mhaim is steep, long and narrow, but its crest is a mere walk. The second-longest ridge is that of the Angel's Peak referred to above. Other ridges are short *fiacails* separated from the mountain mass by the encroachments of neighbouring corries. Most of them are of no climbing interest and can be tackled by any hill-walker with a little experience. The only exceptions are the Fiacail Ridge, which divides the Snowy Corrie of Cairn Gorm from Coire an Lochain, and the nameless (as far as I know) *fiacail* between Coire nan Clach and Coire an Dubh Lochain in Beinn a'Bhùird. The so-called Mitre Ridge is certainly a fine piece of rock, but hardly a ridge and ought properly to be classed as buttress.

The Sgorans, the Lurcher's Crag and Sròn na Lairig display some rock features approximating to ridges, but it would be more appropriate to describe them as shoulders or ribs.

The Devil's Point from Càrn a'Mhaim across the Lairig Ghru " mounth "
The Shelter Stone Crag

The Fiacail Ridge is crowned with a short arete of moderate difficulty, a scramble rather than a climb for the most part which, moreover, can easily be evaded altogether by the scree and grass slopes on the west side. It is, nevertheless, very exposed on the side of the Snowy Corrie and demands caution in view of many loosely perched boulders though, on the whole, the rock is sound for the Cairngorms. The Beinn a'Bhùird *fiacail*, which I have not climbed myself, wears a more formidable look. The arete can be reached without undue exertion by the grassy ledges from the Black Lochan, but the approach from the other side involves serious climbing. The rock seems fairly reliable.

All the remaining Cairngorm climbs are definitely of the face type, with the usual variety of mural precipice, slab, buttress, short arete, pinnacle, chimney, crack and gully. By the hill-walker's standards, the corrie-faces appear very intimidating, and some of the rock-bluffs are inaccessible enough by any standards; but in most cases closer scrutiny will soon reveal a number of practicable climbing routes, which have at first been obscured by the sharp optical contrast with the gentle character of the surrounding hill vistas. Thus, at the beginning of a Cairngorm climb, the scales are tilted in our favour: we have almost certainly overestimated the difficulties that lie ahead. And a good thing it is, too, for while there may be no need for hanging on our eyelashes or performing staggering acrobatics, many factors will be against us.

Cairngorm granite is of the rough, lumpy variety, with joints far apart and apt to be remarkably poor in good holds. In the worst cases, especially where pre-glacial features have been preserved, it has weathered into "pillows", "bolsters", "Aztec sculptures", "fish-bodies" or "cheese-rings", round of edge and often of monumental proportions. When steep, such "Egyptian rocks" become altogether unscalable. Their surface is very rough and sometimes consists of easily detachable grit, so that once, during some practice climbing of Stac na h'Iolaire, I was literally able to dig my toes into the rock. It is not always, nor indeed often, as bad as all that. Usually the roughness of the

o

Malcolm Slesser's party exploring the great slab

" *Over my right shoulder I could see the Black Pinnacle, which seemed to be floating midway down—a dark spire in an airy flood* " (p. 221) surface is a help: where no holds are available, it yet provides sufficient friction to prevent the climber from slithering off, and by jerks and diminutive frog-leaps he can make progress up such features. So far as safety goes, an "Egyptian" ridge is worse than a clean "Egyptian" face; it offers few, if any, secure belays or stances, and the best thing one can do if a member of the party goes off is quickly to jump on to the opposite side—an experience which I have so far been mercifully spared. In vertical climbing the danger is less pronounced, as the "cheese-rings" end from time to time in knobs or platforms which provide good stances and occasionally excellent belays, but a great responsibility rests on the leader, who must cut out all risky antics.

If the rocks look pink or grey it is usually a bad sign: it means that they have been worn by sand-blast down to the "bone" and cleared of the protective layer of lichen. Fine-grained dark granite is more trustworthy; even when not visibly differentiated, it will often abound in small firm holds.

The vegetation of "Egyptian" rock consists mainly of moss—black-moss and golden-moss (the latter easily recognizable by its grey colouring). If the weather be dry, the moss follows suit and adheres to the rock as best it can. In most cases it will stand the pressure of a nailed boot but yield to the fingers of an eager hand. When present in large cushions it offers a strong temptation to use one's knee and, not being a purist, I see no harm in yielding to it within reason, as the knee is less likely to tear off the cushion than either the hand or the toe. In wet conditions it is dangerous to entrust one's balance to a mossy hold and one is well advised to clear it beforehand.

Grasses and other plants soon get hold of decaying granite and the Cairngorms offer many examples of that abomination of all cragsmen—the "vegetable climb". Very typical of the Cairngorm faces and gullies is the structure where grass-and-moss-grown stretches of reddish gravel, with thin edges of protruding rock-joints and loosely embedded stones, are traversed by a series of steeper rock-bands forming short pitches of varying difficulty. Alternatively, one encounters slabby inclines of forty-five to eighty degrees, where slabs are arranged like bricks or tiles with a regular system of vertical cracks, partly filled with moss and gravel, and wider horizontal ledges strewn with debris. Such configuration involves little technically difficult climbing, but neither does it afford much opportunity for using one's rope to advantage and requires great circumspection. Sharp-nailed boots are generally preferable to any other kind of footwear.

Gullies and some of the chimneys, here as elsewhere, owe their existence either to direct action of water on firm rock, in which case they are sound though often deficient in large holds, or else to a band of weak rock which has yielded to the elements more rapidly than the tougher stuff on its sides. Not infrequently the weakness is produced by the sliding of the adjacent strata on one another, which results in what is known in geology as "foliation". Along the surface where the lateral pressure and friction have been strongest the granite has been transformed into flakes or foils and resembles a squashed book. Such rock decays very easily, is breachy and unreliable, with small sharp-edged holds which tend to crumble under the climber's weight.

Yet, although by and large the Cairngorm rock is poor and not very suitable for climbing, there are also considerable stretches of good sound granite, especially where it is of a later, glacial or post-glacial sculpture. This is usually true of the lower part of corrie-faces and buttresses which may, however, terminate upwards in holdless "Egyptian" rocks. The buttresses, low as they may be by Alpine standards, are often greatly exposed in their upper portions, where caution is recommended both for reason of loose debris and lack of secure belays. Some of the pinnacles are just heaps of boulders, crazily perched on one another like a small child's brick tower. It is no small wonder how structures of this kind can withstand the violence of the gales—sometimes they do not.

3. *The Main Climbing Areas*

The main climbing areas of the Cairngorms are associated with the great corrie systems of the big peaks, but some of the glens are crag-bound and offer varying possibilities for climbing.

In the west, there are a few minor crags in Glen Feshie which, however, can at best provide limited practice. Coire Garbhlach contains considerable cliffs of gneiss and schist which, as far as I know, have never been attempted. On the other hand, the Einich side of the Sgorans has been subjected to intensive glacier erosion by the ice descending from the vast gathering grounds of the Great Moss and is very rocky, offering continuous stretches of crag up to 1,200 feet in vertical drop and the longest, if not the most impressive, climbs of these mountains. The Sgoran crags fall into five distinct buttresses, up which various climbs have been made in summer and winter. The rocks of Sgòr Gaoith are broken up into a series of ribs or ridges, of which the one with A'Chailleach is known to climbers as "The Pinnacle Ridge". The ridge is of no great difficulty except for the Pinnacle itself, and climbing it has something of make-believe about it, as at most pitches one can stroll in reasonable comfort a score of yards on either side. Sgòran Dubh Mòr displays a more compact rock-face, comprising two buttresses which are divided by a funnel-shaped depression running into a narrow gully at the base and throwing up pre-glacial aretes of a low angle towards the summit. The rock, as usual, is fairly good to begin with but deteriorates with the ascent, to end eventually in holdless slabs and precarious block structures.

The corries of Braeriach facing the Sgorans across Loch Einich have only fragmentary rock-friezes and Coire Odhar at its head rises to the Great Moss in some slabby and hummocky buttresses, which by themselves might have been of climbing interest had they not been dwarfed by the far mightier Sgorans.

Braeriach's north-west corries, with the exception of Coire Lochain, have little and poor rock and lend themselves mainly to snow-climbing. Coire Lochain is contained by a semi-circle of cliffs, attaining some 400 feet from base to top. The rock is said to be quite good and the tarn below adds to the pictorial interest of climbing. Yet it is on the other side that the peak possesses a magnificent array of corries, two miles across from

Coire Bhrochain to the Angel's Peak. These corries, with their walls of cliff, buttresses, gullies and pinnacles, form the most impressive rock scenery of the Cairngorms, above which the Angel's Peak and Cairn Toul tower gracefully, isolated into tapering shapes by the optical recession of the intervening high ground.

The deepest part of the recess, known as the Rough Corrie, is divided by a short, blunt *fiacail* into the Great Rough Corrie (An Garbh Choire Mòr) and the Rough Corrie of the Dee (Garbh Choire Dhàidh), over whose "grisly cliffs" the young river shoots down in a thin waterfall, 400 feet high. It is along it that the first recorded Cairngorm climb was made by Dr. Skene Keith in 1810, who, as he explained, was anxious to make sure that it was the Dee and no other river all the way through. He completed his ascent over a snow-bridge which often spans the waterfall at the upper edge of the cliffs. The rock in the Dee Corrie is sound but little differentiated and inclined in parts to be broken up with grass and scree. Its quality markedly deteriorates in the adjacent Great Rough Corrie, which is mainly of the slab-grass-and-moss formation, with some smooth and rather holdless gullies and buttresses. The 500-foot Choke-stone Gully, mossy and wet, is the main climbing route up the slabby north face of the Angel's Peak on the Cairn Toul side of the corrie.

But the climbing palm belongs to Coire Bhrochain (Porridge Corrie), the easternmost of the great Braeriach corries. Unlike most crags on these hills, its three buttresses enjoy a good reputation for the soundness of their rock. The West Buttress, it is true, is somewhat deficient in this respect. It is the easiest and the least attractive of the three, offering mainly chimney and gully routes encumbered with scree. The East Buttress, on the other hand, is fine black granite with vertical drops of 600-650 feet, somewhat broken up at the top but compact in the lower pitches. The main rock-face, known as the Central Buttress, leads direct to the summit of Braeriach. The initial 200 feet have been skirted by the climbing routes, though there is no reason to believe it unscalable. Probably the most characteristic feature of the buttress is the Black Pinnacle, which shows clearly in midday sunshine about the centre of the face. The Braeriach Pinnacle, higher, bulkier and less finely shaped, faces it across a gully which forks between them. The main climbs have been made through this gully over both pinnacles, involving some 650 vertical feet of continuous rock-work, " moderate " to " difficult " in grade, perhaps a little more in places. The Braeriach Pinnacle has also been climbed from the gully between it and the East Buttress. This, however, does not exhaust either the actually completed or the possible climbs; and both the Central and the East Buttress have a wide choice of routes of any degree of technical difficulty.

The main peak of Cairn Toul, despite its brave outline, has little rock and that mainly fragmentary, but farther south the inlet of Glen Geusachan is bound with flights of slabby, ice-polished cliff. Beinn Bhrottain on the south side has a considerable, though uninteresting, rock-face, which apparently still awaits a conqueror. The Devil's Point, north of the glen, is much more impressive and affords fully 1,000 feet of rock-climbing, which seems to be of no great technical difficulty but exposed and dangerous. Strictly speaking, to make a climb of this kind reasonably safe, one would require pitons for rope-anchorage, but this, of course, is " not done ". I have never been there and have no personal comment to make.

Across the watershed, the Lairig Ghru is flanked by the rocks of the Lurcher's Crag (east) and Sròn na Lairig (west). These are divided into a series of buttresses, ribs or ridges, slabby pitches and grassy gullies with steep walls of live rock, reminiscent of the Sgorans. On the whole, however, the rock, shaped during and after the Ice Age, is better than on the latter and, save in some gullies, fairly reliable. The height of the buttresses varies from 200 to 500 feet, possibly a little more. The Lurcher's Crag is definitely the more interesting of the two hills and, breaking out of the Cairngorm norm, its south-westward scarp is the higher and the more rugged.

The Snowy Corrie and Coire Lochain, divided by the Fiacail Ridge, are the most rocky features of the Cairn Gorm massif.

The late Sir Henry Alexander dismisses them somewhat sweepingly with the statement that "the rocks are rounded and not suitable for climbing".[1] This is, however, taking too severe a view of the matter. There is much rotten rock in both corries and in the Snowy Corrie in particular; the upper pitches are encumbered with loose blocks; and, especially in Coire Lochain, some pillow-shaped rocks appear; but there are also reasonably sound buttresses with angular rock structure. The best and most climbed of these is the Aladdin Buttress, which stands out clearly and massively about the middle of the Snowy Corrie. It is divided by a narrow gap from a short ridge with three pinnacles which connects it with the summit plateau. The central gully above the great slab at the base of the Coire Lochain cliffs forms a natural climbing route to the summit of Cairn Lochan. Both ascents involve some 400 feet of climbing.

The Loch Avon climbing area may be said to be pivoted on the Shelter Stone. The buttresses of Cairn Gorm, north of the lake, are of the pink, nasty variety, but those of Beinn Mheadhoin, and Ben Macdhui, facing north and, therefore, of a younger geological age, are "black" and sound. The main feature of the cliff-scape is the abrupt bluff of Càrn Etchachan at the head of Loch Avon, divided by the Castle Gate Gully into the higher, but less uniform and formidable, pyramid-crowned crag of Càrn Etchachan proper and the fiercer-looking, square-topped Shelter Stone Crag. Both contain some 600 feet of live rock. The main face of the Shelter Stone Crag is very smooth and sheer, but it has been climbed round the edges and by the flanking gullies— the Castle Gate and the Forefinger Pinnacle Gully—which are of only moderate difficulty but require caution, owing to loose debris. The cliffs are very airy and as near to perpendicular as possible, though even the Shelter Stone Crag averages no more than 70 degrees at its steepest.

The Corrie of the Red Spouts in Ben Macdhui has a slabby rock-face of nearly 800 feet and a few quite imposing buttresses which, however, are out of favour with climbers in view of adverse stratification. The main face is not particularly difficult

[1] Sir Henry Alexander: *The Cairngorms* (1928), p. 138.

but poor in belays and with much loose stuff about, which makes it more suitable for winter than summer climbing.

In the Eastern Cairngorms, Ben Avon has only fragmentary rocks, mostly of very dubious quality, and such climbs as have been made there are on its numerous tors, thus being only a glorified edition of bouldering. Beinn a'Bhùird, on the other hand, has a fine system of corries, well deserving of a cragsman's attention.

A'Chioch is fully 800 feet high but the rock, especially in the upper part, is distinctly "Egyptian" and I am not sure whether it would "go". The same applies to the most cliffy south-west corner of Coire an Dubh Lochain, which is made up largely of a palisade of monumental "bolsters", though the dividing chim-. neys might yield to the back-and-foot or back-and-knee technique. The *fiacail* between this corrie and the neighbouring Coire nan Clach has been referred to elsewhere. The crags composing the *fiacail* and bordering on it in the latter corrie are of the "European" type, rock fairly well differentiated apart from some glabrous slabs at the base, and several climbs have been made from that side. In the north part of the corrie the rock-frieze is low and of little climbing interest.

Across the wide isthmus of table-land between the North Top and Cnap a'Chlèirich lies the Rough Corrie of Beinn a'Bhùird, second only to the big corries of Braeriach. In good agreement with the general principles of snow accumulation and its influence on the development of rock-faces, the finest crags of this corrie face north-east. It is here, about midway between the North Top and the Cleric's Knoll, that the Mitre Ridge shoots up from the screes; 600 feet high, it is a formidable cliff bearing a strong family resemblance to the Shelter Stone Crag, from which it will be gathered that it can hardly be a ridge. Its eastern aspect is not very encouraging but on the west side it offers a practicable, though difficult and very exposed, climbing route with one or two variants. The rock is sound but somewhat holdless and poor in good stances and belays.

Facing it across the corrie frowns another buttress or *fiacail*, which looks very stern from the distance but on closer acquaintance proves of an easy angle and moderate climbing difficulty, comparable in some ways to the Fiacail Ridge of Cairn Gorm, with the difference that its pitches are not so easy to evade. The corrie presents other climbing possibilities. It is, however, rather difficult to get at and only seldom visited by climbers.

4. *Braeriach, Some Others and Myself*

My acquaintance with the rocks of Coire Bhrochain had a somewhat unorthodox beginning.

It so happened that one hot sunny day I was persuaded to act as a climbing instructor and take a party of two beginners up Braeriach. In itself the proposition was unexceptionable enough and I had done such things once or twice before; but, having had no serious climbing training for several years, I did not feel too happy about it despite the manly assurance that " it was going to be all right ". To make matters worse my climbing boots were in a very sorry plight, with most of their nails gone or polished flat and one sole cracked through the middle.

The night in a tent at the Pools of Dee was slightly chilly and, when trying to sleep, I had to manœuvre so as to get an un-removed stone under the small of my back where it was relatively harmless. Off I dozed and woke up in turns, to hear the March Burn sing its eternal song in the dark stillness and see a star or two twinkle in the tiny chink under the tent's flap. Then accommodation with the stone was achieved once more and my eyes closed wearily upon my hopes and my doubts, until the sun had painted orange the upper half of Braeriach and the smoke of the camp fire was rising shaggily into the expectant morning air. There was heavy dew on the ground and my boots (aye, they had known better days!), left outside, were richly moistened.

On the way to the corrie I was faced with the double psychological problem of instilling into my charges, a young lady from Surrey and a young man from Cheshire, as well as into myself the conviction of my own infallibility. The sky was clear and pale, the sun already hot despite the early hour, and the blae-berries among the boulders—tempting. We made a rapid traverse of the steep slopes as I wrestled with my thoughts and danced over the stones to test my remaining nails and my sense of balance. It worked. Conviction seemed to grow in the three of us and my own mind attained the pellucid repose of a mountain tarn.

Now the three buttresses of Coire Bhrochain were before us and, after some mental calculation, I voted for the Black Pinnacle.

I was hard put to it to prove that my method of contouring, to avoid loss of height, was superior in speed as well as effort to following the more obvious course; but, with a little additional haste, we managed to arrive at the foot of the rocks at the same time as the other parties.

The climb began some 200 feet above the lowest reach of the rocks, at the foot of the slabby incline which gave access to the central gully cleaving the hill-face half-way up. Here we, that is to say, Malcolm Slesser's and my own party, paused. Ropes were uncoiled and sandwiches munched. Having re-examined the nailing of my boots, I discarded them resolutely and decided to climb in my very "concentrated" ski-socks, which had shrunk to about half their original size and correspondingly increased in thickness. I tied the bootlaces round my insteps and ankles to prevent the socks from slipping off, and was ready. Slesser's party started off at ten o'clock and we followed a few minutes later.

The dry slabs were child's play and, for encouragement, I led the first three pitches with my pack which, having acquired a pair of boots in addition to our food and reserve clothing and my camera, had a fairly respectable bulk and weight. Very soon we were at the foot of the gully, where Slesser asked us to wait for fear of dislodging loose debris on our heads. We did. In looking for a suitable perch I had an opportunity to see that "condensed socks" were inappropriate for dried-up black-moss, as my foot slipped off at once as soon as I tried to use a mossy foothold. This was not dangerous there but might have been quite fatal in another place, so that I was grateful for the warning.

Seconds were ticking over. The flotsam of climbing memories

passed across the pool of my mind. Then Slesser appeared, fore-
shortened, gathering the rope over his back and shoulder on the
ridge above the gully. I moved on, the moist sweet bitterness
of grapefruit in my mouth. My feet avoided the wet moss. The
rope was up; the coolness of stone enclosed me as, wedged into
a narrow cleft, I passed the rough coils over my shoulder.

Above, the gully narrowed down and steepened into a short
wall. I was again on the move. My socks denied me the use of
the insecure mossy footholds on the wall and I took instead to
the somewhat overhanging rocks on my right—up sideways, a
seat-hold and again, and a small traverse to the edge of a beetling
block, back into the gully. This was the first difficult place. I
swung round the block and out into the void with a kind of un-
reflecting automatism: it was a plunge not into the unknown,
but into the abstractedly remembered. Yet the device worked
with precison. My left foot and hand landed firmly where expected, and over the lip of the rock I went into the spacious
cavity where the gully forked towards the small gaps at the back
of the Black and Braeriach Pinnacle respectively. Both arms of
the fork were quite easy.

My companions followed faithfully and well, and we could
now engage the short arete leading to the Black Pinnacle, which
promised more interesting climbing than the gully.

To begin with the holds were somewhat adverse in inclination,
but ample. The ridge itself, however, was one of those rounded,
featureless things, almost a monolith of rough weathered granite,
with few holds and no belays as I was shortly to find out.

The first step offered a good stance and I was satisfied that my
companions were secure on the rope—besides, exposure was
slight. Not so on the ridge, which broke away towards the corrie
in a 400-foot precipice. It resembled an uncomfortably large and
steepish horseback, at the beginning of which we came upon our
second difficult pitch. There were scarcely any holds on the
"rump" of the "horseback" and I did not dare to entrust my
weight to the dubious cakes of mica extruding above the wind-
worn granite on the corrie side. One had to push oneself upwards by the pressure of one's palms on the rough rock and

elbow leverage, clinging to the arete with one's knees—by little jerks, up and up, until the top of the "rump" was reached, where the hands got a firmer purchase. The exercise was gritty but not unpleasant. The ensuing awkwardness, however, resided in the fact that I could find nothing remotely similar to a belay and was lured on by the hope of finding one farther up. Thus a moment arrived when my whole party was strung out on the 120 feet of rope, all of them on the same side of the arete and holding on to precisely nothing. So there we were, myself nearing the Pinnacle, Allan bestriding the rock in the middle and Beatrice creeping up the holdless "rump". With experienced climbers the danger would have been trifling as, apart from the "rump", the ridge did not present serious difficulties. Yet, probably wrongly, I discounted in my mind Allan's ability to hold Beatrice if she slipped clean off the rocks, and glumly resigned myself to jumping down into the gully on the other side should anything go amiss.

There were some dimly anxious moments, stored up in my subconsciousness, before she reached the crest of the arete. Thereupon I asked them to move up a few steps, to give me more rope, and then to stay put while I made a dash for the Pinnacle, overrunning Slesser's party in search for a belay. I found a glorious one and sighed with relief. We were all together again, watching Malcolm Slesser exploring the big slab above the gap. From where I was I could see that its upper part was impracticable and shouted to him words of discouragement. He persisted for a while, then gave in and struck straight up along its edge. We waited to have a clear way.

A few minutes earlier the rope had knit round our lives a warm bond, beyond the reach of everyday social contacts. I still had the other half of my grapefruit and some toffees, which we divided between us. It was good to be sitting idly, caressed by the midday sun, on a lofty watch-tower in a perpendicular desert of rock, grown with sparse oases of moss, sedge, groundsel and Alpine lady's mantle.

One often hears that the cragsman does not climb for views. Nonsense! This may not be his prime motive; nor does he

climb for panoramas, such as can be had from the summit
reached without any danger from another side; but the views
he gets are unique and his own, won by his muscles and his will
from the unyielding rock which, defeated, rewards him with its
intimacy. In the views revealed to him there is fear and exulta-
tion, combined in lofty Gothic beauty. Fear, I said, and fear
is an important element of that beauty, making it all the
sweeter, like a forbidden fruit. We climb for fear and release
from fear. Fear is our inseparable companion. It may be completely forgotten in the effervescence of the struggle, dissolved
in fellowship, or overlaid by technicalities—prospecting for the
route, paying out the rope, search for holds or adjustment of
balance. But make no mistake: even when our eye glides without emotion over lethal precipices at our feet—and a precipice
need not be high to be lethal—fear is there, lurking in a dark
corner of our mind.

Meanwhile Slesser's party had reached the grassy ledge above
the big slabs and we followed—down onto the gap, easily, over
a short, sharp arete likewise, and on to the edge of the slabs
where the rock overlapped them, forming a kind of very steep,
obtuse rib, made up of a succession of rounded bumps. This
was, as I later discovered, a considerable straightening of the
original route, which led over the gap and by an easy traverse
to a gully farther west.

I encountered no difficulty in following the rib, climbing now
directly over the bumps, now with one foot on the slab. The
face of the buttress below fell away to the screes in one magnificent sweep of some 700-800 feet, with nothing to hold the eye.
Over my right shoulder I could see the Black Pinnacle, which
seemed to be floating midway down—a dark spire in an airy
flood. Stances and belays were good, my hands moved in an
easy concerted rhythm and I felt that my charges were quite
safe, though simultaneously the nervous strain of the Pinnacle
arete began to bubble up from my unconscious mind.

My party climbed nicely, without let or hindrance of any
kind. In a matter of half an hour we stood on the top of
Braeriach, not far from the summit cairn. It was one o'clock.

I had certainly enjoyed the climb, but not the responsibility of it, which I was glad to have discharged and done with.

On dry rock, in fine weather, the ascent seemed safe and easy; the holds were sound; apart from the gully, there was no dangerous debris to dislodge. But in adverse weather, when the moss is soaking wet, it might well have been a very different story. Anyway, I would hesitate to grade the route—" difficult " would probably be about right.

The distances were pale and shallow. The sun cast a skein of silver ripples on the dull mirror of Lochan Uaine.

Emperor moth

XI

STUDIES IN WHITE

The snae that lies lang lies on ither snae.
(A Scottish Proverb)

1. *Snow Conditions*

IT was in January. A fresh fall of snow had spread its glittering mantle over the countryside and the hills stood white against a blue sky with scattered clouds.

When, however, I set out on ski I soon discovered that the road was barely negotiable, with gravel coming through the thin layer of hard-rolled snow, bringing me every few seconds to a sudden and unwelcome halt. The Braemar path through Rothiemurchus had a deeper covering, but it still lacked a foundation of snow and the soles of my ski were grinding pitifully on grit and stones. Only beyond the Cairngorm Club footbridge did conditions improve sufficiently to make my progress less irritating, if not much more rapid.

The forest was still and the frosted heather was edged with silver flame against the low glare of the sun, poised in a misty halo at the top of Càrn Eilrig's blue triangle. Crested tits were flitting along the road, alighting ahead of me for a few acrobatics on the heather twigs and the rough meanders of cracked pine bark and again taking wing at my approach, as though determined to keep me company on the way.

The lower part of the Lairig path, up beyond the cairn, defeated my resolve to proceed on ski. No sooner, however, had I taken them off than it proved that, although the snow was too shallow to ski on comfortably, it was rather too deep for walking, so that I had to reverse my tactics.

The sharp blizzard blowing in the Lairig hung a white veil across the V-shaped gap. To the left, the rocks of the Lurcher's Crag loomed up, dim and very steep in the turmoil. But along the path there was hardly any wind and limp fluffy snowflakes came spiralling down out of an unbelievably blue sky, tinged with watery green by the fine snow-dust which the wind was whipping up from the High Tops.

The truth was that early winter seldom offered good ski-ing, and the game was largely a hide-and-seek with the wind that would create here and there in the lee large or small cakes of hard, drifted snow which might occasionally attain the thickness of several feet and even yards and, the configuration of the ground being favourable, extend for a mile or more along or athwart the hill. Upon these the later falls would settle a layer of soft powder-snow, which would in turn be packed to the gypsum-like windslab by the next blowy day.

There seemed little point in going much farther up the glen and I turned towards Castle Hill on the left, which displayed a chain of sizable " cakes ". My luck held. The top layer was still soft, though somewhat deep for quick turning.

I pushed upwards in an untroubled zigzag.

The half-veiled sun cast a creamy sheen upon the snows. The Rothiemurchus Forest and Strathspey lay at my feet. The scene was one of stark beauty : rough of edge, limited but powerful in tint, like a four-coloured woodcut. The heather rising above the snow was bright maroon with a purplish bloom; the pines—harsh blobs of dark, burnt greenery—merging in the distance into a livid ink splashed along the river; and the sky above a glowing Cambridge blue. The raucous call of a capercailzie was like the sound of a wooden knife cutting a sheet of Whatman paper.

It was my first day on ski that year.

I bent my knees as deep as I could without raising my heels, and with a twist of my body the wonder of the past came to life leaving the flourish of a christie between the boulders. It was good to be alive, though my knees were quivering with the effort when I reached my pack at the edge of the long heather.

Snow conditions in the Cairngorms are dominated by two factors: wind and heather. They make and mar your ski-ing. The heather performs the important task of binding the snow

Rothiemurchus under snow

to the ground, opposing the efforts of the wind to dislodge it and eliminating more or less completely all avalanche danger on the lower slopes, while higher up any perilous accumulation of the snow, save cornices, is unlikely owing to the strength of the winds. Thus a large avalanche is a rare happening in these mountains; and I have never seen one yet, though I have heard of some from people whose experience in these matters I am inclined to doubt. So far so good. It requires, however, a good deal of snow to plaster over the heather so as to produce a good ski-ing surface. Most hills are grown with heather up to about 3,000 feet, from which it follows at once that the matter is of no small importance. At the upper range of its growth a foot of snow, which, as meteorologists will tell us, is equivalent to an inch of rain, is generally speaking sufficient for this purpose; but at lower levels at least a yard will be needed to make a uniform snow-slope and it takes a lot of snowing to build up such a layer, more particularly so as the wind constantly blows the snow from all the exposed features of the ground into hollows, cracks and nicks, and windless snowfalls are rare.

For these reasons an open Cairngorm slope in winter presents at most times a speckled appearance. All crests and humps are very nearly bare. Heather protrudes above the snow and only the sheltered declivities, gullies and corrie-beds sport a uniform whiteness. There the snow will often lie very deep and I have seen drifts the thickness of which, as disclosed by the water gurgling down through icy caverns, was sufficient to engulf a two-storied building. This situation is welcome to white hares, rabbits, ptarmigan, grouse and deer, which need never be totally deprived of food during the winter, but less so to a skier whose dream of a continuous and carefree run down the hill is not easy to attain.

It is possible to ski over snow-covered heather. I have done this often enough. Even with only a few inches of snow you can move fairly fast down heather-grown ground, reasonably free from stones; but this is a special art, bearing little resemblance to ordinary ski-ing, and requires time and practice to be mastered. In most cases you have to lean back rather than for-

P

Speyside in silver filigree

ward to avoid a nasty nose-dive and regulate your speed by a judicious use of sticks, now checking it, now giving yourself a push. Any turn other than a jump is practically out of the question, though a telemark might come off on short heather.

With a deep layer of hard snow, the heather sprays sticking out above it offer by themselves little resistance to a straight run. Nevertheless, such ground is not to be trusted, for it often conceals pockets of soft snow among hard crust and gaps roofed over only by a thin crust which collapses under the skier's weight, thus forming a perfect man-trap.

However, the snow is not all as bad as that. The corries, gullies and slopes sheltered from the prevailing winds will soon accumulate a considerable depth of snow and in favourable weather offer prospects of good running. Owing to the force and frequency of winds and fluctuations of temperature, various forms of windslab and crust, ranging from the thin breakable sun-crust to sheet ice, are the most likely condition of the snow to be found on the High Cairngorms. At the lower and middle altitudes the snow covering is seldom continuous and one is mostly confined to a definite course, while the intervening ground is just negotiable on ski, sometimes not even that.

From this it follows at once that it is absolutely indispensable to have the ski equipped with steel edges. I still remember my first winter in the Cairngorms when I tried to ski on a pair of borrowed boards without steel edges and the harsh treatment meted out to me by the icy snows of the High Tops. At each turn I used to slide interminably to the side, quite unable to control my direction.

This does not mean that powder-snow does not occur. It does, usually in the form of drifted powder superimposed on hard windslab or crust, which provides easy turning and excellent running; and occasionally one finds large fields of it. Yet this is an ephemeral phenomenon, as the snow soon becomes patchy or develops a breakable wind-crust in which any turn but the jump turn is very doubtful. Sometimes a few hours are sufficient to complete the transformation. We may begin our ascent on most enticing powder-snow and on the return find our hopes dashed to the ground. It is a bad sign if the ridges are smoking and our ski and feet suddenly disappear in a low flood of rushing snow-dust which, incidentally, is a very fine sight. The whole slope seems to be flowing down with extraordinary rapidity, with ourselves buoyant, floating up a shimmering cataract.

With a sharp change in the direction of the wind it is by no means unusual to see a whole snow-slope shifted, as it were, bodily from one side of the mountain to another. Where yesterday there was an excellent run we may find on the morrow but bare ground, gleaming with ice sheets and lined with those arrow-like formations of windslab produced by a persistent high wind which are known under the Siberian name of *zastrugi*; while the hitherto naked hillsides in the lee have acquired, without any snowfall, a fine coating of sifted powder-snow.

Thus winter snows in the Cairngorms are rather fickle and unreliable, providing a wide scope for surprises, pleasant and unpleasant, as well as for testing our mountain craft and weather wisdom.

As the day lengthens and the sun rises higher in the sky the upper layer of the snow begins to thaw up during the day, to freeze hard once more during the night. By this process of superficial melting and regelation it gradually assumes the granular structure of the *névé* or spring-snow, and in this form is much less subject to unexpected changes. It can freeze to the consistency of a " cheese-grater ", on which a skier rattles down like a tank rolling over an asphalt roadway. It can also melt in direct sunshine to a slushy " pap ", which no wax can cajole into yielding a glide. But it can do nothing else : neither wind nor sun have any permanent effect on its structure. It is, so to speak, " heart of oak ", though sometimes too literally so, and we can depend on it.

With the proverbial changeability of insular weather spring-snow may form at any time of the year, but it is certain to be found in spring and there is no other snow to be seen in summer, apart perhaps from some occasional and ephemeral fall on the summits.

Generally speaking, a dull, windless day with a fairly high

and uniform temperature of the air is best for ski-ing on spring-snow, as then both the "pap" and the "cheese-grater" effects are eliminated and the running is smooth and easy, if somewhat slower than on good winter-snow. Though, of course, it is much more fun to let the sun see what we are about. The combined sensation of hot sunshine and cold snow has about it something of the taste of ice-cream on a blazing afternoon in June or July. The rounded, concave snow surfaces, with their high reflecting power, act as magnifying mirrors, and the heat of the air in a sheltered, snow-filled gully or corrie in April or May can be excruciating, so that bad burns, blisters and sun-sores on the lips and nostrils may result from reckless exposure.

2. *Months and Winters*

On the High Tops a light snow shower may be expected at any season, but as a rule a few hours later the last trace of the snow has gone and, however cold the air may be, the temperature of the ground is well above freezing-point. But beginning with the second half of October snow gets a footing on the Cairngorm heights and a heavy fall may bring it even on to the lower ground for a day or two, making some ski-ing possible on the grassy slopes and flats in the glens and above the range of the heather. Yet although the hills may look speckless-white to the eye, the game is seldom worth the candle: the snow has no foundation and much climbing is necessary before any depth of it is reached. In November and December there may be considerable precipitation at the higher levels, as a rule accompanied by high winds, but Old Yule is more often black than white (to which the winter of 1944-5 forms a notable recent exception) and the heavy snows do not come till the second half of January, sometimes not even then.

Winters vary greatly from year to year, both in the amount and timing of the main falls of snow, and snowless, or nearly snowless, winters occur. The common malignity of the deities presiding over wintry matters will have it that whenever a conscious effort is made to utilize the snow for human pleasure or convenience it invariably fails to come. Thus when, in the winter of 1909-10, the Scottish Ski Club, encouraged by the copious snowfalls of preceding years, set about equipping the postmen of Braemar and the neighbourhood with ski, the snow instantly receded high up into the Cairngorm glens and stayed there for several years, so that the whole venture collapsed before it had time to get into its stride.[1] Similarly the attempt at organizing winter sports in Scotland on Swiss lines was nipped in the bud by the snowless winter of 1932-3, and ten years later the Snow and Mountain Warfare Training Centres in Braemar, Glen More and Glen Feshie were faced with an equally difficult situation, which made ski-ing training very trying for trainee and instructor alike.

On the average, however, there is sufficient snow in the Cairngorms between mid-January and mid-April to make ski-ing possible at least in some parts of the hills; and after a hard winter one can ski till the end of May, though by that time much carrying is necessary before the snow is reached.

The early part of the winter is normally characterized by south-westerly winds which, mild and very strong, are unfavourable to ski-ing and mountaineering, hampered as these also are by the low visibility and the short day. At this season the best snow is found on the north-eastern slopes and Deeside will have a better snow-cover than Speyside. Later, with the prevalence of southerly and easterly winds, the situation is reversed. These winds seldom attain the violence of a Sou'Wester, are bitterly cold on high ground, and associated with clear or lightly-veiled skies and hard night frosts.

March has a bad reputation for winds, but I cannot support it from my experience, and the suspicion is that it has been formed by those who have not tried ski-ing earlier in the year and have thus missed most of the blowing. There are, indeed, many considerations against ski-ing earlier. Cold, wind and short daylight hours, combined with the great distances that must be overcome and the difficulties encountered by wheeled

---

[1] W. H. Higginbotham: " Ski-ing in Scotland," *The British Ski Year Book*, 1943, pp. 109, 110, 118.

transport on the snowed-up roads, are enough to discourage any-one from ski-ing in the Cairngorms in early winter. But of ski-ing on spring-snow in April, when the Scottish Ski Club holds its annual meet at Aviemore, loud peans are sung, and again I beg to dissent; for, pleasant as this may be, in most Aprils the snow is reduced to " wraiths " (wreaths), that is to say isolated fields, streaks and patches, which afford good opportunities for turn practising and " circus " running but will not satisfy those who look upon ski-ing as primarily a form of mountaineering. In fact, I would place the optimum ski-ing season a few weeks earlier, in March. Later, though quite enjoyable, the enterprise becomes unduly laborious, and I personally have little en-thusiasm for carrying heavy loads over heather-slopes and boulder-screes.

The greatest difficulty of ski-ing in the Cairngorms is not so much the climate or the lack of snow as the approach to the hills. The few derelict bothies in various stages of disintegration may give shelter from rain in the summer but are of little use under wintry conditions; and in the whole of the Cairngorm Moun-tains there is nothing however remotely resembling an Alpine hut. In fact, there are only two such in the Highlands: the Scottish Mountaineering Club Hut on Ben Nevis and the small "lunching hut" maintained by the Scottish Ski Club on Ben Ghlas—both uninhabited. The villages are several miles from the foothills. Sometimes it is possible to obtain accommodation sufficiently near to the snow. In most cases it is not. Therefore, to enjoy ski-ing in such conditions it is advisable to have a car, which helps to eliminate at least some of the tedium of the approach. Otherwise one must just plod on. If there is enough snow in the valleys well and good, you can at least get along without carrying your ski, but more often than not this is not so.

In the past ponies and mules were used for carrying ski-ing kit, and during the war half-track vehicles proved most success-ful in negotiating Scottish mountain ground and were a great help in military ski training. It has since become the ambition of the Scottish Ski Club to acquire one of these, but no substantial

progress has been made in this direction at the time of writing
(1947).[1] Still, with more interest and a little organization, ski-
ing in the Cairngorms need not be quite so strenuous as it is
to-day: but in this case, as in others, the gregarians who enjoy
things and suffer in huddles have an easy life, while "the cat
that walks by himself" gets the worst deal.

After the intermezzo of the Lambing Storms, there is usually
little snow left in the second half of April; though, as in other
parts of Britain, heavy snowfalls occur in the Cairngorms towards the end of May. Seton Gordon records than on 29th
May, 1923, the snow was continuous upwards from the 2,200-foot
contour, and ten years later the tops were again white with about
a foot of snow in the middle of May. There seems to be a fairly
distinct ten-year weather cycle, probably associated with the
sun-spot period, with a correction for the annual revolution of
the earth. Most of the May snow is just "froth" and does not
stay long, but it serves to revive and reinforce the shrinking
"wraiths" and may help to extend the ski-ing season into
June.

In the recesses of the hills sheltered from the sun and the
warm winds minor fields and "pockets" of snow survive well
into the summer and are often still there at the winter's return.
The largest of these and the only one with a claim to eternity is
the "Old Snow" of the Great Rough Corrie of Braeriach, which
is said never in living memory to have completely disappeared,
though the flaming summer of 1945 reduced it to a narrow
crescent. It may be taken to represent the last remnant of the
glaciers of the Ice Age, albeit Seton Gordon does not support this view.[2] The other notable summer snows are: in the
north-east face of Ben Macdhui, some 200 feet below the summit,
in the Snowy Corrie of Beinn a'Bhùird, Coire Creagach of
Monadh Mòr, Horseman's Corrie in Braeriach, and Ciste Mearaid (Margaret's Coffin or Chest) a little below the top of Cairn
Gorm. They are, however, of no practical interest to the skier.

[1] I. W. Rutherford: "The 1945-46 Season in Scotland," *The British Ski Year Book*, 1946, p. 128.
[2] Seton Gordon: *The Cairngorm Hills of Scotland*, p. 179.

3. *On the Wintry Heights*

A winter ascent in the Cairngorms is on the average a tougher proposition than it would be in other mountains of comparable size, but less exposed to winds, which offer more or less uniform snow-slopes.   Here, if this is to be done wholly on ski, great care must be exercised in the choice of the line to avoid imperfectly covered ground, loss of height and unnecessarily long traverses.   Whenever possible the best course is to choose a gully on the side of the mountain which has suffered least from the depredations of the wind in the last fortnight or so.   The knowledge of the weather record will be helpful, but a few minutes' study of the general distribution of the snow on the surrounding hillsides, of the cornices and windslab formations ought to suffice for making the right choice.   There is, however, this compensation that we need not worry about avalanches, save perhaps a superficial slide of wet snow which can easily be countered by driving a ski-stick, handle first, into the underlying stable layer. A portion of windslab lying on hard crust or ice might become detached but I have never seen this happen, because at least at some points windslab will as a rule rest directly on the hillside and is thus strongly anchored.   Moreover, fret as we may over the inconveniences encountered in climbing on ski, it is well to bear in mind that our progress is in most cases both much easier and more rapid than it would be on foot over the same ground in the summer-time.   In the worst case we could try H. G. Wells' method of consoling himself with the thought that he might have been sitting in the dentist's chair instead.

At any time, and in midwinter in particular, a sharp eye should be kept on the weather.   However promising the morning may be, there is no telling how the afternoon will develop and high winds have a disconcerting trick of springing up suddenly about three o'clock, just as the winter sun begins to lower for the setting.

Thus, for instance, it was cold but sunny, without a trace of wind, when I left Glen Feshie with two companions in the morning of 6th January, 1946, heading for Càrn Bàn Mòr and the

Great Moss, with Monadh Mòr as our final objective. The hard crust of the "cheese-grater" type was trying on the way up, but yielded good running. After a few trial runs about Ciste Mear-aid, we set forth across the Great Moss. Monadh Mòr's rounded shoulders were speckless-white against the blue sky. There was nothing but a light air coming over the snows from the gap of the Eidart as we slid fast over the hummocky ground.

When we were about to cross Allt Luineag the binding of one of my companions got out of order. The other was rather tired after a long train journey from the south the previous night and they both decided to return, while I continued alone. The wind was freshening as I put on my ski-crampons and struck a straight line towards the summit of Monadh Mòr. By the time I had climbed some three-quarters of the way up, which had not taken long, it was already half a gale and my windjacket was flapping around me like a loose sail. I unbuckled my crampons and turned to schuss back. Yet, though the snow was icy and very fast and the incline not less than twenty degrees, I had to push myself along with my sticks to make headway against the wind.

The hollow part of the plateau about Loch nan Cnapan was fairly sheltered, but the way up Càrn Bàn Mòr in the teeth of a raging Sou'Wester was an experience that I would not care to repeat. The spikes of the crampons held the easy incline well, but I do not know how I would have fared without them. My hands were completely numb inside my thick waterproof mittens. Yet at the same time my shirt was wet with perspiration from the effort of ploughing up through the icy blast. I found it extremely difficult to breathe. Take in air I could easily enough—in fact, it rushed into my lungs chilling them on the way—but I had to pump hard to get it out again, till my chest ached. The strain on my lungs and heart became almost unbearable, and never had I been so thankful to see the filthy bothy of Ciste Mearaid, where I could gain a few minutes' respite before escaping into the safety of the glen.

Now, though a military medical board has stigmatized me with Grade III, I am no weakling and I have little doubt that many a less well-trained skier would have succumbed to the strain.

So beware of dawdling on the high plateaux of the Cairngorms in midwinter and remember the *tertia hora!*—the time when the Devil used to get at the monks.[1]

Nothing saps your vitality so quickly as a mountain wind. Scottish winter is in this respect particularly treacherous. In this climate, however lightly you may dress, you always feel too hot when climbing or langlaufing. Yet if you rashly succumb to the illusion that you will still be warm when resting you will soon discover your mistake, for the relative dampness of the air has now a chilling effect. On the whole, therefore, it is better to overdress than to underdress. The warmth we experience on the way is our own and is gained at the expense of our precious calories. Thus our power of resisting the cold is being squandered and we are left defenceless once our sustained effort ends, as happens when we are resting or running down. This is, of course, generally true, but the effect is less marked in the dry air of the Alps or other Continental countries. With still air one can get away with a lot, but with a strong wind the matter is not one for joking.

To make good the loss of bodily warmth we must eat. No merit attaches to the exploit of doing a day's ski-ing on a sandwich and an orange—it is just plain unhealthy. But it is not easy to consume icy food, held in numb fingers, amid an arctic blast feeling for our soft spots. Those crumbling sandwiches with which we are usually equipped become particularly unpalatable.

Cornices, rocks, drifts and trees provide natural shelter but, unfortunately, are not always available, and I have found that it usually repays trouble to construct an artificial one.

Find some deep snow, preferably windslab, of which as a rule there is no shortage on the Cairngorms, even though it may be overlaid with powder, make in it a round hollow by trampling the snow to a hard floor, cut a few large snow bricks with the heel of your ski, and build with them a semi-circular wall on the

---

[1] This properly refers to 3 a.m.

windward side of the hollow, sufficiently high to cover you when sitting on your skis inside it. In doing the latter take care that there should be a space between your improvised bench and the floor. It does not take two people working together more than fifteen minutes to construct such a half-igloo, though, of course, one can spend any amount of time on improving and embellishing it. A single skier may require more time but, on the other hand, he needs a smaller shelter.

If the site has been well chosen you will be immune to the most biting blizzard and can rest and eat your lunch in peace. Should the day be sunny it will be warm and cosy inside your temporary "home". It is what the ptarmigan do: when they feel cold they bury themselves in the snow.

Windblown as the Cairngorms may be, they know quiet spells. Long before April rings its silver bugle, in February and March there will come still, sunlit days, all aglow and aglitter with crisp, frosted snows. The open-skied, star-spangled night will be cruelly cold, and the morning will awake bristling with ice-crystals, the trees by the burnside coated with rime, and bushy fern leaves adorning the inside of the windows. But by ten or eleven o'clock, and in March even earlier, the sun will get the better of the frost and, though the temperature of the ground may be many degrees below freezing-point, the air will be warm and springlike. Icicles will begin to drip and housetops to steam.

This is the time to enjoy the mountain winter, in its blaze of light, its deep-blue shadows, and its great stillness.

Your ski will carry you fast and, if it be powder-snow as well, you will seem to float above the ground with only the *shee*-hiss of the parting snow to restore to you a sense of reality.

And don't forget the sunset, for it comes every day, though days may vary, when the light yellows and the shadows lengthen, but the heights incandesce all the brighter under the wan sky.

A few minutes will pass. The sky will turn paler still and a greenish tinge will rise from the east. Then the sun on the lower hills will change to orange and the shadows will be of a dull purplish-blue. This is the signal that the magic of the evening is at work.

There will be purple and green reflexes on the glens. The orange glow will creep up, increasing in brilliance as it ascends, to be replaced by flame and blush-rose set in frames of turquoise shadow. Now the eastern sky is pale yellow jade and the peaks are like the giant petals of titanic flowers crowning the alabaster cup of the Earth. An ethereal sheen of magenta and purple, deepening to mauve and blue, spreads over the foothills, growing fainter and fainter, with shadows of glaucous green, as the blue eyelid of the night closes upon the passing day. A moment comes when the highest peaks, for a short precious while, brighten up against the darkening sky and then fade to the last parting blush, which gradually yields to the ghostly pallor advancing from below.

Another day of sunshine and snow has died, and the High Cairngorms tower above, cold, stern and hostile in the tightening grip of the frost.

Keep away, keep away, Sons and Daughters of Man!

Shut your doors, draw your curtains, pile blazing logs on your hearths! It's the world where the stars wander and the comets glide.

XII

A-SKI-ING ON THE TOPS AND "WRAITHS"

1. *In the Lee of the East Wind*

IT all depends, in ski-ing as in politics, on which way the
wind blows, and whichever way it may blow it is always the
wrong way; so watch the vane or, even better, the clouds,
and look for the lee. The two quarters of the sky of particular
concern to us are the north-east and the south-west which, as
a Chinese might put it, are the Houses of the Big Winds; but
winds oscillating between east and south are frequent in winter
at periods of high pressure and may attain considerable strength.

The action of the sun is most intense on the south-east and
south inclines, which are to be avoided unless we are on the look-
out for early spring snow; and on the whole the north-eastern
slopes and gullies offer the fairest prospects for ski-ing. Yet with
a strong easterly wind, the west faces are in the lee and therefore the most likely to have a good and even snow cover. Should
you at such time happen to be on the Spey side of the hills, go
to Glen Feshie, which is easily accessible by the new road from
Insh, itself connected by roads with Kingussie, Kincraig and
Aviemore. There is also an old road on the east side of the glen,
running from Feshiebridge to Achlean, but it is barely negotiable by car and not to be recommended, especially after a
heavy fall of snow.

The best ski-ing grounds in Glen Feshie are found in the
hills about Achlean, and the Balachroick croft, some two miles
down the glen, makes a good starting-point for the Sgorans.
Those motoring along the main road will find it convenient to
park their cars by the school-house at Stronetoper and cross the
river by the foot-bridge below, which gives access to the stalking
path to Càrn Bàn Mòr.

The middle of the glen is wooded on both sides, but some

237

good ski-ing can be had on the hummocky sides and in the corries of Mullach Clach a' Bhlàir which can be reached over the bridge below the head keeper's house.

Finally, late in the season, when the snow, except for a "wraith" or two, has already gone from the western hillsides, the Great Moss can be relied upon to produce some ski-ing, and after a hard winter will be under snow well into May. Combined with Glen Geusachan, the Moss makes a practicable route from Glen Feshie to Glen Dee and Braemar. Another interesting, though strenuous, tour is from Ciste Mearaid across the Moss to the Wells of Dee and Braeriach with a descent to Aviemore, best made over Sròn na Lairig. Thence those who do not mind a little intricate wood running may take the Lairig "mounth", though there is usually better snow on the flatter and treeless moorland tracts which spread from the Sròn to Gleann Einich, connected by a cart-track (sometimes accessible to light cars) and a driving road with Coylum Bridge. The tour can, of course, be also done in the opposite direction, but this entails a rather heavier climb. Settled weather is essential for the crossing of the Great Moss and the extensive summit plateau of Braeriach.

In exceptionally good conditions with thick snow, one may follow the broad ridge of the Sgorans all the way from Càrn Bàn Mòr to Creag Dubh above Loch an Eilein and run down to the lake by the main depression in the north face of the hill. Creag Dubh is wooded in the lower reaches but rough timber tracks zigzag up Inchriach and can be used for the descent. Once more it is hardly worth attempting the tour in the reverse direction.

The 1945 Christmas was "black", or—to be precise—a mixture of brown and yellow hues with those stark, ominous blues and purples peculiar to the Highland hills. Only after the New Year did a few white showers skim the Cairngorm tops, putting some "icing" on their cake-like faces.

Hopefully, I had left my ski in Glen Feshie and watched from Kingussie how the ribs of the Sgorans and Càrn Bàn Mòr

were swept bare on a different side by each successive change of
the weather and how the drifts in the gullies deepened, until
one Saturday brought a quiet, grey canopy of cloud from which
a steady stream of snow was descending on the earth. White
carpets were soon spread over the road, though the heather-lands
remained speckled.

This was the time to try my luck.

As if to damp my enthusiasm, Kincraig greeted me with a
sleety drizzle; but by the time I reached Insh the drizzle had
turned into white floccules pouring down densely from the overcast sky. The road to Glen Feshie lay ahead, bleak and
deserted: no transport—no lifts. I passed the shattered battle-
fields of trees—thin bare trunks pointing mournfully upwards
into the belly of the sluggish cloud.

A deep hush had blanketed the world. Now and then a dim
hill vista would open among the mists and float away like a
mirage. The birches stood in a silvery trimming over the dark,
swirling flow of the Feshie. It continued snowing, but as yet
the snow cover was just sufficient to take away the unpleasant
sting of the hard road from under my feet without, however,
impeding the walking itself. Nevertheless, miles stretched out
long, as though diluted in the mist and falling snow.

At Achlean there was a great show of ski waxing that night.
The wee laddies were most intent on polishing their improvised
contraptions, in which Granddad took a more than sympathetic
interest. The B.B.C. announced next day that it had been the
coldest night of the young year, which may well have been so
to judge by the way I had felt under my multiple blankets.

The morning came sparkling with frosty sunshine. My only
possible companion was prevented from joining me, so up I went
alone, without undue hurry. To make a brave show, I started
out on ski, but soon the stones proved inimical to their welfare
and on their loud protests I had to take them off.

An icy blast, curving in from the south-west round the knob
of Meall Dubhag, struck me in the face as I emerged above the
"Wee Woodie". Still, heated by the exercise, I was feeling
much too warm for my hood and scarf. The snow grew deeper

but the stones, cleverly concealed under the powdery covering, were extremely difficult to locate and made the traverse of the long south face of Càrn Bàn Beag very trying. Eventually, however, about an hour and a half after leaving Achlean, I reached the nick between the Little (Beag) and Great (Mòr) Càrn Bàn, and struck off across the shade of the steep icy snowfields above the Red Corrie towards the Sgorans. This, though it robbed me of the well-earned sunshine, brought me into the lee. The frost was keen and my hood and scarf came in handy.

It was rather reassuring to see two frail snow buntings fluttering up in spurts towards Ciste Mearaid with a ringing chirp in the teeth of the arctic wind. Surely I would not be beaten by a couple of snow buntings!

A lone ptarmigan " periscoped " its neck from behind a snow-drift. Otherwise there was no sign of life, not even a fox track.

A half an hour's traverse brought me onto the flat saddle leading to Sgòr Gaoith, the highest point of the Sgorans (3,658 ft.). The surface was ice with *zastrugi*. The sun and the wind returned to give me their mixed blessings. But, having them on my back, I gained the rocky promontory of Sgòr Gaoith in a matter of minutes. This is always an exciting moment, for here, invariably present yet ever fresh, a topographical surprise awaits the climber.

First, the sprawling dome of Braeriach came into view, looming above the brim of a cornice, and then a scene of stern grandeur, far mightier than at any time in the summer, unfolded before me. Loch Einich's spring waters had not yielded to frost, except for a few floes near the sluice at the bottom end, and lay jet-black at the foot of the massive mountain-sides, wrapped finely in the fluted mantle of snows dropping in pleats from the verglassed crags of the corries. The bastions of the Sgorans stood out, dark and forbidding, oversteepened by the downward sweep of the surrounding whiteness which had swallowed up the rivers of scree and streaks of grass. A'Chail-leach, huddled up in a grey habit, was stooping gravely from

Near the summit of Sgòr Gaoith

her lofty battlement; beyond the rock rampart at the head of
the glen, steeped in shadow, still greater heights, eerie-white and
polar, rose above the billowy tundra of the Great Moss.

The contrast with the mild undulations of the approach could
have hardly been more complete.

The sheerness of the summit snows promised the unwary a
shuddersome glissade. I took off my ski and warily stepped
onto the edge of the cornice to record (alas, unsuccessfully) the
scene on photographic emulsion. The bitter wind assaulted me
with fury and I was glad to remount my "wooden horses", as
the T'ang chroniclers used to describe ski.

With an easterly wind one could count on a fairer climate and
better snow on the west side of the hill; and, indeed, my expecta-
tions did not deceive me. Beyond a patch of ice and stones,
some fifty yards wide, the snow shone smooth and even, stretching well below the 2,000-foot contour. Again the contrast was
complete.

My ski were now gliding softly over glittering crystalline
powder. From a fierce blast the wind had changed to a gentle
breeze sweeping down a low veil of snow-dust. The sun was
dazzling and hot. Here was a slanting square mile or two of
a real ski paradise!

Time and again I ran down a few hundred yards over perfect
snow to where I had left my pack. My lunch "pieces", though
still frozen and involving unpleasant gulping, had become pass-
ably edible, which helped to revive my somewhat waning
strength. I was just beginning to find my ski legs and each
successive wave mark I had left on the snow was more stream-
lined, when my watch reminded me that time had not been
idle. "*Nous ne somnes pas d'ici*"—I repeated to myself the
famous remark of a French mountaineer, picked up my Bergen
and climbed to the summit for my last run. Lower down the
gully the snow was deep and heavy and had reached the unpleasant stage when it was no longer powder and not yet definite
windslab. Turning in it was like sawing wet wood with a blunt
saw, and after a few stem-christies my legs seemed to be all flesh
and no bone. I went through various movements, totally dis-

Q

A scissor-christie in heavy set snow (the author)

regarded by my ski, and landed ignominiously in a sitting posture. In the end I was only too pleased to escape sideways from the gully over some half-covered heather, which was held by ptarmigan in great strength.

The birds were undisturbed by my approach. What seemed to be their sentinels were spaced regularly along the gully, rattling away their wooden calls to one another from prominences of stone and heather. I stopped near one of them, so near, in fact, that I could see the bird's throat swell and vibrate as it emitted a croak, a gurgle, a croak and the prolonged *tr-r-r-r-r-r*.

I made a clumsy attempt at imitating the noise, but could not get the right interval between the beats. To my surprise, however, the ptarmigan replied in a chorus, which might have been a sign of alarm, but it appeared to me that their sound identification left much to be desired.

The Red Corrie was a cold and draughty place and I re-ascended Càrn Bàn Beag without delay.

In the rays of the declining sun the hills were a pastel composition in pink, blue and lilac, edged with the dark, colourless streaks of heather. On the snow there were numerous tracks of foxes, rabbits and white hares. With a characteristic chuckle a brace of grouse rose near the ridge, which marked another sharp transition—from a realm of shadow and numbing frost to the soft glory of sunset. On the west side the air was warm above the snow and I could once again enjoy a comfortable rest and a bite of chocolate.

Chrome-yellow light was flooding the gentle braes, where each smallest thing threw a long clear shadow of luminous blue beside which the blue of the sky paled to a dull pigeon-grey. The glowing orb was sinking in an amber haze behind the hills of Lochaber.

There followed some miles of wobbly navigation over snowed-up heather, and about half-past four, just as the last magenta after-glow of the day was dying out on the tops, I arrived back at Achlean.

2. *The Aviemore Cairngorms*

The broad front which the Cairngorms present to Aviemore is made up mainly of the massifs of Braeriach and Cairn Gorm and their outliers, divided by the deep gap of the Lairig, in which Ben Macdhui shows distantly as an inconspicuous oblique dome. The only important outsider is Creag Dubh, rising in a sprawling, stepped pyramid above Loch an Eilein. At the north end of the panorama a chain of lesser heights, facing towards Boat of Garten, stretches from Pityoulish to Ryvoan.

The last named hills are rather exposed to the winds, densely wooded in the west and, owing to their moderate elevation, seldom get a sufficiently deep snow cover to afford really good ski-ing. Even during the exceptionally snowy winter of 1946-47 I found them very patchy. Nor is Creag Dubh a good ski mountain. One can obtain some enjoyable runs in the gully above the tree line, but the latter is high and reaching it from Loch an Eilein requires a stiff pull over difficult forest ground and very deep heather, of which I have had a rather gruelling experience. Thus the skier's list is reduced to Braeriach and Cairn Gorm, both of which have excellent ski slopes and gullies.

Braeriach is scooped out on both its north and south sides into a system of rocky and precipitous corries, for the most part totally beyond the skier's reach, though they have a few weak points that might in favourable conditions be assailed on ski by an experienced ski-mountaineer. This structure of the mountain rather restricts the number of runs Braeriach has to offer in any weather; but in bad visibility it may prove dangerous to those unacquainted with the terrain and great care must be exercised in ski-ing about the summit plateau.

The descent of a few hundred yards from the Wells of Dee to the Great Moss is practicable till late in the season, but not very exciting when other parts of the hill are under snow. The corries above Loch Einich are steep and afford good snow runs of Alpine proportions, with vertical drops of over 2,000 feet. Their slopes, however, cannot be regarded as safe in all weather and snow conditions. On hard crust one risks a nasty slip that might result in serious injuries, while after a heavy fall of snow an avalanche cannot be ruled out.

The shoulder on the west of Coire Lochain is badly exposed to the prevailing winds and more often than not blown clear of snow, inclining at best to be icy and patchy. The northern corries and hillsides below them offer varying possibilities for ski-ing. Yet the best runs are down Coire Beanaidh from the col between Braeriach and Sròn na Lairig and from Sròn na Lairig itself, whose north face is grooved by a gully that collects and preserves the snow. Once on the high moorlands beneath the peak, one can follow either the course of the burns towards Gleann Einich or turn east to the Lairig Ghru.

The Lairig Ghru can be easily crossed on ski, but to make this really worth while there must be sufficient snow on the lower ground on both sides of the pass; otherwise it is all sweat and very little fun.

Cairn Gorm is largely free from the limitations of Braeriach and undoubtedly " takes the cake " as a ski mountain. Being sheltered from the north-east and south-west alike, its array of corries and gullies is particularly well placed for the accumulation of snow. Coire Lochain and the Snowy Corrie are mountaineering propositions, rather more formidable than the corresponding corries of Braeriach; but Coire Cas and all the corries north of it present no difficulties to an experienced skier and give direct access to the summit of Cairn Gorm. The sloping upland of Cairn Lochan and the Lurcher Crag's Meadow with its northward gully also afford good and easy runs.

Ben Macdhui can be gained either by way of Cairn Gorm or Cairn Lochan and crossed to Glen Dee by Coire Etchachan or Glen Luibeg, the latter being the shorter and easier route. In the first case we follow the summer path more or less all the way through; in the latter up to a point overlooking the centre of Loch Etchachan, where we cross the shoulder to the south and drop onto the wide saddle leading to Derry Cairngorm. In good visibility the ground presents no difficulties, but there are many rocky steps and bluffs that could be dangerous in the fog, and the long sojourn on the high, exposed plateaux will be very trying on a windy day.

The south-east face of Cairn Gorm is very steep and partly rocky, which together with its unfavourable situation with regard to wind and sun, makes it uninviting to a skier. If one intends to do the Lairig an Lui on ski it is better to follow the course of the young Nethy up to The Saddle and pick up the summer track in Glen Avon. The north side of the Bynacks has as a rule a good snow cover but is rather out of one's normal reach.

The morning of 25th February, 1947, was sunlit and frosty, the mercury having just risen from a headlong drop to 30° below freezing-point. The trees were silver with rime and the scene was a lace of tender lights and shadows as I left " Shunem " and slid down the oak-grown hillock onto the road to Aviemore and the tops.

My plans were far from crystallized when a timber lorry gave me a lift to Glen More and thus set my course for the day. About 11.30 I was standing above the white expanse of frozen Loch Morlich. The ice was so thick and solid that somebody had cycled over it and there were footmarks going right across it. It was rare fun to be able to cross the loch and, without thinking twice, I pushed off from the shore.

A silent blaze of white light closed round me. The snow on the loch was coated with hoar-frost and the sun, low over the hills in front, lit in it myriads of prismatic beams. Red and green, blue and purple sparks were twinkling, dancing and quivering everywhere—whole patches and fields of them, as though of the fairy flowers of winter, poised on the leaf-like crystals of ice.

On the other side I crossed the forest fence and struck straight up towards Coire Cas. A sad stretch of forest it was, devastated by a fire which had consumed many young trees. Blackened roots bulged up from under the luscious pillows of snow. Charred stems stood forlornly about the hillside. Only here and there had the summit of growth enough vigour left to throw up a thin plume of reviving greenery.

It was so gloriously hot that, in glaring defiance of my own precepts, I undressed to the shirt and even rolled up my sleeves. My watch said twelve. The choice before me was Cairn Gorm or the Lurcher's Crag; it was difficult to decide which until I had a clear view of the approaches. Meanwhile the trees grew denser, the snow deeper and the air chillier. One by one I had to don the discarded clothes and was pleased to see the fence at the other end of the forest.

There, old Scots firs were scattered sparsely over a long transverse depression which must have been dredged by the waters of glacial overflow when Glen More had been buried deep under an ice sheet. The snowy glades, with their network of blue shadows, the small idyllic slopes, dressed in perfect powder-snow resting on hard crust, and the great sunny stillness had almost succeeded in seducing me to spend the day among them. Yet the *fiacail* of Coire Cas stood above in dazzling whiteness, like a finger raised in admonition, and I durst not sin. So on I pushed towards the open, inhospitable heather-slopes. It soon transpired that I could not reach the corrie without considerable loss of height, whereas the Lurcher seemed near at hand.

I clamped on my ski-crampons and took a southward course, climbing quickly up the well-covered hillsides, and about one o'clock was in full view of the snow-laden corries of Cairn Gorm and Cairn Lochan. However, a fairly deep gully, its sunny side free from snow, divided me from the ground swell that rose into the apparent cone of the Lurcher's Crag. Spurning the long footslog to the pass, I ran down to the nearest snow and was once more on ski.

The gully was packed many yards deep. The winds had blown the snow into fantastic pockets with overhanging rims which, following one another in intersecting surfaces of light, penumbra and shade, made a perfect arctic composition. The hard crust, overlaid with fresh falls, was good for running and climbing alike. The most sensible line would have been towards the pass, but I yielded to the temptation of wider views and made for the ridge above, which involved me in some clambering over awkward stones and soft drifts.

I flushed a few grouse but, in marked contrast with the preceding winter, there were no ptarmigan anywhere about.

The air was dead still. The gullies, well filled with snow, descended towards Glen More in white highways and my eye followed the promising sweep of whiteness down from the Lurcher Crag's Meadow to Allt Mòr and the forest.

Coire Cas and Coire na Ciste, in which the Scottish Ski Club often holds a spring slalom race, with their greater vertical drops and steeper angles offer more exciting runs, but this gully, though gentler in its lower part, is also longer. As far as I could make out there were in it some four miles of downhill ski-ing.

Nearer the summit the snow was hard and icy but it still had on it that fraction of an inch of rime which took the edge off the crust and on the Lairig side the coating of powder was several inches deep. The incline steepened and I had to meander between outcrops of rock and patches of boulder-scree now on the one, now on the other side of the ridge. One snow-field above the Lairig fell away at something like 60°, rather an alarming angle when combined with jagged rock ribs below, though the spikes of my crampons bit well into the crust and there was no real danger of slipping. I admired the nerve of the fox which had come right up the steep snow—pad after pad —in a fine dotted line from the rocks to the ridge. Seeing how helpless a dog usually was on mountain snows, this seemed a remarkable performance. A blue hare was the other sturdy mountaineer that had blazed a trail up the gleaming back of the hill.

And gleam it did. When I first emerged onto it from the shaded side I was overwhelmed by an avalanche of light, blinding even through my very scratched visor. The snows were an incandescent blaze, underlined by the darkness of the rocks. The domes and *fiacails* of Braeriach had on them a frosty bloom and shone on the edges like folded satin held against the light. Farther west, above a wide white expanse, the Sgorans soared up in cones of blue shade, framed with sickles of sunlight.

The sun had a bite in it and lay scorching on my cheeks.

By three o'clock I had reached, entirely on ski, the lower cairn of the Lurcher's Crag, where the hoary rocks of Coire Lochain suddenly peeped at me over the snow-covered boulders. They seemed so near that it would be enough to stretch one's hand to touch them. The whole scene had about it the unreality of a lunar landscape.

I dug a hole in a deep drift, made a stool with my ski and sticks[1] and, being fairly starved, flung myself upon my un-buttered rolls and several prunes, which were the only foods I had been able to get on the way (this being the thin end of the rationing week). It was comfortably, and even uncomfortably, warm in the sunshine, but when for a short while I had held my gloveless hands in the shade they were instantly numb with cold.

The stretch of ground below the main summit was too stony for ski-ing and I proceeded on foot, leaving my ski a little short of the topmost cairn.

The sight I had been looking forward to was now before me.

The rocks were thickly decked with snow, which had filled in the irregularities of the hill's face, giving it a terrifying steep-ness. The bottom of the Lairig glen appeared enormously remote beneath the heavy shadow of Braeriach. Ahead, Ben Macdhui was glowing in speckless whiteness and the hills beyond the pass stood out sharply against the blue sky.

I climbed a little way down the main buttress—rather gingerly, as my slippery ski-ing boots got little purchase on the snowed-up holds—to photograph the Lairig Ghru. It was 3.30 p.m. and I could not linger, the more so as I was hoping to catch the last lorry leaving Glen More for Aviemore about five. I hurried back to my ski and tackled the awkward field of boulder-scree which lay between me and the Lurcher Crag's Meadow. The snow was deep enough but it would have needed

---

[1] The " ski-stool " is made by planting the two ski, heel first, vertically in deep snow at a man's width from one another and passing the two sticks through the bindings on the outer sides of the ski. If one then covers the sticks with a pair of mittens, a scarf or the like, a quite comfortable seat is obtained. The snow, however, must be sufficiently firm, otherwise the ski tend to collapse.

yards of it to cover up the huge stones. The best I could do was to clamber up them on ski and then jump down on the little snowy pathways that would offer me a few yards' free run. This was a laborious affair and I was too engrossed in it to stop to listen to the strange noises which seemed to be coming from the pass. I heard something like the yapping of a small dog and, quite distinctly, the squeal of an eagle, but could see nothing about substantially different from the stones.

By the time I reached the Meadow I had had enough of this exercise and the promise of a cup of tea in the workers' canteen at Glen More acquired in my thoughts peculiar warmth. Once more I did the wrong thing and turned north instead of running down into the Lairig Ghru.

The snow in the gully was deep, frosted powder on breakable windcrust, somewhat dull in the glide and heavy for turning. I was running much more timidly than I would have liked to picture myself doing and stopped twice for a breather. Yet when I finally abandoned stem-christies and launched myself into parallel swings these proved delightfully easy, and I could have certainly taken the whole run straight with a few check slips. Now I had to content myself with an indifferent schuss, which gave my knees some rest from turning and brought me down to Allt Mòr. After an unspectacular turn I fell on nearly flat ground from sheer exhaustion and grouse chuckled, it seemed, in derision.

In the forest the snow was fast, lapping under the soles of my ski as I whizzed in among the trees, but the path below had been spoiled by deer and the gamekeeper who had reduced it to the consistency of Swiss cheese. This cost me further delay and it was just about five o'clock when I finally skied into the lumber camp.

There—the object of my desire—a lorry was standing, painted a bright, vernal green. I took off my boards and made straight for it. The driver received me civilly and we had a chat about the weather, at the end of which he remarked that if I wanted a lift to Aviemore I had better hurry to the sawmill where the other lorry was being loaded—he wasn't going. I did hurry but, alas, there was no lorry at the sawmill; I was one minute too late.

Three cups of tea were not enough to drown my disappointment. Underdressed and hungry, I skied nine miles along the patchy and gritty roads, through the crimson fires of sunset and the darkness of the icy night, moving automatically, without pain or pleasure, like a ghost driven along by the memory of a decision. Next day I was in bed with a bad cold . . .

3. *The Ski-ing Grounds of Dee- and Avon-side*

If starting out from the villages of Glen Dee, the skier has a wide choice of grounds worthy of his attention. Morven is one of the customary objectives and Glen Clunie is well patronized by the ski-ing folk; so far, however, as the Cairngorms proper are concerned, the choice is somewhat restricted by the latitudinal direction of the glen, which contrives that the most accessible slopes and gullies of the Eastern Cairngorms all face south. They are thus exposed to the sun and warm winds and can seldom maintain a continuous snow cover for long, especially in the spring. In fact, in April, 1946, when the Central and Western Cairngorms still had plenty of snow, there were only a few white patches left on the Braemar faces of the Eastern. These hills are also relatively difficult of access, as there are no motor roads through the glens at their foot and the glens themselves are at most times only insufficiently covered, so that a long foot trek over forest roads is necessary before the ski slopes are reached. For this reason Beinn a'Bhùird and Ben Avon are seldom visited by skiers, though the surroundings of Dubh Ghleann offer some good runs and, after a heavy fall, the descent from Ben Avon over the Sneck to the edge of the forest makes a fine downhill course with a difference of levels of about 2,000 feet or more.

Ski-ing prospects are always very much at the mercy of the winds, and in one way the Braemar hills are favoured, for they are well sheltered from the tepid furies of the west, whence most thaws come. Thus in early winter, when westerly winds prevail, one can as a rule expect better ski-ing on Deeside than at the other end of the Lairig Ghru. On the other hand, when a spell of wintry easterly or south-easterly weather sets in, as is often the case later in the young year, Deeside is apt to prove a distinctly draughty place. The 1942-43 winter was notoriously a bad ski-ing season. Nevertheless, Lt.-Col. F. S. Smythe's summary of the conditions experienced by the Commando training centre established at the Mar Lodge is not irrelevant. He writes:

> "It blew as it does in Tibet. There were five full gales a week and one hurricane. What happened on the seventh day no one cared—it was our rest day."[1]

Of course, this need not be so and there will be periods of windless calm at various times of the year. My own recollections of Deeside are rather of placid, dull weather, with intermittent sunshine and some not excessive wind on the tops.

The corries of Cairn Toul and Braeriach get all the snow that is blown off the Great Moss by the western gales and are well packed till late in May, if not longer; they can, therefore, be relied upon to produce some ski-ing at the end of the season. But the sides of the cauldrons are largely rock and their rims far too steep for ordinary ski-ing; only Coire Odhar can be negotiated on ski without undue difficulty. Glen Geusachan forms the main natural gateway from Glen Dee to the grounds of the Great Moss and in a hard winter is under snow for a considerable time. The bottom of this valley is, however, as flat as flat can be and does not make an interesting run. The eastward gullies of Beinn Bhrotain often hold substantial snow-fields and can easily be reached along the Lairig Ghru track from the White Bridge, connected by a driving road with the Linn of Dee and Braemar. Yet it is Glen Luibeg that enjoys the greatest popularity with skiers who have chosen Braemar or Inverey as their headquarters.

[1] F. S. Smythe: "Mountain Training in the Cairngorms," *The Open Air in Scotland*, Vol. I, No. 2.

This is largely due to the ease with which it can be reached, since there is a driving road as far as the Derry Lodge at the mouth of the glen. But, quite apart from its accessibility, Glen Luibeg deserves the skier's attention. Lying in the very heart of the Cairngorms on the ski route to Ben Macdhui and being protected from the ravages of the winds by the high massifs around it, it offers exceptionally good prospects for the even accumulation of snow. The high plateau of Ben Macdhui is within an easy compass of the glen. The Corrie of the Red Spouts, it is true, is not negotiable on skis, while Càrn a Mhaim and Sròn Riach are rather steep, though not inaccessible to a skier; but the burn between them leads easily to a saddle, whence one can follow the gully of Allt Clach nan Taillear towards the summit of the highest Cairngorm *ben*. As a rule, however, there is better snow along the Luibeg on the gentler slopes, ascending towards a small prominence in a northern shoulder of Ben Macdhui above Loch Etchachan, which make a longer, but easier route to and from the top. The Luibeg side of Derry Cairngorm, though facing west, is protected by the scarp of Ben Macdhui and Sròn Riach, as well as by the high ground beyond them, from the direct effect of the winds blowing from that quarter and, neither too steep nor too gentle, affords a variety of good runs.

Some ski-ing can likewise be had on both sides of Glen Derry, where Beinn Bhreac is the most promising hill.

The hills north of Glen Geldie face south and a long stretch of flattish moorland divides them from the road, but in a snowy winter the drifts along the streams may link up into continuous ski paths, making Monadh Mòr and Beinn Bhrotain worth attempting from this glen. Runs with a vertical drop up to 1,500 feet ought to be possible.

Nearer at hand, the foothills of the Eastern Cairngorms, and Càrn na Drochaide in particular, will have some fields and "wraiths" of snow that repay the trouble of the climb. However, owing to their low elevation they lie entirely within the heather zone, so that a considerable depth of snow is required to make continuous runs of any length. Also here the most accessible slopes face south and are not likely to hold much snow for long.

The Tomintoul side of the hills is bleak and cold at most times. It is also off the main communication tracks. In consequence it does not attract many visitors even during the " season ", let alone in winter. Yet from the skier's point of view the northern faces of Ben Avon and Beinn a'Bhùird, which are sheltered from the south-west and south-east alike, are exceptionally well placed. They acquire a good coating of snow early in the year and will often sport continuous ski-ing fields long after the snows of the Western and Central Cairngorms have been broken up by the onslaught of the Sou'Wester into scattered " wraiths " and patches. Ben Avon in particular is within easy compass of Inchrory, itself eight miles from Tomintoul with which it is connected by a driving road. The road, it is true, does not enjoy a good reputation with motorists but is definitely accessible to cars. However this may be, Inchrory, though less magnificently situated, occupies with regard to ski-ing possibilities a position similar to that of the Glenmore Lodge.

In midwinter, when north-easterly weather prevails, the place is extremely cold and windswept, but in periods of south-westerly winds, such as are frequent in the months of December, January, the second half of March and early April, it will be found a veritable oasis of calm.

4. *The Hills of Spring*

I was ski-ing along a birch lane with a wide view of the hills, thinking my own thoughts, when I saw a shrew. The little creature was darting about, running over the hard sun-crust, but underneath some two inches of a fresher fall, through which it showed as a grey shadow and which did not seem seriously to impede its progress.

I bent down and caught the shrew in my hand.

The tiny whiskered gentleman with a pair of the minutest eyes, like pinheads, and a long, flexible red nose, to which the species owes its name, sat quietly in my palm. It was warm and he appeared content to abandon himself to the comfortable sensation after the numbing contact with the snow or, perhaps, was just overawed by my enormous presence. The "presence", however, proved harmless enough and soon put him gently down on the snow, into which he buried himself with amazing rapidity, only his stiff tail flicking about in the air.

What had happened to him must have been a strange experience, an incomprehensible intrusion into the world of his realities. Yet, after all, was there such a lot of difference between the range of his and our "worlds"?—a mere shift of an inch or so on the logometer of eternal change.

My hat off to you, Old Friend Heraclitus!—one can't step twice on the same snow.

Yesterday it had been powder with hard crust in exposed places. During the night there had been some cloud and a light downy fall, just enough to reduce a shrew's field of vision without compelling it to stay at home. To-day the frost held, but the Cairngorm forests were inky-blue and the shoulders of the hills were beginning to wear through their white mantles. The long-awaited thaw was coming and with it the time of spring-snow and "wraith" ski-ing.

And, indeed, the snow on the lower ground where it had seemed so well established, was gone in a matter of days. Yet the "Little Summer" that usually marks the middle of March was in 1947 a mere flash in the pan, followed by new heavy falls of snow, so that in early April the Cairngorms were as specklessly white as at any time during the winter. The wet spring-snow which had just begun shaping froze to the "cheese-grater", coated with frosty powder. On the 5th, with bright sunshine and windless calm, the hills were "Switzerland", but the following day, when most members of the Scottish Ski Club arrived in Aviemore for the Easter Meet, the weather underwent a fatal transformation. Grey cloud, driven by a furious Sou'Wester, enveloped the hills, whipping them with rain, sleet and wet snow in the order of increasing altitude.

Nevertheless, a flotilla of cars pushed on towards the Glenmore Lodge and beyond. The Racing Committee prudently never left their car, but some others sallied forth in the direction of Coire na Ciste, where the much-delayed Scottish Kandahar Race was to be held as the main attraction. Faced with such an aspect of the sky, I would have normally stayed at home, but for the sake of company I was now getting a thorough soaking on the lower snow-fields of Cairn Gorm. An unfriendly place it was but, knowing its ways, I kept to a sheltered line. This did not save me from getting wet but it at least freed me from the agony of the wind. I soon came to realize what a boon this was, as my companions had become detached in the blizzard and in an attempt to locate them I made my way up to Clach Bharraig, where a few skiers were dimly outlined, flapping in the wind. When only about two yards from them I found it impossible to keep my eyes open and all my attempts to have a peep at what was showing of their faces were completely unsuccessful, so that I departed without having identified them.

Needless to add, there was no race that day, though the Hird Trophy was competed for next day on Càrn Bàn Mòr in conditions of almost equal ferocity. I demurred, for, after all, I had not come to Aviemore all the way from Edinburgh for a ski-ing week-end and my boots were still steaming before a fire after the last attempt.

On the 8th there was spring-snow at about 2,000-2,500 feet, but higher up it passed through a gamut of climatic gradations into pure winter powder. Again the Queen of the Fairies came travelling on an eddy of the west wind and touched the snow with her magic wand; and when, two days later, I was on my way to Cairn Gorm the world wore a different look.

In an easy way, I had arrived at the Glenmore Lodge by car at about 12 noon B.S.T., and, having left my friends to practise on the lower snows, struck for Coire na Ciste and the summit. They were not to await my return.

I threaded snow "wraith" after snow "wraith" on the rosary of my zigzagging track, but here and there the "rosary" broke and had to be patched up by walking over a stretch of bare ground.

A grouse rose, a little sun filtered through the clouds, hurried over the tops by a lively south-westerly wind, a passing shower or two sprinkled additional moisture on the snow and heather. Without hurry or delay and with no other worry than the weather, I made good progress, keeping well within the shelter of the Aonach shoulder of Cairn Gorm, and soon reached the continuous snows a little below its first step. Here my tracks of two days ago were almost totally effaced and long broad grooves on the steep slope marked the place where some walkers had practised glissading on their seats, which, I should think, was a distinctly wet form of physical recreation.

Anxious not to lose height, I was rather high up above the main gully of Coire na Ciste and the snowy incline was so steep that I instinctively hastened on—just in case it did make up its mind to avalanche, though I knew full well that this was most unlikely, particularly so as the sky was overcast and the temperature of the air fairly low. The traverse was slightly awkward and I had lost the chance of leaving my rucksack to be picked up on the return run. I struck the floor of the main gully some three-quarters of the way up from the bottom of Coire na Ciste and a little below the first band of rock.

Out of the milky haze a ptarmigan soared up gracefully on an ascending air current and, having sighted the approaching danger, veered off and out of sight with a warning "crackle".

After a short "breather", I made straight for the top. The gradient of the gully was not excessive and the snow wet but quite firm. At two I was up on the gentle snows of the summit —a vast, windy, wintry wilderness, with close, indistinct perspectives. It was a damp, cheerless place. I stopped about a hundred yards short of the topmost cairn and, having wrapped myself in an oilskin cape, sat down on a "ski-stool" with my back to the wind to have my lunch.

Below, Mam Suim and Creag nan Gall showed dark through the haze under a menacing canopy of foxy clouds—red foxes, blue foxes, silver foxes. . . . For a moment the mists lifted and a pasty yellowish radiance spread over the snow. Then the ragged curtain was dropped again and it began to drizzle thinly, with tiny, scattered pats on my creaking oilskin.

Cairn Lochan on a sunny day in February
" The sight I had been looking forward to
was now before me " (p. 248)

The snow in the gully was slightly heavy on the turn and, running as I was with a substantial pack, I was wary of gathering much momentum, for a fall in such conditions could be dangerous at high speed. Still, in six minutes I was by the outcrop of rock at the bottom of the corrie, where the snow petered out in a long tongue roofing a rumbling torrent.

The lower "wraiths" were uniform spring-snow and offered much better, though restricted, ski-ing.

By 3 p.m. I was back at the tree line. My friends had already gone.

I sat down below an old, gnarled pine in the lee of a snowy hollow. At my feet red-tipped lichens were pearling out of the ground and bearberries were "preening themselves" after the long winter sleep. The wind was rushing over the heather and soughing in the pine crowns. A huge snowdrift had bridged the deer fence over the space of many yards and buried under it the sapling pines. The snow entered deep into the forest like a piece of sky which had somehow fallen down. Above the greens and madders, Ryvoan rose in a dark, inky gate to yet another realm of diffuse brightness.

I left my ski in Glen More and went back on foot.

It was a long road but I did not grudge it. My mind was at peace. After the days of cars, voices and faces, the stillness around was welcome and soothing. And what of it if the silver bagpipes of the Glenmore fairies should turn by the morrow into a withered puff-ball and three stalks of dead grass?[1] They were silver enough while playing. The solitude became a presence treading softly at my side and whispering into my ear dreamlike, gentle things—of life's passing sweetness, of yearning and content.

The hills of spring were as though clad in dark purple velvet,

---

[1] The legend is that a famous hunter, Robin Oig, was once passing through the Glenmore Forest when he heard sweet music and saw a company of fairies, headed by a piper playing silver bagpipes. Robin Oig took a great fancy to these pipes, snatched the bonnet from his head, threw it among the fairies, and calling, "mine to you, yours to me!", grabbed the bagpipes from the fairy piper. The fairies took no notice of him as he hurried off with his prize hidden under his plaid, but when he wanted to make sure that it was still there he found but an empty puffball and three stalks of dead grass.

R

The Great Rough Corrie of Braeriach
On the narrow snows of Coire na Ciste.
The 1948 Scottish Kandahar Cup Race

showing yellow on the folds where the hairs had parted. Near at hand the winter frosts had singed the heather to rusty red, but behind the vivid greenery of the firs it was glowing claret and cyclamen, interspersed with the pale sienna and ochre of the grass. Through the colonnades of the forest, down the brae, the Luineag glistened and throbbed with curving surfaces of liquid steel.

The turmoil of cloud was fierce on the Lairig heights, but their dark rocks held no threat—they were friendly. . . .

By to-morrow there would be only a few dead pine needles in my pockets and my feet would be sore from walking.

Heavy snows continued to lie in the hills for a long time and the sunny 9th of May tempted me to revisit Cairn Gorm. It was a limpid, soft, drowsy day with a smell of humid soil in the air, the day that had descended like a soothing embrocation on a world bruised by weeks of blizzard and gale. The distances were blurred and hazy, as though overspread with a blue, milky veil.

In the forest it was still, warm and sultry, but, once I had emerged on the open slopes above Clach Bharraig, the large pink erratic which makes a distinctive landmark of the Cairn Gorm path, I had to face a steady current of air hurtling down-slope. It was tepid and not very strong, but it had an awkward way of catching and holding the broad sides of my skis slung over my shoulders, as I pushed, dry-shod, up the path to the summit.

The lower "wraiths" had dwindled to small streaks and patches but the gully of Coire na Ciste, as well as Coire Cas, still had long runs to offer, the former with a vertical drop of some 2,000 feet.

A pair of dotterel came snooping on me when I sat down at the edge of the summit snow-fields to have my lunch. I first noticed the inquisitive birds over a hundred yards away, as they hurried in my direction. Nearer, they grew more cautious, running fast with outstretched necks from cover to cover, having a peep and again ducking behind a boulder, but all the time approaching along a spiral of diminishing radius. The cock-bird was a little apprehensive, but his anxious "purring" was entirely disregarded by the hen[1] until they both stopped some ten yards from me, craning their necks and staring at me with both eyes. This was the limit of their daring but I could well understand the dotterel's Gaelic name, the Fool of the Moss. Their white eye-stripes, white-tipped wings and black bellies were showing clearly, despite the glare from the snow.

When I had put on my ski and begun exploring the summit snows, I could still spy the birds out of the corner of my eye, scurrying along the edge of the snow-field, not to miss the spectacle of a man walking on wooden planks—I say, have you *ever* seen anything like that? . . . Not in *our* village. . . .

Beinn a'Bhùird was solidly under snow and wide white streaks striped the sides of Ben Avon. Nearer at hand, there was much snow between Cairn Gorm and Ben Macdhui; but, though of good quality, the summit spring-snows were of too gentle a gradient to afford a good run without the *Klister* wax, and I floated down in a leisurely *schuss,* as though poised on a downward escalator. Yet, at the funnel-like entrance into the main gully, which had less sunshine, the snow grew firm and fast, so that I had a fine run for three-quarters of the hill's stature.

My next effort was with a pack which, as usual, had far too many unnecessary things in it and was a nuisance in swinging. Still, I was able to improve my previous "record" by two-thirds —what madness, a two hours' climb for a two minutes' run! . . . This did not seem to make sense, so, lest I should be cheated out of the fruit of my toil, I went up once more. This time, however, it was a little too much for me and I did not finish the climb.

As I lay down limply in the sun-warm heather beside a roaring burn, small shiny clouds were defiling through the sky like a succession of steaming silver teapots, croaking ptarmigan were

---

[1] Dotterel are a matriarchal species.

soaring up above the gully, and the rush of the water was full of strange thuds and voices, sudden alarms and restful lulls. . . .

This was my last ski-ing day in the hills that season, though there were still ample " wraiths " till the middle of June.

XIII

LET'S TALK OF PTARMIGAN AND
CHARS-À-BANCS, OF PRESIDENTS AND PARKS

WHEN the long-suffering mountaineer commits the imprudence of asking an hotel proprietor or a land-lady for what is locally known as "pieces" he is, as a rule, promptly equipped with thin slices of the so-called "cut-ting loaf", i.e. loaf of white bread whose unwelcome freshness has been eliminated by "seasoning". More likely than not the "pieces", apart from an evanescent coating of butter-like sub-stance, are richly smeared with the kind of meat paste that comes out of a small glass jar with an airtight lid. After a few hours inside a paper bag inside a rucksack or, which is worse, a pocket, the "pieces", if they fail to disintegrate, acquire for the palate the quality of woodpulp encased in leather.

This may go some way to explain why a president of the Cairn-gorm Club has been known to spend a night, I believe in the snow, above Loch Etchachan without cover of any sort, feeding ptarmigan with his *lunch,* and return in time for breakfast as if nothing was the matter. The experience of having ptarmigan eating out of one's hand is undoubtedly unique, though this does not by itself account for the existence of "lunch" at so late an hour; while the nocturnal solitude under a starry heaven at the elevation of Britain's highest mountain lake must be magnificent and uplifting, if a trifle chilly.

It is hardly to be wondered at that, steeped in the tradition of such manly self-abnegation, the Cairngorm Club should take exception to Miss Janet Adam Smith's innocent suggestion that a hostel should be built on the site of the Corrour Bothy.[1] Though, mind you, Miss Adam Smith is no "softie" and thought little of crossing the Cairngorms, inclement weather

---

[1] *The Spectator,* November 23rd, 1944.

notwithstanding, straight off the train from London to reach Inverey at dead of night, the sparks struck by her nailed boots lighting her lonely tread.[1]

She brushed aside—comments *The Cairngorm Club Journal*[2] —" the prognostics of the pessimists who foresee swarms of trippers, the ruin of the peace of the hills, and so forth. The yodelling tripper is a nuisance to all within earshot, the boulder-trundler something of a danger to climbers, but the hatchet-carrier is the real menace." As for a resident warden, " where to find one anchorite enough to solicit such a post? "

There is no question that " yodelling trippers ", " boulder-trundlers ", " hatchet-carriers . . ." and so forth really exist and can be more than a moderate nuisance. One can also feel sympathy with the mountaineer's desire to keep the crowd out of his sacred haunts. Nevertheless in the present state of affairs the danger is somewhat remote. The scales are weighted on the opposite side, and even if the worst came to the worst the suspicion is strong that the dreaded trippers would find the surroundings of Corrour at least as unfriendly as the hypothetical warden. " Hatchet-carriers " are less exacting and less discriminating: anything that is dry wood is good enough for them, whether it be a bedstead or a door frame. Yet, somehow or other, in other countries, which one must presume abound in antisocial individuals no less than the Highlands of Scotland, there are mountain huts, and in the selfsame Highlands, as already noted, there are two such, the Scottish Mountaineering Club Hut on Ben Nevis and the Scottish Ski Club Hut on Ben Ghlas, both of which have withstood some years of temptation to " hatchet-carriers ". In most cases a strong lock and key, the latter being issued on application against a deposit and a fee, and solid shutters on the windows prove a sufficient deterrent to potential law- and frame-breakers, while it ought not to be so difficult to find a warden for the summer season.

Meanwhile the situation is rather incongruous.

Any suggestion of building a mountain hut, a hostel or even

---

[1] Janet Adam Smith: *Mountain Memories* (London, 1946).
[2] Vol. XV, No. 84, p. 308.

simply a bothy at once encounters a host of objections, sometimes from the very people who, one might think, ought naturally to be in favour of such things—within reason. It is not
only a hostel at Corrour that the "pessimists" viewed with dis-
may; some others holding similar opinions have effectively prevented the refitting of the now derelict Corrour Bothy, which
used at one time to be a welcome *pied-à-terre* for those climbing
in the Central and Western Cairngorms (it is still used despite
its condition). In the Eastern Cairngorms the "Authorities"
have recently burned down the Sluggan Bothy because "some
stolen property" was found there,[1] though one is tempted to
reflect that it would never have been found had it been hidden
in some less accessible place. At the same time warnings are
issued galore on the dangers of climbing the hills. And why,
pray, should this be so dangerous? The answer is simple: the
climate is treacherous, the weather is more often foul than not,
the distances are great and there are no suitable *shelters* between
the villages which lie some thirty miles apart. Not all people
possess the tastes and the constitution of the Cairngorm Club
President referred to above.

Near the Linn of Dee, at about the meeting-point of the right-
of-way tracks of the Lairig Ghru and Lairig an Lui, a notice is
posted to remind people of the risks they run in climbing the
hills and request them to refrain from so doing during the shooting season. This is an understandable request, but the warning
of the "risks" is general and it might have added a note of
sincerity to the statement if its object had been made plain instead of being thinly disguised by an alleged concern for the
climber's safety. Charles Plumb[2] feels indignant at the thought
that one day there may be a place in the Cairngorms where
one can buy beer and lemonade and is moved by gratitude to
the landed proprietors who have preserved intact the natural
condition of the hills from the rush of brazen commercialism.
There may be something in this, as in every genuinely held view,
but the forests of the Cairngorms have not profited by the pre-

---

[1] *The Cairngorm Club Journal*, Vol. XV, No. 84, p. 307.
[2] Charles Plumb: *Walking in the Grampians* (London. 1935), pp. 45 and 47.

servation of deer, and it is not quite clear why the bulky and often ugly barrack of a shooting lodge is to be preferred to a tea shop. What winning graces does it possess beyond its present and future redundance?

The Fort William Borough Council goes one better by proposing to bar access to Ben Nevis to "inexperienced strangers" during the winter months and impose a fine of £5 on those who would climb the mountain on the Sabbath day.[1] One is left wondering how the sponsors of this exemplary motion expected to test the "inexperience of strangers". . . . However, sounder counsels prevailed and this was not to be.

Police notices advising caution in the hills are prominently displayed at hotels, youth hostels and other similar public places, and rightly, for accidents are frequent. In the Cairngorms they are usually due to exhaustion, and the police justifiably objects to being involved in tiresome search parties, as a rule in appalling atmospheric conditions, made particularly strenuous by the lack or inadequacy of *shelters*.

In truth the hills are no more dangerous than a busy road crossing and, although there are reckless people who ought to be made to defray the costs of the search party, as they are in the Lake District, most fatalities are due not so much to defects of judgment or character on the part of the mountaineers as to the utter disregard of their needs by the community, so eager to condemn their failings.

The countryman seldom feels the need of refreshing contact with Nature and, though he may love his hills, it is a quiet feeling that does not become a passion until it has been whetted by separation. He has little understanding for a townsman's yearning for the hills, which strikes him as somewhat ridiculous, and is inclined to view the mountaineer as an unbalanced bloke who will spend "an' meikle time an' meikle cash on some unco' thing" that is scarcely worth one's while and is liable on top of it to get one into all sorts of trouble. The skier is an even greater oddity, associated with that abomination the snow, and therefore naturally comes under his unspoken stricture; although

[1] *The Cairngorm Club Journal*, Vol. XV, No. 84, pp. 306-7.

there has been a considerable change in this attitude since ski-ing was introduced in the Army and many a Heilan' laddie has learned to ski in the Lovat Scouts or some other unit. This has brought ski-ing, so to speak, down to earth, to the level of ordinary realities, even if the old man or woman, always the more conservative of the two, may not approve of the thing; for most of the older generation are firm believers in the teaching that all pleasure is wicked and that in suffering lies the salvation of the soul.

"Aye . . . there is no knowing what these young folk are com-ing to. The Continental Sabbath is creeping in. . . . Aye, it is."

The country as a whole tends to live rather by rumination on the past than by anticipation of the future, which is partly the result of historical circumstances and partly, I suspect, the fault of the schools.

In the future the emphasis will be on mountaineering instead of shooting and on forests instead of sheep, but few people are prepared to come out half-way to meet the change. This, of course, is not so easy to someone who has never left the place where he or she was born, and many a statesman of wide experi-ence has proved no less obstinate in refusing to see the perhaps less spectacular changes in the world around him. So, are they to blame?

Still, all these tendencies combined provide a peculiar accom-paniment to the Scottish drive to encourage "foreign" visitors from home and abroad; and, while a certain amount of opposi-tion is always useful as a balancing force, there surely is a middle way between spending one's night feeding ptarmigan above Loch Etchachan and loads of trippers disgorged by chars-à-bancs in the vicinity of neatly labelled *Sehenswürdigkeiten*.[1]

In fact, the Cairngorm Club has itself recognized this, for it has approached the Duke of Fife's Trustees for a lease of the Derry Lodge,[2] and what difference is there, pray, between a lodge leased to a mountaineering club and a hut? Or, for that matter, a hostel, except perhaps the latter's plebian flavour? But such

[1] Germ.: sights to see.
[2] *The Cairngorm Club Journal*, Vol. XV, No. 84, p. 302.

considerations invariably operate against the young and the poor who, one would think, are the more entitled to the "Hills of Home" as the "Playground of Europe" is beyond the stretch of their purses. . . . However, it appears that the Agents of the Trustees "might be willing to consider" the leasing of the lodge, when this has been de-requisitioned by the military authorities. I am unable to say whether the project has yet been brought to fruition and if so, in what form. The Scottish Ski Club, too, used to lease the Glenmore Lodge from the Forestry Commission for the Club Meet. This, however, is only a short-lived occasion. Although myself a member of the latter body and no lover of promiscuous crowds, I must confess that I temperamentally object to shutting the hills to people not belonging to this or that particular "set", whether it be one of sharp-shooters or of parallel-swingers, and as for boulder-trundlers and hatchet-carriers an appropriate educational campaign in the Press and organizations of youth and, as the last resort, police action ought to have the necessary discouraging effect.

The skier suffers more than the mountaineer from the lack of suitable huts, for his equipment is heavier than the latter's, it can seldom be used to any advantage before considerable altitudes are reached and thus represents a "dead weight" on the approach and, finally, his activities are limited to the period of short daylight and low temperature. For these reasons there is no need to convince him that mountain huts in the Cairngorms, which remain under snow for a longer period than any British hills, would be highly desirable.

Fortunately, the matter has been taken up at a "higher level". The Scottish Council for National Parks has approved the creation of a National Park in the Cairngorms, and the Forestry Commission has decided to convert its Glen More property into a National Forest Park.

The National Parks come under the Department of Health and a Scottish Council for National Parks has been set up by the Secretary of State for Scotland to deal with the matter. In January 1944, a Scottish National Parks Survey Committee was appointed to make recommendations for suitable areas in consultation with the local authorities and other interested bodies. A year later the Committee published a report[1] in which five areas, including the Cairngorms, were recommended for the establishment of National Parks and three additional areas put on the reserve list.

The Cairngorms were classed fourth in the order of suitability, partly owing to their distance from the main urban centres, partly to their " surprisingly low popularity " as measured by the number of visitors to the youth hostels of the district (which, however, must be largely due to the difficulties of internal access), but chiefly as a result of the inflammable nature of their dry-peat subsoils, juniper-heaths and pinewoods, which, in the Committee's opinion, rendered necessary "special provisions for protection from fires ". Indeed, the district has a bad record for forest fires, most of which have been started by the spring heather-burning.

The recommendation of the Survey Committee has since been approved, so that it is now certain that a National Park will be established in the Cairngorms. At the moment of writing another Committee is sitting to make proposals for the management and administration of the Scottish National Parks. In other words, things are moving; but it is salutary to bear it in mind that over eight years have now elapsed since the question of National Parks was officially taken up in Britain and as yet there is not one Park in being. The Cairngorms will probably wait until the other three areas given higher priority by the Survey Committee have been dealt with, and it must be reckoned that much water will pass under the Cairngorm Club's unbeautiful foot-bridge over the Druie before the project condenses from the gaseous state of reports and recommendations to the solidity of fact.

The area of the proposed National Park covers roughly 180 square miles and comprises the whole of the Western and Central Cairngorms as defined above, as well as the "lowland " between the Feshie, the Spey and the Craiggowrie-Meall a'Bhuachaille

[1] *National Parks, A Scottish Survey*, H.M. Stationery Office, Edinburgh, 1945.

ridge. It may even overstep the Spey and extend as far as " the road or railway on its western bank ". The Eastern Cairngorms, on the other hand, remain entirely outside the proposed boundaries, which follow in the east the Lairig an Lui path to the Linn of Dee and thence the course of the Dee to the Geldie, the Geldie and the Feshie.

Such are the confines of the Park, but the country immediately across the " march " will also be affected, as no defacement of the landscape which may be said to form part of the Park views will be allowed.

Several Nature Reserves are planned within the Cairngorm Park, one of these being in the vicinity of Loch an Eilein, including the wooded Ord Bàn and Kennapole Hill and the stretch of beautiful woodland beyond.

A National Park has been defined in the Report as "an extensive tract of country of outstanding natural beauty, preferably also of scientific, cultural or historic interest, owned and controlled by the Nation, accessible to all as a matter of right under suitable regulations, and administered by or on behalf of the Nation to the end that its distinctive values may be preserved unimpaired for the enjoyment and recreation of this and future generations ".

Now the Cairngorms, apart from the Forestry Commission land in Glen More and Inchriach, are not "owned and controlled" by the Nation. Most of the area is privately owned and has yet to be acquired, with which certain difficulties of personal and traditional, as well as legal nature are associated, even though the establishment of a National Park does not preclude the maintenance and extension of such economic uses of the land as are consistent with the objects of accessibility and preservation of its natural character and beauty (a quarry would clearly be incompatible with these). In fact, no restriction of agriculture is contemplated, and the Survey Committee was of the opinion that considerable afforestation could be easily reconciled with the plan, provided the viewpoints were kept clear and a sufficient variety of hardwoods were planted to break the sombre monotony of coniferous plantations.

The report foresees progressive extension of the freedom of access, though access to cultivated land will have to be restricted or forbidden, and a further limitation may be necessary at certain seasons for the extermination of vermin and control of deer and other game.

Construction of paths and bridle tracks is envisaged, and the Report suggests that it may be necessary to provide "hostel accommodation" closer to the hills than is now the case, in view of the excessively long approach. No mountain huts as such are mentioned, though it is considered that "facilities for winter sports would be an advantage". What these would be is left to the imagination of the reader, perhaps because the Scottish Ski Club was not among the bodies consulted on National Parks. The Committee's suggestions include the provision of a camping site somewhere at the confluence of the Beanaidh and the Druie, where, between two rivers, the danger both of straying and of forest fires could be considerably reduced. Camping will be controlled.

The camping site will be the one most "revolutionary" change, for otherwise the transfer of ownership to the Nation will have little immediate bearing on the situation. Its effects will be gradual and cumulative.

The plan for a National Forest Park which is now being put into effect by the Forestry Commission in Glen More (Queen's Forest) is an independent venture, not to be confused with the National Park proper. Their aims and organization are similar in broad outline but not identical. In a National Park forestry is, as it were, "tolerated" inasmuch as it is not incompatible with the objects of accessibility and preservation of its natural character; a National Forest Park, on the other hand, is an area held by the Forestry Commission primarily for the purposes of cultivation and exploitation of trees, but thrown open to the public inasmuch as this is not inconsistent with rational forestry. While in the forest, and in a newly planted area in particular, visitors to the Park are not allowed to stray off the recognized paths and regulations for fire prevention are strictly enforced, but once on unplanted or unplantable land they are free to roam as they list.

In a National Forest Park camping and other facilities are provided, chiefly for educational purposes and such bodies as the Central Council for Physical Recreation, which has already been using the Commission's grounds about the Glenmore Lodge and the Lodge itself to a considerable extent.

According to information received by me from the Director of Forestry for Scotland:

"The immediate proposals include a large camping ground suitable for all types of campers, including caravaners, in front of the Lodge. A separate area will be reserved for boys' organizations. Drinking water will be laid on. Water-flushed lavatories and washing facilities will also be installed.

"Part of the Lodge must be retained meantime for Forest Workers, but the remainder will be made available for special parties, mainly educational. The management of this part of the Lodge will probably be undertaken by the Scottish Education Department.

"The uncertainty of supplies of labour and materials makes it impossible to forecast a date when these facilities will be available, but it is hoped that they may materialize this year (1947)."

The vital difference between the Forestry Commission and the as yet non-existent National Parks Authority is that the former actually holds the land and can do with it as it pleases, so long at least as its actions are consistent with its object. Thus the Glenmore National Forest Park is a reality, or at any rate will be a reality by the time this book leaves the press.

When the National Park proper comes into being it will incorporate the Glenmore Forest Park as one of the cultivated areas with restricted access. The total extent of the latter is 12,500 acres, of which only some 4,000 acres are classed as plantable and reserved for forestry uses, while no more than 1,600 acres have been planted at the time of writing.

Once the Glenmore Lodge is made available to the public, the access to the Central Cairngorms will be materially facilitated, creating a considerable danger of overcrowding during the summer season. On the other hand, the position in the western massif will remain unchanged until the consummation of the National Park scheme, and even then the distances will be sufficiently forbidding to discourage the tripper, if not the " boulder-trundler " !

The Eastern Cairngorms will continue under the present régime, which, if anything, will be the more anxious to exclude the swollen ranks of visitors from its shrunken domains; although, there being no law of trespass in Scotland, access to that part of the hills can never be barred.

The new conditions will, no doubt, create new problems which will in turn demand new controls, and it must be hoped that the " dignity of walking " is upheld and " wheeled transport " kept at a respectful distance from the hills. In particular, the creation of the National Park will remove the threat to Glen Feshie represented by the long-mooted project of a motoring road to Braemar, which would mean not only the ruin of its peace but a physical defacement of the still unspoiled narrow part of the glen.

It is expected that with time the increasing numbers of visitors to the Park and the " staggering " of the tourist season will stimulate the life of the now moribund village communities of the Cairngorm district, whose population has been steadily on the decline for many decades despite the high birth-rate, by expanding the market for local farm produce, creating favourable conditions for the development of folk industries, such as tweed weaving, and other opportunities for employment. Rational forestry will also add to the district's economic possibilities.

To-day the situation here, as in most parts of the Highlands and Islands, is economically and mentally unhealthy. There are far too few openings for local ability, so that the more enterprising of each successive younger generation are forced to emigrate, while the " stick-in-the-muds " remain. There is a sudden flow of easy money during the two or three months of the tourist season, when prices soar and exorbitant rents are paid for indifferent accommodation. This has a demoralizing effect on the people, with the temptation to subsist for the twelve-month on the proceeds of the summer letting. The showy ways of the richer visitors contrast unfavourably with the modest possibilities of the place, encouraging social bitterness and per-petuating the specious principle, once invoked by the " infamous bykes of lawless lymmars" in raiding the farmlands of the plains,[1] that somebody has to bear the cost of the economic in-sufficiency of the Highlands as a matter of course.

These problems are common to many tourist localities in this and other countries and by no means peculiar to the Highlands, but the economic disproportions are seldom equally striking.

[1] W. Forsyth: *In the Shadow of Cairngorm* (Inverness, 1900), p. 211.

Salix herbacea

Cairn Gorm from Ord Bàn, Loch an Eilein country

INDEX

A'AN, *see* Avon
Aberdeen-Angus, 176
Aberdeenshire, 24, 144
Abernethy, 26, 66, 103, 137, 197
A'Chailleach, 68, 73, 81, 181, 212, 240
A'Charn Guirm, 36
A'Chioch, 116, 121, 122
Achlean, 12, 16, 18, 42, 69, 157, 158, 237, 239, 240, 242
A'Choinneach, 86, 94, 107, 108
Acids, organic, 73, 163-4
Alexander, Sir Henry, 20, 140, 142, 207, 215
Alladin Buttress, 215
Allanquoich, 148
Allt, 17
Allt a'Mharcaidh, 168, 202
Allt an Eàs Mhòr, 76, 131
Alltan na Bienne, 120
Allt Creag an Lèth-choin, 91
Allt Dhàidh Mòr, 76, 77
Allt Fhearnagan, 18, 19
Allt Leirig, 139
Allt Luineag, 43, 72-4, 81, 233
Allt Mòr, 91, 101, 247, 249
Allt Preas nam Mearleach, 136, 145
Allt Ruadh, 56, 69
Allt Sgairnich, 72, 75, 81
Alpine lady's mantle, 46, 47, 64, 220
Alpine plants, 45-9
Am Bodach, 62, 69, 181
Am Braigh Riabhach, 62
Amethysts, 36
Am Moine Mhòr (*see also* Great Moss, the), 30, 61, 71-4
An Diollad, 119
An Garbh Choire Mòr, 44, 62, 213
Angel's Peak, 44, 54, 65, 146, 213
An Slugan, 103
Aonach shoulder, 93, 98, 100, 256
Aonachs, the, 23
Arctic plants, 45-9
Argyll, 144
Army, ski-ing in the, 229, 230, 265
Ath nam Fionn, 139
Aurora Borealis, 27
Autumn, 36, 37, 53-7, 166

Avalanches, danger of, 225
Aviemore, 25, 33, 93, 98, 138, 143, 148, 161, 172, 179, 196, 230, 237, 243, 245, 248, 254, 255
Avon, river, 34, 92, 107, 112, 126, 128, 139, 151-6, 164, 192
Avonside, ski-ing on, 250-3

BADAN Mosach, 17, 19
Badenoch, 15
Balachroick, 237
Balguish, 157
Balmoral, 151
Ballater, 151
Ballindalloch, 198
Banff, 24
Bannockburn, 11
" Barns ", *see* Tors
Barns of Bynack, 35, 108, 139
B.B.C., 14, 103, 239
Beanaidh, river, 160, 181, 269
Bearberry, 45, 48
" Beheading " of the valley, 34
Beinn a'Bhùird, 24, 25, 28, 111-34, 151, 165, 208, 209, 216, 250, 253, 259
Beinn a'Chaoruinn, 113, 140
Beinn Bhrotain, 25, 65, 72, 74, 76, 77, 79, 80, 145, 193, 203, 251, 252
Beinn Breac, 113
Beinn Mheadhoin, 25, 85-8, 91-3, 95, 107, 108, 113, 140, 182, 215
Bell heather, 49, 94
Ben Avon, 24, 25, 35, 111-34, 136, 151, 154, 165, 250, 253, 259
Ben Ghlas, 230, 262
Ben Macdhui, 14, 23, 24, 25, 29, 44, 75, 79, 85-93, 101, 105, 108, 109, 111, 113, 140, 146, 182, 183, 215, 244, 252, 259
Ben Nevis, 23, 24, 230, 262, 264
Ben y Ghloe, 131
Big Brae, 125, 129, 130
Bilberry, 48, 131
" Birchfield ", 128, 156
Bird cherry, 166, 171
Black Glen (*see also* Dubh Ghleann), 116, 117
" Black-house ", 14

Càrn Crom and the Derry Forest at sunset (the inclination of the trees attests to the force and persistence of the Sou'wester)

Black-moss, 64, 80, 87, 88
Black Park, 148, 196
Black Pinnacle, 214, 217-22
Black Sgoran, *see* Sgoran Dubh
Black Tarn (*see also* Dubh Lochan), 121, 122, 165
Blaeberry, 48, 95, 159
Blusher, 51
Boat of Garten, 25, 93, 104, 201
Bog asphodel, 54, 94
Bolets, 51-2
Boletus edulis, 52
Boletus scaber, 52
" Bolster ", 209
Bonaparte, 181
Bonnie Prince Charlie, 11
" Boss ", 28, 112
Bothies, 66, 101, 138, 145, 160, 181, 198, 233, 261, 263
" Boulder-trundlers ", 262
Braemar, 25, 26, 66, 112, 115, 131, 142, 150, 156, 196, 229, 238, 251
Braeriach, 15, 23, 29, 30, 31, 33, 48, 54, 62-4, 67, 69, 73, 74, 79, 146, 148, 161, 195, 213, 214, 217-22, 238, 243-5, 251
Braeriach Pinnacle, 214, 219
Britain, 23, 197, 231, 261
British Edible Fungi, 53
British Ski Year Book, The, 21
Broo, 180
Broom Moss (*see also* Moine Bhealaidh), 111-15, 133, 134
Brose, 180
Bruach Mhòr, 116, 124
Builg Burn, 128, 153-6
Burton, John Hill, 24
Bynack Beg, 107, 139
Bynack Lodge, 158
Bynack More, 25, 86, 107, 108, 111, 138, 139, 245

CAILLEACH Bheur, 14
Cairn Gorm, 23, 25, 30, 57, 85, 86, 92, 93, 97-9, 103, 170, 173, 217, 243, 244, 245, 246, 258, 259
Cairngorm Club, the, 87, 143, 223, 261, 265
Cairngorm Club Journal, The, 21, 207, 262
Cairngorm Hills of Scotland, The, 20
Cairngorms, the, boundaries of, 23-6; Central, 25, 85-110, 243-50; climate of, 39-44, 54-9, 114, 223-6; Eastern, 25, 40, 111-34, 151-6, 250-3, 268; geology of, 27-37, 73, 97-9, 111-3, 135, 136, 153-6, 164, 165; Southern, 74, 75-9; Western, 25, 61-83, 237-42
Cairngorms, The, Scottish Mountaineering Club Guidebook, 20, 207
Cairngorm stones, 35, 36
Cairn Lochan, 97-101, 170, 173, 183, 244

Cairn Toul, 15, 23, 30, 44, 61, 62, 64, 65, 67, 74, 78-80, 109, 145, 146, 183
Calart Hill, 170, 175, 177
Caledonian Forest, 71, 185, 188, 189, 192, 197, 203
Caledonian Mountains, 27, 112, 136
Camberwell Beauty, 19
Camping, 269
Canadian foresters, 17, 69, 200, 202
Caochan Dubh, 72
Caol Ghleann, 128
Càrn, cairn, 61, 62, 85
Càrn a'Mhaim, 29, 90, 145, 192
Càrn an t'Sabhail, 62
Càrn Bàn Beag, 240
Càrn Bàn Mòr, 12, 15, 16, 42, 43, 67, 70, 73, 81, 237
Càrn Drochaid, 127
Càrn Eas, 125, 151
Càrn Eilrig, 29, 147
Càrn Eilrig Mòr, 124
Càrn Etchachan, 91, 92, 95, 108, 215
Càrn na Drochaide, 115, 252
Carpathian shepherds, 199
Castle Gate Gully, 215
Castle Hill, 224
Ceilidh, 14
Central Council of Physical Recreation, 270
Chanterelle, 51
Chars-à-bancs, 265
Circumdenudation, 27, 28, 34, 112, 135
Cirro-velum, 41
Ciste Mearaid (Càrn Bàn), 15, 42, 74, 80, 94, 233, 240
Ciste Mearaid (Cairn Gorm), 91, 231
Civil War, the, 144
Clach Bhan, 126, 127
Clach Bharraig, 93, 255
Clach Bun Rudthar, 129, 130
Clach nan Taillear, 59
Clais Fhearnaig, 117, 118
Clark, John, 12, 16
Clearances, 180
" Clegs ", 53
Climbing, 64, 99, 205-22
Clip, 198
Cloudberry, 47, 84, 72, 80, 105
Club-moss, 43
Cnap a'Chleirich, 116, 132
Cnapan a'Mheirlich, 155
Coire an Dubh Lochain, 121, 122, 216
Coire an t'Sabhail, 65
Coire an t'Saighdeir, 65
Coire an t'Sneachda, 93, 97, 98, 99, 101, 208, 214, 215
Coire Bhrochain, 63, 213, 214, 217-22
Coire Cas, 100, 245, 246, 247, 258
Coire Cath nam Fionn, 74, 76
Coire Creagach, 231
Coire Dhondail, 66

Coire Domhain, 96, 103
Coire Etchachan, 48, 108, 109, 113, 140, 182, 193
Coire Garbhlach, 70, 212
Coire Laogh Mòr, 100
Coire Lochain (Braeriach), 63, 212, 244
Coire Lochain (Cairn Lochan), 98, 99, 208, 214, 215, 249
Coire na Ciche, 121
Coire na Ciste, 100, 247, 255, 256, 258
Coire nan Clach (Stony Corrie), 116, 121, 208, 216
Coire Odhar (Cairn Toul), 67, 80
Coire Odhar (Gleann Einich), 67, 72, 73, 160, 180, 181
Coire Raibert, 103
Coire Ruadh, 16, 63
Comyns (Cummings), 33, 170, 171, 177
Continental Sabbath, 265
Cooke, M. C., 53
Corndavon Lodge, 151, 152
Corrie Beanaidh, 45, 63
Corrie of Red Spouts, 192, 215, 252
Corries, origin of, 29, 31-2
Corrour Bothy, 67, 79, 80, 143, 145, 261
Couch of the Yellow Stag, 131
Coutts' Stone, 127, 131
Covenanters, 144
Cowberry, 48, 54
Coylumbridge (Coylum Bridge), 66, 143 144, 175, 180, 195, 196, 238
Craig, creag, 61, 69, 85
Craig Derry, 113
Craiggowrie, 103, 104, 105
Craiggowrie-Meall a'Bhuachaille ridge, 165, 172, 200
Cranberry, 48
Craobh an Oir, 109
Crathie, 148
Crathie and Braemar, History of the United Parish, 24
Creagan Gorm, 104
Creag Bhalg, 113, 118
Creag Chaisteal, 175, 177, 201
Creag Dubh, 69, 169, 243
Creag Ghiubhsachan, 69
Creag, Ghreusache, 201
Creag Leathan, 69
Creag Mhigeachaidh, 56, 69, 167
Creag na Caillich, 168
Creag na Gaibhre, 71
Creag nan Gall, 106, 173, 256
Creeping azalea, 46, 54, 120, 131
Creeping willow, 46, 55, 86
Crossleaved heath, 49
Crowberry, 46, 48, 49, 54, 131
Cuillins, 88, 123
Curlew, 42
Cyclopean building, 34

DALNADAMPH Lodge, 153

Dante, 97
Dee, Chest of, 79, 143, 159, 189
Dee, Linn of, 76, 78, 112, 117, 124, 142, 143, 149, 150, 251, 263, 268
Dee, river, 33, 34, 44, 117, 141, 143, 146, 148, 149, 150, 158, 164, 178, 213, 268
Deer, 55, 74, 75, 78, 80, 81, 129, 133, 134, 185-7, 189
Deer forests, 26, 90, 186
Deeside, 67, 115, 144, 229; ski-ing on, 250-3
Delnabo, 155
Denudation, 27, 28, 112
Derry Burn, 141, 182, 193
Derry Cairngorm, 88, 89, 108, 109, 111, 140, 244
Derry Forest, 193
Derry Lodge, 67, 143, 252, 265
Devil's Point, the, 55, 65, 75, 79, 80, 90 214
Diollad Coire Eindart, 70
Disney, Walt, 185
Distilling, illicit, 137
Don, river, 34, 153, 154
Dotterel, 259
Douglas fir, 194, 195, 196
Drovers, 136
Druie, river, 85, 143, 198, 269
Druim nam Bò, 71
Drumguish, 156
Drumintoul Lodge, 175
Drumochter, 11
Dubh Ghleann (*see also* Black Glen), 119, 124, 192
Dubh Lochan (*see also* Black Tarn), 165
Duchess of Bedford's Tree, 202
Duke's Chair, 77
Dwarf cornel, 123
Dwarf juniper, 46

EARL of Mar's Punchbowl, 151
East Buttress, the, 213
East Green Finger, the, 129
Edible bolet, 52
Edward I, 11
Egypt, 16
"Egyptian rocks", 121, 122, 209, 210, 211, 216
Eidart, river, 14, 72, 74, 157
El Alamein, 17
Emeralds, 36
Emperor moth, 45
English language, 12, 18
Erosion, 28, 31, 69, 72, 97, 112, 150, 153-6, 165
"Erratic stones", 29
Espalier, 46
"Everlasting battle", 68

FAINDOURAN Lodge, 155
Fairies, 14, 29, 45, 50, 174, 257

Fawns, 80
Fèith Buidhe, 90
Fèith Laoigh, 125
Fèith na Sgòr, 145
Felspar, 36, 88
Felspar porphyry, 35
Feshiebridge, 12, 157, 195, 202
Feshie, river, 12, 24, 34, 61, 69, 71, 157, 160, 164, 167, 239, 267
Fiacail, 121
Fiacail Ridge, the, 93, 98, 99, 209
Fife, Duke of, 119, 265
Fingal, Lady of, 126, 139, 140
Fingalian legends, 74, 126, 139
Fingalians, 74, 139
Fionnar Choire, 70, 71
Fires, forest, 104, 188, 193, 245, 267
Föhn, 57
Foliation, 211
Folk-lore, 14, 45, 50, 68, 69, 126, 174, 181, 182
Forefinger Pinnacle, the, 96, 215
Forest Lodge, 137
Forest of Glen Avon, 192
Forest pine, 194
Forestry Commission, 104, 195, 200, 201, 266, 269, 270
Forests, 17, 26, 104, 124, 141, 143, 168, 172, 185-203
Fort William, 23, 264
Fungi, 51-3

Gaelic, 17, 18, 28, 29, 40, 62, 105, 123, 137, 198, 259
Gairn, river, 112, 152
Garbh Allt, 98
Garbh Choire, 87
Garbh Choire Dhàidh, 64
Garbh Uisge, 92
Geal Chàrn, 56, 69
Geikie, Sir Archibald, 29, 111
Geldie Burn, 24, 34, 71, 72, 76, 149, 157, 268
Geldie Lodge, 157
Geology, 27-37, 69, 73, 97-9, 111-3, 121, 135, 136, 153-6, 164, 165
Germans, 16, 199
Giant Spectre of Glen More, 26
Glacial drift, 29, 164, 167
Glaciers, 29, 31, 112, 154, 155, 165, 175
Gleann an t'Slugain, 115, 117, 151
Gleann Einich, 32, 67, 72, 160, 172, 196
Gleann Fèisidh (*see also* Glen Feshie), 158
Glen Avon, 32, 116, 126, 127, 153, 155, 192, 245
Glen Builg, 115, 151, 153
Glen Clunie, 250
Glen Dee, 25, 28, 30, 55, 62, 78, 79, 85, 143, 145, 149, 238, 244, 250, 251
Glen Derry, 109, 140, 188, 189, 192, 252

Glen Eidart, 75
Glen Feshie, 11, 12, 15-7, 25, 30, 33, 35, 66, 68-71, 78, 81, 157, 158, 185, 202, 203, 212, 229, 232, 237, 238, 239
Glen Geldie, 76, 78, 156, 157, 158, 203, 252
Glen Geusachan, 65, 66, 74, 75, 79, 108, 143, 145, 188, 189, 214, 238
Glen Lui, 85, 140, 141, 192
Glen Luibeg (Lui Beag), 89, 150, 189, 192, 251, 252
Glen More, 14, 26, 33, 91, 93, 96, 98, 196, 229, 245-9, 257, 268, 269
Glenmore Forest, 172, 195, 199, 270
Glenmore Lodge, 93, 102, 253, 255, 266, 270, 271
Glen Quoich, 115, 118, 124, 125, 151, 189, 192, 193
Glen Tilt, 158
Glen Tromie, 158
Globeflower, 47
Gold Bug, The, 109
Golden eagle, 71, 96, 122
Golden-moss, 43, 56, 64, 86, 159
Golden plover, 43, 55, 56, 81
Gordon, Seton, 20, 47, 142, 231
Gorm, 105
Graham, Henry Grey, 191
Grampians, the, 20, 23, 24
Granite, 35-6, 209-11
Grant, Allan, 166
Grant, Lady Elizabeth, 180, 197
Grant, Sir George MacPherson, 195
Grant family, 144, 170
Grants of Rothiemurchus, 170, 180, 195
Grantown, 26, 174
Graylag geese, 178
Great Bynack (*see also* Bynack More), 107
Great Gully, the, 68
Great Moss, the (*see also* Am Moine Mhòr), 16, 24, 30, 43, 55, 61, 65, 66, 71-4, 78, 86, 107, 131, 157, 160, 182, 212, 233, 241, 243
Great Rough Corrie (*see also* An Garbh Choire Mòr), 44, 62, 63, 213, 231
"Great Steep" (*see also* Bruach Mòr), 116, 118, 123
Green Lochans (Tarns), 64, 65, 89, 106, 109, 138, 173, 174
Grey Mountains, the (*see also* Monadh-liath), 36
Grouse, 186, 242, 247, 249
Gymnadenia orchis, 118

Haig, Col., 156
Half-igloo, 235
Hare, blue (white), 40, 46, 242, 247
"Hatchet-carriers", 262
Hawk, 82

Heather, 49, 50, 104, 106, 180, 190, 225, 267
Heraclitus, 254
Higginbotham, W. R., 21
Highland Table-land, 111, 112, 125
High Plateau, 111, 112
High Tops, the, 26, 29, 30, 32, 40, 41, 46, 47, 57, 58, 77, 112, 205
Himalayas, the, 28, 205
Hogmanay, 14
Horseman's Corrie, 231
Huntly, Earl of, 144
Huts, 25, 230, 261-4, 265, 269

ICE Age, 29, 31, 46, 79, 154, 155
Iceland, 40
Inchriach, 195, 202
Inchrory, 127, 128, 151, 153, 154, 192, 253
Inchrory, Lodge, 156
Industrial Revolution, 52
Insh, 157, 239
In the High Grampians, 20
Invercauld, 194
Inverey, 25, 74, 150, 262
Inverness, 137
Inverness County Librarian, 21
Inverness-shire, 12, 24

JACOBITES, 11, 141
John of Corrour, 160, 180

KAME, 29
Kelpie, 14, 178, 181, 182
Kennapole Hill, 170, 268
Kincraig, 12, 13, 25, 33, 156, 157, 167, 168, 195, 237, 239
King George V, Silver Jubilee of, 195
Kingussie, 15, 16, 25, 156, 161, 167, 237, 238
Klister, 43, 259

Lactarius deliciosus, 52
Lairig, 24
Lairig an Lui, the, 25, 89, 92, 107, 108, 112, 113, 114, 135, 136, 137-9, 142, 245, 263, 268
Lairig Ghru, the, 25, 28, 33, 40, 54, 57, 59, 79, 85, 86, 89, 90, 97, 105, 135, 136, 137, 142-9, 158, 214, 223, 238, 248, 251, 263
Lakes (*see also* Lochs), 32, 163-84
Lambing storms, 41, 42, 213
Landseer, Sir Edwin, 157, 202
Larch, 166, 194
Lauder, Sir Thomas Dick, 148, 200
Ling (*see also* Heather), 49, 102
Linn of Avon, the, 155
Linn of Dee, the, 76, 78, 112, 117, 124, 142, 143, 149, 150, 251, 263, 268

Lochaber " reivers ", 106
Loch Alvie, 33
Lochan a'Bhainne, 139
Lochan Buidhe, 90
Loch an Eilein, 33, 66, 165, 169-72, 174, 175, 195
Lochan nam Bò, 71
Lochan nan Gabhar, 126, 129, 130, 165
Lochan Oir, 178
Lochans, 33, 63, 73, 91, 99, 123, 128, 140, 163-84
Lochan Uaine (*see also* Green Lochan or Tarn), 64, 65, 109, 173, 174, 183, 222
Loch Avon, 88, 91, 93, 97, 103, 153, 178, 179-82
Loch Builg, 112, 126, 165, 178
Loch Coire an Lochain, 183
Loch Einich, 55, 62, 73, 160, 166, 179-82, 212
Loch Ericht, 11
Loch Etchachan, 88, 89, 91, 92, 108, 182
Loch Gamhna, 165, 168, 169
Loch Insh, 12, 56, 167
Loch Mhic a'Ghillie Chaoile, 172
Loch Morar, 164
Loch Morlich, 33, 66, 85, 97, 104, 138, 164, 165, 172, 173, 174, 245
Loch nan Cnapan, 43, 67, 72, 73, 75, 182
Loch nan Stuirteag, 65, 74, 182
Loch of Black-headed Gulls (*see also* Loch nan Stuirteag), 80
Loch Pityoulish, 33, 85, 104, 165, 174-8
Lochs (*see also* Lakes), 26, 32, 163-84
London, 11, 25, 158
Lovat Scouts, 265
Luibeg Cottage, 134
Luineag, river, 196, 258
Lui Water, the, 141
Lunar Alps, 143
Lurcher's Crag, 54, 91, 105, 143, 208, 214, 223, 246, 248
Lurcher's Crag Meadow, 99, 244, 247
Lus a'chraois, 123

MACBETH, Lady, 69
MacDuff, 23
Màm Suim, 103, 138, 256
Mar, Earl of, 141, 151
Mar, Forest of, 26, 73, 90, 107, 188, 192
Mar Lodge, 117, 119, 124, 151
March Burn, 91
Margaret's Coffin (*see also* Ciste Mearaid), 15, 94, 231
Marsh violet, 75
Meall a'Bhuachaille, 103, 104, 106
Meall an Lundain, 113, 118
Meall Dubhag, 16, 43, 70, 239
Memoirs of a Highland Lady, 180, 197
Midges, 53, 105
Midget marsh marigold, 74

Milkwort, 118, 152
Mitre Ridge, the, 132, 216
Moine Bhealaidh (*see also* Broom Moss),
    111
Monadh, 28
Monadhliath (Monadh Liath), 36, 86,
    158, 195
Monadh Mòr, 15, 25, 72, 74, 75, 203,
    233, 252
Monadh Ruadh, 36
Monadnock, 27
Mons Graupius, 11
Monte Rosa, 35
Montrose, 144
Monty, 17
Moraine, 29, 32, 165, 167
Moray Firth, 26
Morven (Morrone), 26, 250
Moss campion, 46, 47, 64, 74, 76, 88, 94,
    120, 133
Moss-carder bumble-bee, 106
Moss of Kincardine, 188
Mossy cyphel, 43, 46
Mountain indicator, 87
Mountain pine, 194
Mounth, 90, 135, 136, 137, 139, 149, 151,
    152, 156, 158
Muckle Slock (*see also* Slòchd Mòr),
    115, 116, 125, 126, 127
Mullach Clach a'Bhlàir, 70, 238
Mullach Lochan nan Gabhar, 115, 130,
    131
Munroes, 127
Mushroom, 52, 53

Nairn, 127
Napoleonic Wars, 199
National Forest Park, 269-70
National Parks, 266-9, 270, 271
Nature Reserves, 268
Nethybridge, 25, 26, 107, 137
Nethy, river, 107, 138
Névé, 31, 227
Newtonmore, 174
Nor'Easter, 41, 44, 114
Norsemen, 11
Northern eggar moth, 45
North Top (Beinn a'Bhùird), 115, 116,
    131, 132, 133

Oak, 166, 176
Ogilvies of Elgin, the, 177
Old Man, the (*see also* Am Bodach), 63,
    68
Old Man of Ben Macdhui, the, 14
Old Yule, 57, 228
Orange lactary, 52
Ord Bàn, 170, 268
Ordnance Survey, 21, 91
Osbourne and Dodsworth, 200
Osprey, 171

Peneplain, 61, 112, 116
Perry, Richard, 20, 87
Picts, the, 11
Pityoulish, 170, 196, 243
Plumb, Charles, 20, 267
Poe, Edgar Allan, 109
Pools of Dee, the, 33, 57, 142, 147, 217
Potholes, 30, 126
" Pot Luck ", 148
Ptarmigan, 15, 42, 81, 100, 242, 247, 261
Purkinje effect, 49
Purple saxifrage, 46, 47

Queen's Forest, 104
Quick-fir, 14
Quoich, 151
Quoich Water, the, 117, 125, 141

" Race of the Trough, the ", 144
Rathad nam Mearlach, 107
Reafforestation, 191
Red deer (*see also* Deer), 185, 186
Reindeer, 185
Richmond and Gordon, Duke of, 199
Ridges, 29, 208, 209, 210, 216, 217, 219,
    220
Right of way, 66, 107
Robertson, Dr., 148, 149
Robin Oig, 257
Rock-rose, 118, 152, 153
Roe-deer, 129, 185, 186
Roseroot, 47
Rothiemurchus, 26, 54, 109, 143, 161,
    172, 192, 197, 199, 223
Rough Corrie, Beinn a'Bhùird, 132, 133
Rough Corrie (*see also* Garbh Choire),
    Braeriach, 33, 64, 143, 213
Rough-legged bolet, 52
Ruthven, 156
Rynettin, 138
Ryvoan, 85, 98, 103, 106, 138, 165, 172,
    243, 257

Saddle, The, 103, 245
Saxifrages, 47
Schists, 35, 71
Schuss, 259
Scots fir, 194
Scottish Council for National Parks, 266
Scottish Kandahar Race, 235
Scottish Mountaineering Club, 20, 230,
    262; *Journal*, 207
Scottish National Parks Survey Com-
    mittee, 266, 267
Scottish Ski Club, 100, 229, 230, 247,
    254, 262, 269; *Journal*, 21
Secretary of State for Scotland, 266
Sgoran Dubh Mòr, 68, 69, 212
Sgorans, the, 67-71, 136, 147, 161, 166,
    205, 212, 237, 238, 240, 247
Sgòr Gaoith, 68, 212, 240

Shaw family, 105, 144, 177
Shaw, Farquhar, 170
She Devil, the 62, 205
Shelter Stone, 92, 95, 96, 103
Shelter Stone Crag, 96, 215, 216
Shipton, E. E., 180
" Shunem ", 245
Silurian Age, 27
Sitka spruce, 194, 195
Skating, 171
" Sketofax ", 134
Ski-crampons, 233, 247
Ski-ing, 16, 17, 21, 43-4, 171, 223-60, 264, 265, 269
Ski-ing in Scotland, 21
Ski-stool, 248, 256
Slalom, 100, 247
Slesser, Malcolm, 218, 219, 220
Slochd Mòr (*see also* Muckle Slock), 125, 126
Sluggan Bothy, the, 263
Sma' Glen (*see also* Caol Ghleann), 128, 155
Sma' still, 136, 137
Smith, Janet Adam, 261
Smith, William, 109
Smith of Baltiboys, Elizabeth (*see* Lady Grant)
Smythe, F. S., 16, 251
Sneck, the, 116, 125, 127, 132, 251
Snow, 15, 31, 39, 40, 41, 43, 44, 57-9, 114, 207, 223-60
Snow and Mountain Warfare, 173, 229
Snowy Corrie (*see also* Coire an t'Sneachda), 208
Social Life in Scotland in the 18th Century, 191
Soldier's Corrie (*see also* Coire an t'Saighdeir), 65
South Top, the (Beinn a'Bhùird), 115, 116, 117, 120
Sou'Wester, 41, 114, 229, 233, 253, 254
Spey floaters, 198, 199
Spey, river, 15, 25, 33, 34, 105, 154, 165, 166, 175, 178, 195, 267, 268
Speyside, 25, 33, 88, 114, 156, 197, 229, 237
Spring, 39-45, 255-60
Spring snow, 227, 255, 257-60
Sròn an Aonaich, 100
Sròn na Lairig, 45, 57, 63, 86, 143, 214, 244
Sròn Riach, 90, 252

Stac na h'Iolare, 139
Statistical Account of Scotland, The, 36
Stirton, Rev. John, 24
Stob an t'Sluicht, 127
Strath, 25
Strathspey, 57, 61, 69, 142, 147
Subdued hills, 28
Summer, 46-50

TARNS, *see* Lochans
Thieves' Road, the (*see also* Rathad nam Mearlach), 172, 173
Thrift, 122
Thyme, 152
Tibet, 251
Tit, crested, 223
Tom Dhu, 167
Tomintoul, 25, 26, 127, 151, 153, 156, 181, 253
Tom na Bat, 128
Topazes, 36
Tors, 35, 63, 125 *et seq.*
Tree of the Return, the, 161
Trollius (Globeflower), 47
Tsampa, 180

Uaine, 105
Uisga, 14

VALLEY of the Pines (*see also* Glen Geusachan), 188
Vermin, 186-7
Victoria Bridge, 150

WATER, colouring of, 163, 164
Water of Ailnack, the, 154, 155
Weather, 15, 19, 39-42, 50-1, 53, 54, 57-9, 228-31, 235, 236
" Wee Woodie " (*see also* Badan Mosach), 17, 18, 202
White Bridge, 78, 158
" White Burn " (*see also* Allt Fhearnagan), 18
White Dryas, 47
Winter, 15-20, 223-54
Wintergreen, 45
Wraith ski-ing, 254-60

YELLOW saxifrage, 54
Young, G .W., 94
Youth Hostels, 267

Zastrugi, 227, 240